the heritage of
biblical faith

J. PHILIP HYATT

the heritage of biblical faith

AN AID TO READING THE BIBLE

CBP PRESS
St. Louis, Missouri

preface

THE PURPOSE OF THIS BOOK IS TO ENCOURAGE THE reading of the Bible, and to give the reader certain basic aids in understanding it as he reads.

In spite of the fact that the Bible is a perennial best seller, and is very widely distributed throughout our country and in other lands, there is widespread ignorance concerning the Bible and failure to take its teachings seriously for our corporate and individual life. Survey after survey has revealed an amazing ignorance about simple facts of the Bible, even among those who have grown up in Sunday church school and church and have graduated from college. More important is the contemporary failure to see the relevance of the Bible to modern life, and to wrestle courageously with the task of applying the biblical faith to the problems of the twentieth century.

For the Christian a minimal knowledge of the Bible should not be considered as optional but as absolutely required. How can we be genuinely Christian if we do not know the essentials of the biblical story, and of the biblical demands upon faith and life? When it is not grounded in the Bible, our Christianity is prone to become a halting commitment to a vague Christ and a superficial religiosity. The church becomes a means of human fellowship, hardly distinguishable from many secular associations. The New Testament writers sought both to win commitment to Christ and to promote Christian maturity in faith and life. We simply *must* know what God has done for us, what he requires of us, and how we can fulfill his demands and come to have a genuine knowledge of him.

We often fail to read and ponder the message of the Bible because we do not know how to read it, or we do not know what questions to bring to the Bible. We can expect too much from the Bible, and think that possession of a copy of it or perfunctory reading of it can have magical effect. Sometimes the best friends of the Bible have done much harm to potential Bible readers by promising too much or making the Bible appear too simple. Many of its parts are not easy to understand, and its message is by no means easy to translate into faith and action. Yet, it is not a book of mysteries and secrets, but a volume that invites reading and can be understood.

A fundamental insistence of the Protestant form of the Christian faith has been that the Bible should be available for reading by the common man in his own language, and that he has the right and duty to read it, interpret it, and appropriate its message. His interpretation should not be "private," but it must be intensely personal. Within the Roman Catholic form of the Christian faith there is a remarkable renewal today of interest in the Bible, and in promoting its reading by laymen as well as clergy. In this renewal lies one of the most promising seeds of hope for ultimate Christian unity.

The present volume is not intended to take the place of the Bible itself, but to accompany it. I have tried to set forth here some of the facts concerning the way in which the Bible has come down to us; the reasons why it has the form in which we now have it; an introduction to its history, literature, and theology; and the method we should follow as we read and study it, and seek to find for ourselves the authority that resides in the Bible.

The contents of this volume are necessarily varied, and the reader should take from it what meets his need. I hope that no one will fail to read carefully the first chapter, for it sets forth the approach that is basic to the whole discussion.

I wish to dedicate this book to the memory of my son, James Lee Hyatt, whose untimely death occurred a few months before I completed writing it. Our family is grateful for the gift of his twenty-six years of life. Since his passing we have felt special gratitude for the love of many friends, and above all for our Christian faith and hope.

J. PHILIP HYATT

The Divinity School
Vanderbilt University
Nashville, Tennessee
August 5, 1963

contents

9

I

a modern approach to the bible

THE BIBLE IS THE WORLD'S BEST SELLER, AS everyone knows. It has been translated into more languages and dialects than any other book. Yet, the Bible is not read as often or with as much understanding and appreciation as its wide distribution might suggest. Many Bibles and Testaments lie on tables and shelves, unread and unused, sometimes brought out or dusted up to impress a guest.

Yet the only Bible that is truly valuable to anyone is a read Bible. Sentimental stories have been told about the lives of soldiers or others being saved by a Testament carried in the vest pocket. But, to tell the truth, would not any other book of the same size and thickness—even a comic book—accomplish the same purpose in the same place? Our Bible is not an amulet, a magical charm, but a book to be read, marked, inwardly digested, and translated into life.

The Bible is not easy to read and understand. Many a person has started out to read it, with a good will and noble intentions, only to become bogged down in difficulties not of his own making. Mortimer J. Adler once wrote: "The problem of reading the Holy Book—if you have faith that it is the

Word of God—is the most difficult problem in the whole field of reading. . . . The Word of God is obviously the most difficult writing men can read. The effort of the faithful has been duly proportionate to the difficulty of the task. I think it would be true to say that, in the European tradition at least, the Bible is *the* book in more senses than one."[1]

Some of our difficulties in reading the Bible arise from the fact that it is, as Adler says, a holy book. The Old Testament is the sacred book of Judaism, and we Christians look upon the Old and New Testaments together as our Scripture. To us it is in some manner divine in its origin, and authoritative for our belief, worship, and life. We have to face the fact frankly, however, that various branches of Christendom and individual Christians have various ways of understanding the divine origin and authority of the Bible, and varied ways of interpreting it.

Our difficulties in reading and understanding the Bible may arise also from the fact that it is not really so much a single book as a small shelf of books, written over a period of some twelve hundred years by writers and editors so numerous that they cannot now be counted. Fifty years ago Charles W. Eliot, president of Harvard University, compiled a long shelf of books called *The Harvard Classics,* fifty volumes in all, that he said would provide that knowledge of ancient and modern literature "essential to the twentieth century idea of a cultivated man." In more recent times, under the influence of Robert M. Hutchins and Mortimer J. Adler (formerly of the University of Chicago), many people in America have been engaged in reading and discussing the Great Books, selected from the literature of the world.

We may appropriately call the Bible the "Classics" or the "Great Books" of the Christian faith, which every Christian

---

[1] *How to Read a Book* (New York: Simon and Schuster, 1940), p. 288.

ought to know. Erasmus, the Catholic humanist of the early Reformation period, once suggested that a man is no more entitled to be called a Christian if he has not read the Scriptures than to be called a Platonist if he has not read Plato.

Some of the difficulties we encounter in reading the Bible are inherent in its nature. It is made up, as we have just noted, of many separate little books, which were written by many men over a long period of time. Some parts of it are not well organized. It has much diversity within it, and its unity and primary message are not immediately apparent. But some of the difficulties in Bible reading are imposed upon it by our false attitudes toward it, or inadequate doctrines about it. We often set the Bible completely apart from other books, and consider it to be unique and different. Or, we think that because it is Scripture we must believe every word of it, and some parts we have honest difficulty in understanding and believing. Or, we may think there are mysterious secrets in it we should not try to understand, or that there is some single magical key that will help us to unlock all its secrets.

The purpose of the present volume is to help those who would read and study the Bible to do so as intelligently and sympathetically as possible. Because this is a book *about* the Bible, we must warn that it is never sufficient only to read about the Bible, but the Bible itself must be read.

Reasons for Reading the Bible

The Bible may be read for a variety of reasons. Different people will read or study it with various purposes in view.

Some read it for its literary qualities. They admire the beauty of its writing. There can be no question that the Bible does contain passages and books of very high literary merit. Any anthology of the world's masterpieces must include selections from the Bible. In English the King James Version has many passages of unusually high literary quality; some critics have even said that as literature it ranks higher than the Bible in the original languages. Furthermore, this version has had deep influence upon English and American literature.

Much of the Bible, however, is not of high literary quality. Some parts of it are in poor prose, and some of its poetry is of disappointing quality. Any honest reader must confess that parts of it are dreary reading, and some are quite obscure. When the Bible does exhibit high literary merit, it is not because the writers were consciously seeking to compose great literature, but because they had a message to convey, and had the genius to write well. In the Old Testament the Book of Ecclesiastes has many well-written and memorable lines, but its message is in parts cynical and out of harmony with the main stream of the Old Testament faith. Cynics and skeptics sometimes can write exceedingly well.

Some read the Bible as a sourcebook of history. For this purpose it is very valuable. The history of ancient Israel and early Christianity is an important part of the history of the world. Tiny Palestine was of little significance in the ancient world for its natural resources or its political or economic power, but it was very significant as the homeland of two great faiths. The history which the Bible records is sometimes very authentic history, yet some of it must be studied and sifted carefully before its historical value can be assessed.

Very little of the Bible relates history for its own sake, or for the purposes that a modern historian would adopt. Its history is the record in the main of what God has done in the events of which it tells, and of man's doings in response to God's activity. It is, therefore, history of a special order, designed not simply to inform the reader, but to awaken in the reader a response to what the Lord of history has done.

Still other readers turn to the Bible as if it were a manual of ethics. It tells them what is the right way to live, and instructs them concerning the wrong ways they must avoid.

It proclaims great moral principles of justice, righteousness, and compassion. But when one reads it in detail as a guidebook for daily living, it turns out to be a strange book. Many of its injunctions are completely outdated and therefore ignored by Christians today—injunctions telling them what they should wear, what food they should avoid, how they should plough their fields, and so on. What does this book tell us about many of the most pressing ethical problems of our twentieth century? What does it say about the relationships between labor and management, about the limits to which a government ought to go in managing our lives, about war and peace in a nuclear age, about the ethics of outer space? No doubt we can find help in all of these problems from the Bible, but not without a lot of hard thinking on our own part.

When we look more clearly at the morality of the Bible, we find it always closely connected with a religious faith. Why should man do good, and avoid evil? The Bible says it is because the God of justice and love demands it, and wants man to be like himself. Where does man find the motivation toward the good? The Bible says he does not find it within his natural desires, but in a sense of gratitude toward the God who created him and eternally redeems him.

As valuable as these various reasons may be for reading the Bible, we are driven to see that not one of them, or a combination of them, is fully adequate unless we unite them with the most compelling of all reasons for reading it. We should read it because it is our Scripture in which we find a record of what God has done in history for his chosen people and for mankind, and of what God requires of men in response to what he has done that they may be saved.

We may read the Bible to enjoy its literature or to be informed about its history, but most of all we ought to read it in order that we may have an encounter with the God who discloses himself as Sovereign Love, as our Creator and Redeemer, as Judge and Savior. We find mirrored in it the experiences of many kinds of men—some were stubborn and rebellious and rejected God's demands and his way, and some responded in faith and obedience. Some misunderstood him, or understood him only in small part; others saw him or understood him more clearly and accurately, and were dimly conscious of the glory and greatness that would always be hidden from their full vision, but they were willing to follow him as they knew him. Thus, in addition to telling us of the actions of the God we ought to serve, it tells us of some men whose ways we may emulate, and of others whose ways we must reject.

Reading the Bible like Other Books

There is a basic principle of the modern approach to the Bible that may seem at first to be contradictory to what we have just been saying, but it is not really so. This principle is: *we must read and study the Bible as we would any other book.*

This principle does not imply that the Bible is *just* another book, no better and of no greater value than other books we can read. It does not deny that the Bible is unique in some respects. What this principle insists upon is that we should not approach the reading of the Bible with a theory or doctrine that we impose upon it without knowing what is in it. As we read it in a manner similar to that in which we read other books, we shall discover its value, and learn whether or not it is unique. Our belief concerning the nature and authority of the Bible can then rest upon a knowledge of what is actually in it, and not be imported from the outside.

In reading the Bible as they do other books, scholars have learned that they should approach the Bible with two forms of criticism: Lower Criticism and Higher Criticism. The names were derived from the study of the ancient classics. It is very important to understand at the outset what we mean by these two terms.

Let us be careful to see first that the word "criticism" as used here does not mean censure or adverse judgment; it does not imply that we set ourselves above the books of the Bible and their writers, and look down upon them in a censorious mood. Criticism, as applied to a literary document, means intelligent and open-minded reading and study of that document, with a readiness to devote to it all the knowledge and fair judgment to its understanding that we can muster.

Lower criticism is so called because it is logically the first step in the systematic study of a book or document. This type of criticism has a clear-cut goal: to recover, so far as may be possible, the actual words written by a given author. Lower criticism is therefore often called textual criticism.

Textual criticism is important because, if we are to study intelligently what someone wrote, we want to know what he actually did write, free of mistakes or changes made by copyists or printers or anyone else. This kind of criticism must be applied to nearly every piece of literature. There is textual criticism of the plays of Shakespeare which seeks to recover what Shakespeare himself wrote. It is sometimes applied even to contemporary authors, especially when books or poems or the like have passed through several editions, or when there may be some question as to what the author himself originally wrote.

In the case of the Bible, the importance of textual criticism should be obvious. The Bible was written over a space of about twelve hundred years, and was completed long ago. We do not have a single book, not even a single verse, in the handwriting of the author, but only copies of copies of copies, and so on. Textual criticism of the Bible requires a knowledge of the languages in which the Bible was written, Hebrew, Aramaic, and Greek, and often of other languages.

Hence it can be carried on only by experts in the field; among professional biblical scholars there are some who are specialists in lower criticism. It is an exacting and often tedious type of work, but it is necessary.

In a later chapter, when we come to discuss early manuscripts of the Old and New Testaments, we shall give a little attention to the procedures of the textual critic (pp. 284-7). Here we shall point out only that every reader of the Bible in English profits from the labors of the textual critics. We can illustrate this best from the Revised Standard Version (abbreviated RSV).

The Gospel of Mark ends abruptly at 16:8 with the words "for they were afraid." The RSV has a footnote saying, "Other texts and versions add as 16:9-20 the following passage," after which it prints in small type verses 9-20. A second footnote says, "Other ancient authorities add after verse 8 the following," with a few additional lines. All of this means that textual criticism has shown that the authentic Gospel of Mark ends abruptly with the words quoted, and that the two endings which have been added to it in some manuscripts—not the best ones—are not authentic. They are not in the style of Mark, and are made up of selections from other Gospels and possibly Acts. The textual critic says to us, therefore, that these two endings of Mark should not be taken as belonging to the Gospel in its original form. We do not know whether the Gospel ended abruptly, or the original ending was very early lost.

A second illustration is 1 John 5:7. The King James Version of this verse is somewhat longer than RSV and some other versions, naming as three witnesses in heaven "the Father, the Word, and the Holy Ghost." RSV omits these entirely, and does not even contain a footnote calling attention to their absence. The reason is that the additional words of the King James Version occur in *no* Greek manuscript before the fifteenth century; they are found first in a Latin manuscript of the fourth century. It should be obvious that they formed no part of 1 John in its original form, and were added so late and in such a manner that they do not deserve even a footnote in RSV.

Whereas New Testament textual critics must devote much care to comparing the numerous Greek manuscripts of that Testament, the Old Testament textual critic gains little help from comparing Hebrew manuscripts that have survived, because they are fairly uniform. His primary resource is comparison of the Hebrew text with the text of the various ancient versions of the Old Testament, some of which were translated long before the date of our surviving Hebrew manuscripts (or the great majority of them). The RSV contains numerous footnotes indicating that the translators have sometimes followed the wording of one or more of the ancient versions rather than the standard Hebrew text. These abbreviations, which will seem quite cryptic to the reader, are explained in editions of the RSV immediately after the Table of Contents of the Old Testament at the front. One illustration will be sufficient.

Genesis 44:4 ends with the question of Joseph to his steward, "Why have you stolen my silver cup?" In RSV the last word has a note *q,* and the footnote says: "Gk Compare Vg: Heb lacks *Why have you stolen my silver cup?*" This note means that the italicized words are not found in the standard (Masoretic) Hebrew text, but occur in the Greek Septuagint (abbreviated Gk). "Compare Vg" means that similar words, but not quite the same, occur in the Latin Vulgate. The words somehow dropped out of the Hebrew text, but have been preserved in the Septuagint. A careful reading of verses 4-5 will show that they are necessary to the meaning.

Sometimes the textual critic of the Old Testament secures no help from the ancient versions, but the Hebrew text appears to him to be meaningless, and he thinks it has suffered damage or corruption at some point in the long process of copying. Then he may make an intelligent conjecture as to what stood in the text, on the basis of his knowledge of the shape of the ancient Hebrew letters, the kinds of errors that scribes did make, and the like. In the RSV these conjectural changes or emendations in the text are marked in the footnotes with the symbol "Cn," an abbreviation for "Correction." An excellent example is in Hosea 11:9. The second half of this verse in RSV reads:

> for I am God and not man,
>> the Holy One in your midst,
>> and I will not come to destroy."

Note *e* on the last word explains this as a correction, with an indication that the Hebrew text says, "I will not come into the city." The last three words are meaningless here. RSV has corrected the text with the conjecture that it read as quoted.

The average reader of the Bible cannot concern himself with the details of textual criticism. He should understand, however, that its purpose is always to recover the very best text possible, and that means the most nearly original text; its purpose is not to improve the Bible and make it say what some modern scholar thinks it ought to say. The average reader benefits from the work of the textual critics, and may be grateful for what they have done to provide him with more accurate versions of the Bible than he would have without their labors.

Higher (Historical) Criticism

The second type of criticism used in the study of the Bible is called higher criticism. There is much popular misunderstanding as to the meaning of this term, and the word "higher" is particularly misunderstood. It does not imply a sense of superiority to the books being studied, or to other scholars; it should not suggest a spirit of arrogance or egotism on the part of those who employ the method. "Higher" is used simply in contrast to "lower." It is ideally the second step in the study of a book or literary document. After the lower or textual critic has established the original text, the higher critic goes on to consider certain questions regarding that text which are necessary in understanding it. Higher criticism is not intentionally destructive in nature. Though it may lead to the questioning of generally accepted or traditional opinions, it has a positive purpose, seeking to establish a solid foundation for the interpretation of the Bible.

Furthermore, higher criticism is not a set of conclusions, but a method. The method may be applied rigorously or loosely; it may seek to judge all the evidence objectively, or it may ignore important facts. Those who employ the method of higher criticism differ in their conclusions. If a person says that Moses wrote the Pentateuch in the year 1400 B.C. shortly before his death in Moab, for the purpose of providing the Hebrews with the laws they would need in the land of Canaan, he is making a statement within the area of higher criticism; he may be basing this statement upon careful study which he believes to be in accord with all the facts. We sometimes speak of "the assured results of higher criticism," but such a phrase shows that higher criticism is a method rather than a set of conclusions.

The type of criticism we are talking about has been called by other names: historical criticism, or literary-historical criticism. Higher criticism is sometimes divided into literary criticism and historical criticism. In reality we cannot make hard and fast boundaries between these various terms. For practical purposes we consider it best to use the designation *historical criticism,* since it is not subject to the misunderstandings concerning the word "higher" that we have discussed, but we must include in the term all of the questions sometimes treated separately as literary criticism.

Historical criticism must ask and seek to answer certain specific questions regarding a given book of the Bible, or a portion of the Bible (either a part of a book, or a group of books together). These questions are:

Who wrote it?
When did he write it?
For what purpose did he write it?
To whom did he write?
What sources did he use?
What did the first author actually write, and what was added later?

It is not always possible to answer every one of these questions, and they are not equally important. It is a little artificial for us to speak continually of writers and writings in dealing with the Bible. Often it would be better to think of speakers and of what they spoke. The prophets were primarily speakers to the people of their time; only after they had spoken did they, or their disciples, make collections of what they had said. In narrative sections, stories were sometimes recited or sung over and over by wandering minstrels before they came to be written in connected narrative form. Hymns were sung in worship before they were collected in books. In the New Testament, the Gospels record the oral teachings of Jesus, and Paul's letters were written to be read aloud in the churches to which they were sent. We must often ask, therefore, who said and who heard parts of the Bible rather than who wrote them and who read them. However, it is impossible for us to get away from talking about writings and writers because we have the Bible only in written form (and no phonograph records or tapes).

We probably have difficulty in realizing the extent to which most people in antiquity learned through what they *heard* rather than through what they *read*. Few people could read and write; those who could were mostly priests and professional scribes. The people could listen to what was spoken by prophets and teachers, and what was read or recited in religious ceremonies. We must often ask, then, what the words meant to those who first spoke and heard them, rather than to those who first wrote and read them.

Concerning the authorship of portions of the Bible, we must often confess that we cannot determine the name or identity of the individual author. This is especially true in the Old Testament, where the prophets form the main exception. The Israelites had little or no pride of authorship; the writer of a given book or section was often content to remain anonymous. Some parts of the Old Testament should be looked upon not so much as the products of individual authors as the products of the experiences of the people over a period of time, the final composition being done by an individual or by several persons. There was, however, a tendency to attribute books of specific types to certain individuals in Israel's history. To Moses the lawgiver were attributed most of the legal materials of the Old Testament. To David, "the sweet singer of Israel," were ascribed many of the individual Psalms. Solomon was claimed as the author of wisdom literature—most of the Proverbs, the Book of Ecclesiastes, and the Song of Solomon. In each case there was historical justification for associating these men with these types of literature, for Moses was indeed a lawgiver, David a poet and musician, and Solomon a man of wisdom. Yet, it is most improbable that all of these ascriptions are correct, as we shall see in surveying the Old Testament.

In the New Testament, names are attached to the various books. In many cases these are correct, but in some they may not be. The early Christian church was inclined to attribute all of its authoritative writings to an apostle, or to someone closely associated with an apostle.

Consideration of the last question listed above is often of great significance, and biblical scholars frequently find themselves talking about whether a given verse or passage is "genuine" or "secondary"—that is, whether it was written by the person to whom it is attributed, or whose name stands at the head of the book. Such questions are not merely academic and abstract. If we wish to study Amos and his message, we should know what Amos himself said or wrote, and distinguish his own words from those of a disciple or editor. In the New Testament it is of real importance for us to know which letters Paul actually wrote, and which he did not, if we are to study Paul and the early Christian church intelligently.

In ancient times there were no copyright laws, as well as no printing presses. There was, as we have said, little pride of authorship among the people of the Old Testament; perhaps there was more in New Testament times. Furthermore, as we shall see when we discuss the formation of the canon (pp. 258-78), books were not written in order to be known as Scripture or to be included in a Bible. The formation of the canon of Scripture was a long process.

All of this means that it is somewhat artificial to think of a book as being finished and published at a specific time. A book was often a growing organism, or—to change the figure—it might be a literary magnet to attract additions to itself. For example, the long book of prophecy that goes by the name of Isaiah is an anthology of prophetic utterances and writings by several different "Isaiahs" (we cannot really count the number), who lived over a long period of time. There was an original collection of the utterances and deeds of Isaiah of Jerusalem, which formed the nucleus to which many additions were made, probably because of the prestige of the prophet Isaiah.

The serious student must, therefore, try to distinguish between what is on the one hand original or genuine in the sense that it comes from the first author or speaker, and that which is secondary in the sense that it was added at a later time. For the latter type of material some modern writers have used the adjective "spurious," but that is most misleading. An addition to a book may be as valuable as the words of the first author, or even more valuable. At any rate it is still a part of the Bible, and must be read for its own sake.

What we have just been saying is more appropriate for the reading of the Old Testament than for the New, but by no means irrelevant to the latter. Many readers of the Bible are frightened away by facts such as these, and do not like to think that they are true. The biblical scholar can only reply that these readers must study the Bible as it is, and that they must deal with it as honestly as they can. They must face the facts as they see them, and hope that others will do likewise. In the long run most modern readers of the Bible find the modern, historical approach exceedingly helpful, and believe that it answers more questions than it raises.

In summary, we may say that the goal of historical criticism is to enable us to place the various parts of the Bible in their concrete historical setting, and to allow the authors and speakers within the Bible to speak for themselves. It should help us to become contemporaries of the various personalities and events found in the Bible. We can seek to place ourselves in the position of the first hearers or readers of various parts of the Bible, and determine what the words meant to them. This is the best way to begin to understand what the words can say to us in our own lives in the twentieth century.

Let us give two specific illustrations. One will be drawn from the Old Testament, and one from the New Testament.

The prophet Amos lived in the middle of the eighth century B.C., toward the end of a period of prosperity and peace for the northern kingdom, Israel. He was a shepherd and

dresser of sycamore trees who heard the call of God to prophesy to Israel.

Imagine that you are an Israelite living at that time, and
that you have an opportunity to hear Amos as he speaks in
the court of the temple at Bethel and elsewhere. You hear
him say that the God of Israel will punish Damascus, Tyre, and
other surrounding nations for their cruelty in time of war,
and you give assent to what he says. But then he goes on to
denounce Israel for what Israelite has done to Israelite—the
rich selling the poor for a pair of sandals, and the people
committing vile practices in the name of religion. You hear
him proclaim God's message directed against various groups
within the nation: the women, "cows of Bashan," because
they egg their husbands on in acts of oppression and they want
more money to spend on drink; the merchants because they
cheat their customers and are so concerned with business they
do not want to close for holy days; unjust officials who accept
bribes; and the many people who bring abundant offerings
to the temples while they ignore the moral demands of their
God. Amos says the Israelites are truly God's chosen people,
but this places on them a burden of special responsibility, not
special privilege. Because their God has done so much for
them and they have been ungrateful, they must bear a great
punishment. The Day of Yahweh to which they have joyfully
looked forward as a time of light and victory will in fact be
a time of darkness, defeat, and destruction. They can find hope
for the future only if they are willing to turn to God, seek
good and not evil, and establish justice in their land. Amos
goes so far as to say that God speaks to Israel in these words:
"Are you not like the dark-skinned Ethiopians in my sight,
O Israel?"

After hearing Amos speak in this manner, what would be
your reaction? Would you hail him as a true prophet speaking
God's word? Or, would you applaud the priest of Bethel who

chased him out of Israel and told him to go back to his native Judah? Returning in your imagination back to the present, as you recall the message of Amos, would you think he really spoke the words of promise assigned to him in Amos 9:11-15? What message would you see in the words of Amos for yourself and for America in the middle of the twentieth century?

Now go in your imagination to the first century A.D., after Paul has begun his missionary career. You are a member of a little Christian church in Galatia, in Asia Minor. You have heard Paul preach on one or more occasions; maybe you were converted to Christianity through hearing him preach the gospel, and he may have founded the church of which you are a member. You have heard Paul insist that a man is saved by his faith in Jesus Christ, not by doing works of the Law.

After Paul left, dissension arose in your Christian congregation. Some people—maybe they came from Jerusalem—have been insisting that it is necessary for you as a Christian to keep the Jewish Law; everyone must be circumcised and then undertake to keep the whole Law. These have come to be known as "Judaizers"; they are Christians, not Jews, but maybe they had been converted from Judaism to Christianity. Along with their insistence that you must keep the Law, they have cast aspersion upon Paul: he is not a real apostle; at best he is a secondhand apostle, and does not know the true gospel. Yet, others in your church are saying the opposite: as a Christian you are above the Law. You do not have to keep any Law, because you are spiritual, you have been saved by faith in Christ, and that is all that is necessary. The people who maintain this position are probably former Gentiles, who have not known the ethical standards of Judaism, but were converted to Christianity from a non-Jewish pagan religion.

Along with some of your fellow Christians, who have also become confused, you decide to write a letter to Paul (or send a messenger to him) to report what you are experiencing, and to ask his opinion.

One day you hear that a letter has come from Paul in reply, and on the following Sunday you go to the meeting of Christians, where Paul's letter is to be read. You hear a letter that Paul has written with great vigor, even in anger. He dictated or composed it so rapidly and with such emotion that his words tumbled over each other and sometimes his grammar got mixed up.

As this letter is publicly read, you hear Paul insist he is a true apostle. He preaches a gospel that is not man's gospel, but one that has come to him by revelation of Jesus Christ. He summarizes various events in his life, and shows that he had gone up to Jerusalem to talk with the pillars of the church; they agreed that his point of view was correct, and that he should be a missionary to the Gentiles while others would seek to convert Jews. Yet, on one occasion in Antioch, Paul had rebuked even the Apostle Peter for his wavering on the matter of eating with Gentiles.

Then he turns to speak to the "foolish Galatians." "Who bewitched you," he says, "so that you have turned against me and the gospel I preached? Don't you know that you received the Spirit and have been justified by faith in Christ, not by keeping the Law? Christians who have faith are the true sons of Abraham, who was justified by his faith." Paul appeals to the Old Testament scriptures and to the experience of Christians.

Paul begs the Galatians who have been set free from the Law by their faith not to submit again to a yoke of slavery. What really matters is faith working through love. The people of Galatia must not suppose they are above all law. There is a law of Christ which can be summed up in the single commandment to love your neighbor as yourself. Paul closes his letter with practical admonitions which show that a Christian is not so spiritual that he is above all law.

As a Galatian Christian, what would you think after you heard this letter read? Would you continue to be confused, or would you think Paul had really settled the matter? Would you be convinced that, when a man is justified by faith in Christ, he will find himself able to keep Christ's law and his life will produce the fruits of the Spirit? Coming back in your imagination to the middle of the twentieth century, would you see in this fervid letter a message for yourself? You are not worried about whether you must keep the rite of circumcision and observe the Jewish Law, but have you not been disturbed sometimes about the crucial problem of the relationship between faith and works?

Values of the Historical Approach

The historical approach to the study of the Bible has many values. We believe that it is the only approach with which a modern student of the Bible should begin, if he wishes to understand the Bible, though his interpretation may go beyond the historical approach at some points. Let us here enumerate and discuss four primary values of the approach to the Bible through the method of historical (or higher) criticism.

(1) The historical approach enables us to avoid the pitfalls and vagaries of the allegorical method of biblical interpretation.

The allegorical interpretation of the Bible has a long history among both Christians and Jews. In the early period of Christianity it was widely employed, and the church fathers used many long names to describe or subdivide it—tropological, anagogical, typological, mystical, and so on. For practical purposes we may designate all of these methods as allegorical. The essence of this method is that it sees in a scriptural passage a meaning that is different from the plain or literal meaning; the true meaning, according to the allegorist, is veiled and presented in a mysterious and secret way. One person stands for another; a given event really symbolizes another event, and so on.

We cannot deny that the Bible does contain some allegories. For example, Isaiah 5:1-7 presents the allegory of the vineyard and its interpretation. A similar allegory concerning a vineyard is found in Matthew 21:33-43 and parallels. The apocalyptic literature in the Bible—such as the books of Daniel and Revelation—abounds in symbolic use of numbers, veiled presentation of certain events and persons, and a large use of allegory in the broad sense. This kind of literature can be described as "underground" literature intended to inspire in the faithful hope and courage in a time of hardship and persecution. In Daniel the faithful are the supporters of the Maccabean revolt and the persecutors are the Seleucid rulers; in Revelation the faithful are the Christians, and the persecutors are the Romans. The apocalypses, though they make use of allegory, should by all means be studied in their historical setting and be interpreted in the light of that setting.

Furthermore, the allegorical method of interpreting the Old Testament is used in some parts of the New, particularly by Paul. In this the early Christians were using very much the same kind of interpretation that the Jews used in studying their Scripture.

We cannot deny that allegory and allegorical interpretation have their place. Yet, we cannot today use this type of interpretation just because it was used in the first century; we cannot turn the calendar back. In skillful and careful hands allegorical interpretation may have some validity, but it should generally be avoided. Its great danger is that it usually has no objective controls, and becomes completely subjective. Once you start with the assumption that a given passage does not mean what it says, but rather "something else," you open the cover on a Pandora's box of wild imaginings and bizarre interpretations.

Allegorical interpretation has frequently been practiced in the past for two reasons that are closely related: to harmonize some parts of the Bible with other parts when the plain interpretation makes them inconsistent or contradictory; and to find Christ on virtually every page of the Old Testament. Both of these lead to artificial results, and are undesirable for that reason. We can find Christ in the Old Testament, but in a way that rests upon a historical approach; if we can find him only by the method of artificial allegorizing, we do an injustice both to him and to the Old Testament. As for the first reason, we should not subject the Bible to an artificial and irrational harmonization, but understand and accept it for what it is.

Historical criticism has as its purpose to let the biblical writer speak for himself in his own situation. It seeks to start *where the biblical writer is.* It searches for the meaning which has been called plain, or simple, or literal. Allegorical interpretation, on the other hand, *starts where the reader is,* and is often inclined to make the biblical writer say what the reader thinks he ought to have said and meant. The historical method makes possible true *ex*egesis, which means drawing the meaning *out of* the passage; the allegorical method often leads to *eis*egesis, which reads a meaning *into* the passage. One method has controls derived from the study of the historical setting and the context; the other very often has no controls to set bounds to the imagination and the desires of the interpreter.

(2) The historical method helps us avoid the danger involved in using the Bible largely as a manual of prediction concerning events which are taking place today, or are expected to occur in the near future.

As an example of this type of use, let us cite the interpretation that is sometimes given to Gog of the land of Magog, or Gog and Magog, as found in Ezekiel 38—39, Revelation

20, and related passages. We are told by some interpreters that these represent Russia; that the Russians will invade the land of Israel and there be defeated; then will occur the second coming of Christ, the end of this world, and so on. Much weight is placed upon the fact that the nation of Israel has been in existence since 1948. Some biblical interpreters only assure us that the defeat of Russia, as foretold in the Bible, is "near," whereas others set the date rather precisely.

What is wrong with this kind of use of the Bible? Perhaps the greatest harm is the implication that man is only a puppet in the hand of God; all was foretold and planned long ago, and man can only wait for what God will do. History is like a play, of which the script was written long ago, and man is simply required to act out his part. The belief that God is sovereign over history and over our lives does not require such a view as this. Man is a person, created in the image of God, and he has relationships with a divine Person. He is not a puppet or automaton, but a decision-making creature of God.

This kind of interpretation of the Bible has been going on for a long, long time, and has over and over proved to be illusory. Many different persons in history have been identified with Gog and Magog, or the Beast of Revelation, and the end of the world has been predicted many times. In the twentieth century we have been told that both Kaiser Wilhelm of Germany and Adolf Hitler, as well as various Russian rulers, are the Beast or the Antichrist. Disillusionment with this kind of interpretation of the Bible has led some people to give up the Bible entirely; it has led others only to set the date forward a few more years.

No parts of the Bible are more difficult and puzzling than the apocalyptic portions. We shall see that in Christian history there were serious questions concerning the acceptance of the Revelation of John into the canon, and some branches of Christendom have never accepted it as fully canonical. Yet, it is precisely this kind of literature that we can understand best in the light of the historical circumstances which produced it. Every reader should give careful attention to the historical crises out of which books such as Daniel and Revelation arose, and interpret them in the light of their background. Also, one should always make a careful distinction between this type of literature and that which is in the genuine sense "prophecy." Prophecy in the Old Testament sense does not mean primarily prediction of the future, certainly not of a remote future, but proclamation of God's message to the people of the prophet's own day.

(3) Historical criticism frees us from the necessity of defending, or literally believing in, the whole of the Bible.

The Bible is the product of some twelve hundred years of history and of numerous writers, and it contains within its covers varying viewpoints and emphases. The Bible should no longer be thought of as existing on a level plane, with all parts of it equally inspired and of equal value. Artificial harmonizing is not necessary.

The Bible is the record of the wondrous deeds and saving acts of God in history; the sending of his Son was the mightiest, the climactic act. It records also man's understanding of God, and his responses to God's word. We can, with proper safeguards, speak of a progressive revelation of God in the Bible. That revelation must not be understood as proceeding in a straight-line, evolutionary fashion. We do not get on the bottom steps of an escalator with the first chapter of Genesis, and get off the escalator at the top with the final chapter of Revelation (or whatever may be the latest book in the Bible). Man's understanding of God proceeded in an up-and-down fashion, sometimes reaching heights that were later abandoned. The understanding shown by Second Isaiah in the sixth century B.C. was not excelled, and indeed seldom reached, before the beginning of Christianity.

In this long record, there are examples of inadequate understanding of God and passages that are undeniably "primitive," not all of them being at the beginning of the history. There are sections of the Old Testament that are sub-Christian. With a historical understanding of the Bible we have no need to defend or apologize for such things in the Bible; nor should we try to harmonize everything that we find in it.

A historical approach to the reading of the Bible should enable us to see the various parts of it in perspective, and accept the Bible for what it is.

(4) Historical criticism provides us with a solid foundation on which to build a religious and theological understanding of the Bible.

We cannot wholly separate a historical understanding and a religious understanding of the Bible. As we read it with the historical approach, we cannot avoid seeing its religious message. Yet, the historical approach can be fragmentary, concerning itself too much with individual writers, events, periods, and the like. We should go on to see the meaning of larger units and of the Bible as a whole.

We should seek to know the meaning of whole books, and in some cases of bodies of literature. The book of Isaiah, we have said, is an anthology of the writings and sayings of many persons. We want to know what the individual Isaiahs said, but also what the book as a whole means. We should try to find the meaning of the Pentateuch as a unit, as well as of the individual strands that go to make it up. Sometimes our question should be: what did this book signify to its final editor? And we should search for the unity, or the unifying factors, that underly the message of the Bible as a whole.

Some passages in the Bible came to have a more complete or fuller meaning as time went on, sometimes a meaning that may not have been in the mind of the original writer. The same thing can be said of much great literature: it acquires deeper and broader meanings as it is read and used, often going beyond the original intention of the author.

A good example is provided by the work of Second Isaiah, the prophet whose work is found in Isaiah 40—55. He created the figure of the Suffering Servant of the Lord who, through his faithfulness to the Lord and voluntary endurance of innocent suffering even to death, would bring healing to the nations and knowledge of the true God to all the world. It is difficult for us to determine the identity of this Servant in the mind of Second Isaiah; he must have meant Israel in some sense, but he may have meant more. In the first century Jesus Christ came, and he was identified as the Suffering Servant, filling the role Second Isaiah said the Servant would fill. (We shall discuss later, pp. 220-26 whether it was he or his disciples who first made the identification.) In this way the figure created by Second Isaiah acquired a deeper significance. Second Isaiah wrote with a conviction concerning the way in which God brings his purpose to fulfilment among mankind, and he said more than he was conscious of saying; those who saw in Jesus Christ the fulfilment of his words were not doing an injustice to him, even if he did not have Jesus specifically in mind.

Other examples could be given. We shall see them as we read the Bible. Our suggestion is that the historical situation in which a given passage was first spoken or written must be studied, that it may form the beginning of our understanding, but it does not need to end there. Not all parts of the Bible acquired fuller meaning in the course of the centuries; some were of only temporary importance and, though they form part of the message of the Bible as a whole, are not relevant to the religious life of the Christian today.

The historical approach will thus help us see the application which biblical books or passages have for our twentieth-century life. For example, we might ask: does Jeremiah have a message for us, either as individuals or as a society, at the present time? The answer will not come if we look only for "predictions" that apply today, or if we ask whether Jeremiah foresaw the conditions of our time. We must study the life and message of this prophet who witnessed the decline and fall of the kingdom of Judah. Jeremiah lived as a lonely figure in a tragic time. He sought to call his people back to God in repentance; he opposed the dependence upon foreign alliances and military measures for the salvation of his nation. He wanted his people to give up their false gods. In pursuing his mission as a prophet, Jeremiah had severe inner struggles, in which he came even to the point of accusing God of deceiving him. Yet he faithfully delivered his message, with great courage and hope.

As we ask whether he has a message for us, we need to inquire: Are the conditions of our time in any way similar to his? Are our problems like his? Do we need to know the God he came to know? Can we gather strength from his courage, and comfort from his hope? In answering these questions we may find a message for ourselves, but we may find also that in some respects we cannot follow Jeremiah's message or attitude. His attitude toward his personal enemies may seem to us to be sub-Christian. He prayed that God would destroy his enemies, even their wives and children; Jesus prayed for his enemies as he hung on a cross, saying: "Father, forgive them, for they know not what they do." Yet, in many respects Jeremiah will be found to have a word of the Lord for our day, and his life and character can be an inspiration to us. However much civilization may have advanced, philosophical ideas changed, and science progressed, human nature and the basic human problems and needs have changed little through the centuries.

The Role of Biblical Archaeology

A characteristic feature of modern study of the Bible is the wide use made of archaeology in interpreting and understanding it. We cannot here discuss fully the use of archaeology, but make a few remarks that may help the person who reads both the Bible and secondary books that deal with the Bible.

Archaeology is not simply a hunt for treasures to display in a museum, nor is it engaged in for the purpose of "confirming the Bible." Archaeology is the scientific study of past human events and cultures by means of the material remains which have been left and the archaeologist can recover today. As a field of study it does not deal only with the ancient past; it may deal with that which occurred only a few centuries ago. In our own country we can speak of the archaeological study of the early American Indians. The history of every part of the world can be studied archaeologically; in the field of prehistory, archaeology is almost our only resource, since prehistory deals with the time before writing was invented. Biblical archaeology is naturally concerned largely with the findings in Palestine and the nearby lands of the Near East.

Archaeology seeks to recover the material remains of the past. Among those remains are the tools men used, the houses in which they lived, the walls they built to protect their towns, the clothes they wore (if they can be recovered now), the coffins in which they were buried, and the very bodies they left, as well as many, many other things. In the broad sense we can think of archaeology as including also various types of writing which are dug up or discovered by the archaeologist—clay tablets containing cuneiform characters, inscriptions in Egyptian hieroglyphics, Greek papyri, inscriptions in ancient Hebrew, and so on. Archaeology provides the biblical student with a great deal of extrabiblical writing that he can use in interpreting the Bible, in addition to numerous uninscribed objects.

The purpose of biblical archaeology is not, as some writers on the Bible may appear to indicate, to confirm the Bible. As a scientific study its purpose is to discover the facts, and then to see what those facts mean in relationship to the biblical records. Frequently archaeological discoveries *do* confirm the Bible; sometimes they fail to confirm, or they even contradict, specific items in the Bible; very frequently the significance of discoveries cannot be stated simply as either confirmation or nonconfirmation. Archaeology illuminates the Bible and makes it vivid for us. It enables us to reconstruct the conditions of life under which people in ancient times lived, and to understand the background of the lives and writings of biblical personalities. It often helps the history of Bible times "come alive" for us. Archaeology should always be used in close correlation with what the Bible itself actually says.

Some scholars make the mistake of setting biblical archaeology over against the higher criticism of the Bible, and asserting that archaeology disproves higher criticism. When higher criticism is properly understood, and when the discoveries of the archaeologist are rightly interpreted, we do not believe that the two should be set over against each other. Archaeology sometimes serves to correct extreme positions taken by biblical scholars who base their studies too exclusively upon a literary study of the Bible. But usually there is no direct relationship between archaeological discoveries and the results of historical (higher) criticism, since they have different concerns.

Archaeology has a larger contribution to make to Old Testament study than to New Testament study, because Old Testament history spans a much longer period of time than the New. Yet, archaeology enables us to understand better the Roman government and civilization, Hellenistic culture, and some of the institutions of Judaism in the New Testament period.

The modern Bible reader who consults books about the Bible can profit from paying attention to archaeological discoveries. Yet, he should always remember that an archaeological fact—that is, a specific item discovered by the archaeologist—is sometimes subject to widely varying interpretations. In no other area of biblical study is it so important to seek out the mature, experienced interpreters. Field archaeologists, who do the work of exploration and digging, are sometimes good interpreters of what they and others discover, but sometimes they are not. In some cases experienced "arm-chair archaeologists," who study carefully the results of many field archaeologists, are the best interpreters.

Reading with Eyes of Faith

We should read the Bible with eyes of faith, with hearts that are open to respond to the message it conveys. Our primary purpose in reading is not to accumulate information about the past, nor to acquire knowledge *about* God and his former dealings with men, but rather to come to know for ourselves the same God who discloses himself through the biblical record.

The historical approach may seem to require that we read the Bible as a literary document of the past with cold objectivity, in order to analyze it critically. It is true that we must apply our intelligence at its best to understanding the Bible; our minds are the gift of God, and we should use them in our study of the Bible, weak and fallible as they are. But we should read the Bible with the whole self, with intellect and emotions and spiritual insight. Any record of the past should be read with sympathy (or empathy), not with utterly detached objectivity. This is especially true of the Bible if we would find in it a word of God for ourselves.

The Bible is on the whole written out of faith, by men of faith, for the purpose of arousing faith. Such a purpose is most clearly stated in the Gospel of John 20:30-31. The author says that Jesus did many other signs in the presence of his disciples that he has not recorded, "but these are written that you may believe that Jesus is the Christ, the Son of God, and that believing you may have life in his name." The purpose for which this Gospel was written, as well as much else that is in the Bible, was to inspire belief, so that the reader in believing might have life. In this manner the Bible might become truly a word of Life.

Reading the Bible with faith does not mean, however, approaching it with credulity, with a readiness to accept everything and anything in it, simply because it is a sacred book, the Christian Scripture. It means approaching the Bible in an attitude of humility and expectancy, with a desire to hear what it says rather than what we think it ought to say. We shall find much of it to be strange and forbidding, even offensive. Yet, in the strange, new world of the Bible we may find a message for ourselves if we read it with patience, contriteness, and thoroughgoing honesty. We want to know what God has done, but also what he is continuing to do, and what he will do. We cannot rely upon the faith of yesterday, but must find a faith sufficient for ourselves in the twentieth century. Such a faith will be both an acquisition of man and a gift of God.

God speaks to modern man in various ways, frequently outside the pages of the Bible. There is no absolute assurance that he will speak to everyone who reads the Bible, however diligently. But the reader who approaches it in the manner we have been trying to describe, with humility and yet complete honesty, is more likely to find in it a message for himself—even if it is not the message he expects to hear.

Some Practical Suggestions

In closing this chapter, we wish to present some practical suggestions to the reader. We hope that what has already been said has many practical implications, but here we may be very specific.

(1) *Read long portions of the Bible at a time, and not merely small passages here and there in various parts of the Bible.* The reading of well-selected brief passages from various books is suitable for regular devotions, but that is not the best way to study the Bible.

Think a moment of what we have said about reading the Scripture as we do other books. How do we read a novel, or a book of history, or a travel narrative? We do not jump around, reading snippets here and there; we sit down and read it consecutively for an hour or more at a time.

We do not suggest beginning with the first chapter of Genesis and reading consecutively through to the last chapter of Revelation. That is probably the least satisfactory way, for we are likely to become bogged down at some points with trivialities or very obscure passages. The books of the Bible were not written in the order in which they appear in our English Bible. We suggest that you go through a single book at a time, reading it carefully and seeking to know it well. For example, a good book in the Old Testament to read is Amos. It is a relatively short book, and is not very difficult to understand. Or, in the New Testament, you might begin with the Gospel of Luke. You could read through Amos very easily at one sitting, and a thoughtful reading of Luke should require not more than two or three hours. Read through the book itself once with care, but not too slowly, seeking to see it as a whole. Then, go back through it again, and perhaps several times, dwelling upon those parts which are most meaningful for you, or most difficult to comprehend. In the latter case, seek help outside the Bible for an understanding. After reading through a book once or twice, you will be ready to study it carefully with the aid of some of the helps that will be mentioned later.

In this way you could read many books of the Bible. In the Old Testament you would not have great difficulty in reading Genesis, Deuteronomy, narrative books such as 1-2 Samuel and 1-2 Kings, and some of the shorter books of prophecy. Long books of prophecy such as Isaiah and Ezekiel would call for outside help, and so also books such as Job, Ecclesiastes, and Song of Solomon, though the last three can be read for literary merit. You would not miss a great deal if you left unread, or did not read until after many others, books such as Leviticus, Obadiah, and Nahum. The book of Daniel should be read along with an interpretative work which will help you to see the historical setting of the book and understand the symbols used.

In the New Testament, you can read any of the Gospels readily, preferably first at one sitting. Acts and many of the letters are not very difficult. Among Paul's letters, Romans is more of a treatise than the others, and perhaps should be read with an aid. The book of Revelation will require the same kind of outside help as Daniel.

These remarks are not meant to be exhaustive, but only suggestive. Many people will prefer to read the books in a chronological order as suggested by one of the books contained in our Suggestions for Further Reading on p. 340.

(2) *Use a good translation, and be ready to make use of several different translations.* The King James Version is preferred by many people for devotional reading, but it is not the best version to use in serious study of the Bible. It has too many obsolete or obsolescent words, and at many points is obscure. It fails particularly to give with clarity the meaning of difficult passages. Biblical scholarship has made many advances since 1611.

For the average reader, the best version is probably the Revised Standard Version of the Bible. It is in modern language, is based on up-to-date scholarship, and yet is in the tradition of the great English versions. The American Standard Version (1901) is often more literal in its renderings than the Revised Standard, but is less modern in its language.

You may wish to use one of the private, modern-speech translations, and they are frequently very helpful, either for continuous reading or for consulting with regard to particular verses or passages. One of the best is *The Bible: an American Translation,* published by the University of Chicago Press, sometimes called "the Smith-Goodspeed Bible." Many translations of the New Testament are available. Of these we mention especially that of James Moffatt, and *The New English Bible—New Testament* (1961). For further information concerning these and other versions, see below, pp. 312-14.

Since there is no perfect translation of the Bible available, and new ones must continually be made, the reader can very profitably make use of various ones. A good translation is sometimes the best commentary on a passage.

(3) In trying to understand the Bible, especially from the historical standpoint that we have been advocating, *do not hesitate to seek all the aid that is possible.* The Bible is not completely self-interpreting. We can gain much from thorough reading of the text itself, and frequently from comparison of various passages in the Bible. Still, we often require aid from outside the Bible itself.

The Christian Bible has been studied, translated, and interpreted more often and more thoroughly than any other book. Many volumes are at hand with information and various kinds of interpretative aid that any layman can use with profit— books that we consider as secondary sources, for the Bible itself is always our primary source.

We list in the Appendix some books that should be helpful. Some are technically called volumes of "Introduction" to the Bible or to one of the Testaments. Often they carry that word in the title. They treat in a systematic way for the individual books of the Bible the various questions we have listed above under higher criticism, and sometimes also problems of textual criticism. Commentaries offer similar aid in the introductions to individual books, and comment on successive verses or passages. One-volume commentaries will frequently give sufficient aid, but there are longer commentaries that devote a volume to a single book, or to a group of short books of the Bible. Then there are books treating a multitude of special subjects: history of Israel or of New Testament times, biblical archaeology, the history of religion in the Bible, theology of the whole Bible or a single Testament, and so on.

In reading books about the Bible, you may come across statements with which you strongly disagree, or that you think embody wrong interpretations. Do not immediately conclude that the writer is completely wrong, or that he is trying to promote a heresy. Try to understand what he is saying, and consider the evidence on which he bases his statements. Compare what he says with other books, and test it by the Bible itself. You may continue to think he is wrong, or you may be convinced he is right.

The Bible student should be led to strong convictions and ardent beliefs, but there is little room for dogmatism and intolerance. Differing interpretations arise from differing assumptions with which readers approach the Bible, their use of different methods, variations in knowledge or intellectual competence and in spiritual insight, and various other factors. Every reader should seek to study the Bible with all of the dedication, intelligence, and faith that he has, and pray as he reads that he may have the guidance of the Holy Spirit.

II

olò testament
history anò literature

WE EMPHASIZED IN THE LAST CHAPTER THE IM-
portance of the historical approach to the study of the Bible.
The Old and New Testaments were produced over a period
of at least twelve hundred years, and they record events for a
much longer time. Our Christian faith is a historical religion:
it has a history, and it rests upon historical facts. God manifested himself to men upon the stage of history, and they
discerned the action of God in the events through which they
lived.

When we read the Bible, then, we are reading about *our
past.* It is the story of God's dealings with men—individual
men, nations, and peoples—in times long ago, and of their
reactions and responses to God's manifestation of himself.
What he did for them was done also for us, and we should
look upon them as our spiritual ancestors, and see ourselves in
their responses. The history of Bible times is thus far more
than a set of dates, of military battles, of successive rulers and
periods, and the like—though we must often use such facts
as the framework on which to place the story we wish to
learn.

In the present chapter we shall survey in brief manner the history of Old Testament times, giving attention to the general course of events, and attempt to place the literature and religious developments in their historical setting. Before doing this, we must look briefly at the nature of the historical narratives in the Old Testament.

The Historical Books

The narrative books of the Old Testament which set forth the history of Israel are those which extend from Genesis through 2 Chronicles, omitting the little book of Ruth. These books may be divided into three categories according to their times of composition and editing:

1. The first four books of the Pentateuch—Genesis, Exodus, Leviticus, and Numbers—along with Deuteronomy, are often called the "Books of Moses." It is certain that he was not their author; they are the result of a process of compilation over a period of four or five hundred years. This makes them far more valuable than they would be if they had come from the pen of a single man in the thirteenth century B.C. We may distinguish three principal stages in their composition:

(a) In the reign of Solomon—or perhaps somewhat later—a writer whom we call the Yahwist or designate by the symbol J, compiled an epic that began with the creation (Gen. 2) and extended down to the conquest of Canaan. We designate him the Yahwist because he used the name "Yahweh" in the book of Genesis[1]; the symbol J is derived from the name of the Israelite deity (in the form Jehovah or Jahveh) or Judah, because this author lived in that kingdom. The Yahwist was one of the most creative writers in Israelite history. Drawing upon the traditions of his people, which existed mostly in oral form, he wrote a national epic in which he told of the primeval

---

[1] For explanation of the name Yahweh, see pp. 89-91.

beginnings of man and his culture, the wanderings of the patriarchs and the promises made to them, the exodus from Egypt, the formation of the covenant at Sinai, and Yahweh's leading of the people through the desert to the border of the promised land. The Yahwist fixed the basic pattern for the early history, and set forth many elements of the early faith of the nation.

(b) About two centuries later (around 750 B.C.) a second writer, known as the Elohist or E, wrote a similar history, more limited in scope, with emphasis upon the traditions of the northern kingdom, Ephraim. The symbol E is derived from the fact that he used the general word *Elohim* for God in Genesis, and also from the name Ephraim. His work, as now preserved, began with Abraham. Much of the story of the life of Joseph was told by him, but he too covered the whole history down to the conquest of Canaan.

(c) In the time of the Exile, sixth century B.C., or a little later, these narratives were supplemented and edited by a Priestly school of writers, known by the symbol P. To P we owe, among other things, the majestic account of creation in the first chapter of Genesis, and the whole of the book of Leviticus. These writers were interested mainly in setting forth the laws of Israel and the priestly point of view. Their concern with history lay primarily in showing the historical origin of the various rites and institutions of the religion. Genesis 17, which tells of the revelation of God Almighty to Abraham and of the institution of the rite of circumcision, is a good example of P's narrative style.

The work of these three writers or schools, J, E, and P, are now found woven together in the books of Genesis—Numbers. They are a rich mine of information for many periods of history, including both those *about* which they were written and those *in* which they were composed. They contain historical narratives, legends, poems, and legal materials.

2. A second great block of historical narrative is contained in the books of Deuteronomy, Joshua, Judges, 1-2 Samuel and 1-2 Kings. The book of Deuteronomy professes to contain three speeches by Moses on the plains of Moab just before his death and the crossing of the Hebrews over the Jordan. This book (or a large portion of it) was very probably the "book of the law" which formed the basis of the reforms of King Josiah in 621 B.C., as related in 2 Kings 22—23. It had been written some years before that time, and embodied some old materials; it contains both historical narrative and legal prescriptions, civil and religious.

The remaining books of this block are more properly historical narrative, relating the crossing of the Jordan by the Hebrews, their conquest and settlement of Canaan, the establishment of the monarchy, and the history of the united monarchy and then of the two kingdoms of Israel and Judah to the Babylonian Exile. These books were compiled by someone, or a "school," living around 600 B.C., who employed the same style and held many of the same ideas as are found in Deuteronomy. This "Deuteronomist" made use of narratives, many of them very authentic, which had come down to him from earlier times; some scholars believe that some of these materials were from the Yahwist and Elohist who contributed to the Pentateuch. The Deuteronomist selected and edited the older materials in accord with his own ideas. One basic idea was that sacrificial worship should be offered to Yahweh only in the temple of Jerusalem; he therefore condemned all kings of the northern kingdom because they allowed worship in their sanctuaries. Another fundamental idea was that loyalty to Yahweh always brings national success and prosperity, and disloyalty brings punishment and disaster. We can readily see that these books cover a large part of the history of Israel as it is known to us, and that the viewpoint of the Deuteronomic historian had great influence in

interpreting the events that took place in Israel before the Exile.
3. A third block of historical narrative is that found in 1-2
Chronicles, Ezra, and Nehemiah. These books come from an
editor (or group of editors) who probably lived in the fourth
century B.C., known generally as the Chronicler. 1-2 Chronicles
cover the same period of time as the two groups of narrative
described above, beginning with Adam and ending with the
decree of the Persian king Cyrus permitting the Jews to return
to their homeland (538 B.C.). The history from Adam to Saul
is covered in very summary fashion with little more than a
listing of names. The Chronicler devoted many pages to the
life and reign of David, greatly enhancing his importance in
the founding of the temple and its worship. The rest of the
history is necessarily told in abbreviated form. The two books
of Ezra and Nehemiah supplement 1-2 Chronicles by describing the return of the Jews to their homeland, the rebuilding of
the temple, and the careers of Nehemiah and Ezra. A few
scholars believe Ezra himself was the Chronicler. Whoever
he was, he made use of the earlier books of 1-2 Samuel and
1-2 Kings, the memoirs of Nehemiah, and various other
sources now unknown to us. Because it is possible to compare
1-2 Chronicles with the earlier books, we can readily see that
the Chronicler has written idealized history, often omitting
matters that did not fit into his scheme, and rewriting events
to make them accord with his own ideas and interests. He had
a great interest in the music and personnel of the postexilic
temple, and wanted to make of David the founder of the
temple ritual. Sometimes the Chronicler preserves valuable
material not available to the authors of Samuel and Kings, and
the books of Ezra and Nehemiah are of great value for the
history of the postexilic era.

This survey of the historical books of the Old Testament
should show that they are not really books of "history" in the
same sense as books written by a professional historian today.

They do not intend to be objective and to set forth simply a chronicle of happenings. They are interpretations of events, presenting not individual interpretations, but the understanding which the Israelites at various periods had of their own past. Some parts of these books are more "objective" than others; such sections may be used to recover more precisely what actually happened than others. Generally speaking, the Deuteronomist gives a more reliable account of events than the Chronicler, and J is much closer to the events about which he writes than P.

The historical books of the Old Testament are far more valuable as they are than they would be if they sought merely to chronicle in bare and objective fashion "what actually happened." They show us what the events of the past meant to the Israelites; this meaning is important for us, much more important and more interesting than a dry chronicle would be. These historians of Israel saw the action of their God in the events of Israel's life. We should be interested in knowing both what happened and how the Israelites understood and interpreted their history.

The Patriarchal Age

While the history of the Hebrews as a *people* began with Moses, and their history as a *state* began with Saul and David, the Israelites looked back to Abraham as their forefather. They told legends about him and his descendants, Isaac, Jacob, and Jacob's twelve sons, which are now preserved in Genesis 12—50. Above all they emphasized the promises which were made by God to Abraham, that he would give to him a land, bless him with numerous descendants, and through his descendants bless all the families of the earth. Abraham is represented as wealthy, generous, and faithful. His grandson Jacob was a different type of person: religious in his own way, but wily and crafty, not above deceiving his blind father and his father-in-law. Among the sons of Jacob, Joseph stood out as a man of high moral character and great administrative efficiency.

As we read the patriarchal narratives, we should not think of them as factual stories, but rather as legends. Abraham may have lived five hundred years before Moses; even if Moses wrote Genesis (as we have seen is not likely), he could hardly have known the details of the period with great accuracy. Since, as is most likely, the first person who wrote down the patriarchal legends (the Yahwist) lived in the tenth century B.C., he was separated from Abraham by seven or eight hundred years, and the Priestly writer was separated by thirteen hundred years.

Under such circumstances it is difficult for us to assess the historical element in the patriarchal narratives. Some of the figures in these narratives should be considered as representative types rather than as actual individuals. For example, Esau represents the nation of Edom, and stories about him were told to show how the Hebrews got the better of the Edomites (Genesis 25:30; 36:8). Ishmael represents the marauding nomads of the desert, "a wild ass of a man, his hand against every man and every man's hand against him" (Genesis 16:12). Many of the sons of Jacob are little more than names to us, and they probably represent tribes. The wanderings of the patriarchs may represent tribal and racial movements. Furthermore, some of the legends in Genesis may have been told to explain phenomena of nature. The story about Lot's wife turning into a pillar of salt (Genesis 19:26) was told to account for a well-known salt pillar at the southern end of the Dead Sea, and the stories about Sodom and Gomorrah were likely told to account for the strange geological features of the Dead Sea region. Some stories were told to explain the origin of names; the story of Jacob's wrestling with an angel was intended to account for the origin of the place-name

Peniel and the personal name Israel, as well as for a dietary practice of the Hebrews (Genesis 32:22-32).

Nevertheless, we must point out that archaeological discoveries relating to the second millennium have tended to confirm the general accuracy of the background or *milieu* of the patriarchal narratives for that period. Many of the names of persons and places in these narratives have been found in extrabiblical documents (though we cannot in any single case connect the name specifically with the biblical person), and many of the customs portrayed in these narratives are known to have existed in the second millennium. We may affirm that individuals such as Abraham, Jacob, and Joseph *could* have lived in that time, even if we have no confirmation from outside the Bible of a single event or person in Genesis 12—50. While the chronology of this period is uncertain, we may not be far wrong in assuming that the earliest of the patriarchs lived in the ninteenth or eighteenth century B.C.; Abraham may have lived near the time of the great Babylonian king and lawgiver, Hammurabi (1728-1686 B.C.). The stories about Joseph may reflect the career of a Semitic government official during the time when the Hyksos were rulers in Egypt (1730-1570 B.C.). Some scholars would place the patriarchal period much later, but these dates seem to correspond best with the biblical narratives.

The patriarchs worshiped many gods. The narrator we call J says that "men began to call upon the name of Yahweh" in the time of Seth (Genesis 4:26), and he has the patriarchs worshiping Yahweh. This, however, is contrary to the traditions preserved by E and P (Exodus 3:15; 6:3), who assert that the name of Yahweh was revealed for the first time to Moses. The latter tradition is more probable, and we should therefore not think of the patriarchs as followers of Yahweh.

They were polytheists who adopted the religion of the Canaanites to a large extent when they came into that land.

One of the principal deities they revered was the Canaanite high god, El, who is named with various titles or adjectives— *El Elyon,* translated as "God Most High" (Genesis 14:19-20), *El Roi,* "God of seeing" (Genesis 16:13), *El Shaddai,* "God Almighty" (Genesis 17:1; 28:3 etc.), and *El Olam,* "Everlasting God" (Genesis 21:33). Some of these names were later applied to Yahweh, but the patriarchs themselves did not make such an identification.

The distinctive feature of the patriarchs' religion was their worship of special patron deities. The Genesis narratives suggest in several places that each of the major patriarchs received a revelation from a particular deity whom that patriarch considered to be his divine patron and protector, whose worship he passed on to his son and later descendants. Thus, Isaac worshiped a god known as "the Fear of Isaac" (Genesis 31:42), Jacob worshiped "the Mighty One of Jacob" (Genesis 49:24), and Abraham's patron deity was probably known as "the Shield of Abram" (Genesis 15:1). These gods were not attached to places or to particular sanctuaries, but were related to individuals. Such a religion was well suited to the wandering type of life led by the patriarchs, for they could worship these gods in many places, and they looked to them for guidance and protection in their wanderings.

In this age there was no special priesthood; the patriarchs served as priests, offering sacrifice for themselves and their families. They built altars in open-air sanctuaries, and on some occasions erected sacred pillars, either as memorials to the deities or as images of the gods. Abraham is reported to have given a tithe to Melchizedek, the priest-king of Salem (Jerusalem); whether this is in fact an early, authentic report is impossible to determine.

The Israelites looked back upon the age of the patriarchs as a time of preparation, when their ancestors received promises of future greatness. Abraham became to them a prime example of faith, since he went into an unknown country at the command of God, and there remained faithful and obedient to him in his life. Jacob incorporated some of the qualities they admired, but we must not suppose that they admired all of the characteristics he possessed. When in a later ritual they recounted in brief form their history, they said: "A wandering Aramean was my father..." (Deuteronomy 26:5), with reference to Jacob and his wanderings (though some scholars believe they referred to Abraham). Joseph was a model of conduct, and one in whose accomplishments they felt great pride. His life was an example of the guiding providence of God, for Joseph could say at the end of his life to his brothers: "As for you, you meant evil against me; but God meant it for good, to bring it about that many people should be kept alive, as they are today" (Genesis 50:20).

The Age of Moses

"Now there arose a new king over Egypt, who did not know Joseph" (Exodus 1:8). With these words we are introduced to a new period in the life of the Hebrews: their servitude and oppression in Egypt, their deliverance under the hand of Moses, the making of a covenant at Mount Sinai, and their wandering to the border of Canaan.

The Pharaoh who oppressed the Hebrews may have been Ramses II. His character was such that he was capable of the kind of oppression the Bible describes, and the store cities Pithom and Raamses (Exodus 1:11) were apparently built in his time by Hebrew slaves. Ramses II reigned a long time, 1290-1224 B.C. He spent much of his reign having massive monuments—temples and statues—erected for his own glory. At the site of Raamses he had erected a colossal statue of himself ninety feet high. He took over the statues of some former Pharaohs, substituting his own name for theirs. Yet, his buildings were erected hastily and with poor workmanship, and during his long reign his indolence contributed to the decline of the Egyptian empire.

Moses was the Hebrew leader who arose to challenge the Egyptian Pharaoh and lead the Hebrews out of Egypt and mold them into a people bound in a covenant with Yahweh. Moses is a biblical figure who has been deeply encrusted by legend. Yet, through the legends we behold a man who was a commanding leader, one of the handful of geniuses in Israelite history. He was a patient, persistent, and resourceful leader, and a spiritual pioneer.

The general outline of Moses' career is well known. Born of Hebrew parents, he is reported to have been brought up as a son of the Pharaoh's daughter. After an attempt to defend a fellow Hebrew from injustice, he fled to the desert of Midian. There he married, and had a critical religious experience, which is told in Exodus 3. In that experience at the burning bush he became convinced that Yahweh was a deity powerful enough to free the Hebrews from Egyptian bondage, and he was willing in the name of Yahweh to be their leader. After a contest with the Egyptian king and a great Passover celebration, Moses led the Israelites out of Egypt, across the Red Sea, and through the desert to Mount Sinai.

The Hebrews came to look upon the exodus from Egypt as the mightiest of all the acts of Yahweh in the redemption of Israel. Whatever the role of Moses may have been, and whatever the actual circumstances surrounding the exodus, they were convinced that it was Yahweh who, "with a mighty hand and outstretched arm," redeemed them from Egypt.

As modern men we may be interested in seeking to recover what actually happened at this time. The Hebrew name for the body of water which the Hebrews crossed, *yām sûf*, should not be translated "Red Sea," but "Reed Sea" or "Papyrus Marsh." It was certainly not the northern arm of the Red Sea known today as the Gulf of Suez; it was very likely a shallow body of water, or only a marsh, at the southern end of Lake Menzaleh or the northern end of Lake Timsah. In the earliest account of the crossing of the Reed Sea, as told by J, Yahweh drove the sea back by a strong east wind all night, thus making the sea dry land. Yahweh clogged the wheels of the Egyptian chariots in the mud so that they drove heavily, and the Egyptians decided to flee because they saw that Yahweh was fighting for the Israelites. In the morning the waters returned to their usual flow when the wind died down, and Yahweh routed the Egyptians (Exodus 14:21b, 24-25, 27b). This description may sound to us much like a "natural incident," but the Hebrews were sure from very early times that it was Yahweh who led them out of Egypt and through the sea, setting them on the way to Sinai.

The Hebrews had as their goal the sacred mountain on which Moses had received the revelation of Yahweh at the burning bush; they wished to go there to sacrifice to Yahweh. Mount Sinai (or Horeb, as it is occasionally called) is a most important place in the history of Israel, and indeed in the history of the world. It is unfortunate—but relatively unimportant—that we do not really know its location. Since the fourth century A.D. tradition has said it was located at the southern end of the Peninsula of Sinai, at Jebel Musa. This is a late tradition, and does not seem probable. It is more likely that Sinai was located in the northern part of the peninsula, near Kadesh-barnea, a very important oasis at which the Hebrews encamped for a long time; we cannot point out its exact site.

At Sinai the Hebrews made a covenant with Yahweh. As the Pentateuch is now arranged, the long section extending from Exodus 19 to Numbers 10:11 records the events which took place and the laws that were set forth at Sinai. We have seen above (pp. 48-50) that the Pentateuch was produced over a long period of time; much of the material in this long section (including all of Leviticus) comes in fact from the Priestly writing of the sixth century B.C. Because Moses was considered to be *the* lawgiver of Israel, virtually all law was attributed to him. It can readily be shown that most of the laws in this long section originated after the Hebrews entered Canaan, and were designed to regulate their life in that land. Yet, Moses *was* a lawgiver, and very important events did take place at Sinai.

Above all, the covenant between Yahweh and the people of Israel was formed here, with Moses as mediator of the covenant. The ceremony by which the covenant was ratified is recorded in Exodus 24:1-11. The ceremony included the sacrificing of animals, a rite by which the blood of the sacrifice was used to represent symbolically the binding together of Yahweh and the people, and a sacred covenant meal in the presence of Yahweh. At this time Moses read from a "book of the covenant," and the people responded by saying, "All that the Lord has spoken we will do, and we will be obedient."

In the next chapter we shall discuss the teaching of the Old Testament concerning Yahweh as a covenant God. Here we emphasize the fact that the covenant meant a binding together of various tribes and clans to form a people, and the binding of this people in a close bond with their God, Yahweh. At Sinai groups of "Hebrews" came together who had previously been separate in their culture and religious life, and here they became a "people of Yahweh." They agreed together to worship and obey Yahweh, and him only, and they believed that Yahweh took upon himself the obligation to lead and guide them in their life together—in brief, to be their God. From Sinai on, the Israelites were a covenant people, bound to worship Yahweh alone as their deity, and obligated to serve him with moral obedience.

Of all the laws and regulations attributed to Moses at Sinai, the familiar Ten Commandments (Exodus 20:1-17;

Deuteronomy 5:6-21) are the set most likely to have originated at this time. In the time of Moses the Ten Commandments would have been somewhat shorter than they now are. They would have lacked the expansions in Exodus 20:4-6, 7, 9-11, 12, and 17 and corresponding verses in Deuteronomy 5. Thus they would have consisted of ten brief sentences, stating the obligations of the Israelites to Yahweh and to one another, mostly in negative form. The Ten Commandments do not comprise a law *code,* for they do not cover all possible situations and do not stipulate any penalties. The penalty implied for breaking one of the commandments is the wrath of Yahweh and of the covenant community. The Ten Commandments represent the religious and moral terms of the covenant which the Israelites freely agreed to observe; they expressed the will of Yahweh which the people of Israel said they would obey.

When the Israelites left Sinai, they wandered in the wilderness for "forty years," a round number representing a generation. We are not to suppose that they were continuously on the move during this time. They spent long periods at oases, most notably in the vicinity of Kadesh-barnea, immediately to the south of Canaan. They attempted to enter the land of Canaan from the south, but were repulsed (Numbers 14:40-45). Then they decided to attempt to enter Canaan from the east. Going around the lands of Moab and Edom, which in the thirteenth century B.C. were becoming settled kingdoms, they made their first conquests in the hilly, forested region of Gilead, and subsequently crossed the Jordan, not far from Jericho. But Moses died on the border of the promised land. His courageous and deeply devoted leadership had held the Hebrews together in a period that was very creative, but filled with numerous difficulties. Moses had to face both enemies without, and complainings and rebellions within his own people, and his ability was sufficient for his task.

Conquest and Settlement of Canaan

When the Hebrews entered Canaan, they found that land inhabited by a people who had been there a long time, possessing a material culture much higher than their own. When the spies reported that "the people who dwell in the land are strong, and the cities are fortified and very large" (Numbers 13:28), they were relating facts which have been verified by modern archaeologists.

The term "Canaanite" as a designation for the natives of Canaan is not very precise. The Old Testament writers usually employed that name, or "Amorites," to designate the Semitic inhabitants of Palestine at the time of the Hebrew conquest. There were also some non-Semitic inhabitants, such as Hittites, Horites, and Philistines, the last-named coming into Palestine at approximately the same time as the Hebrews. The Semitic Canaanites had been in the land for two thousand years. They were not unified politically, but were organized in numerous city-states; during much of the second millennium their city-states were under Egyptian political domination.

The Canaanites had a religion of their own, and in the course of time it was to have much influence upon that of the Israelites. Since they were an agricultural people, their religion necessarily centered around their life as farmers. They sought through religious rites to secure good weather, abundant crops, plentiful herds, and other needs of their way of living. Their religion was polytheistic, and many of their deities were personifications of forces of nature. Their principal deity at this time was Baal, a god of the weather and of fertility. Among the goddesses mentioned in the Old Testament are Ashtoreth and Ashera, the latter being also the name of a sacred wooden pole or wooden image of the goddess. The phrase "the Baals and the Ashtaroth," found in Judges, stands for the totality of the Canaanite deities.

The Canaanites offered numerous sacrifices in their worship. As farmers they could afford to offer up their animals, since making a sacrifice often entailed little more than slaughter of animals in preparation for religious feasts. They observed festivals that marked the seasons of the agricultural year, particularly at the time of the spring and autumn harvests.

The Old Testament account of the conquest and settlement of Canaan by the Hebrews is found in the books of Joshua and Judges, and the early chapters of 1 Samuel. There is a "standard" account of the conquest in Joshua which describes it as taking place within a short time, by the unified tribes under the leadership of Joshua, after which the land was divided up among the tribes. This simple account of a whirlwind conquest is contradicted, however, by statements in the first chapter of Judges, which are supported by scattered passages in Joshua, such as 15:13-19; 16:10; and 17:11-13. Those passages indicate the conquest was made by individual tribes, and they state over and over that certain Canaanite strongholds could not be taken, for the Canaanite chariots of iron were too much for the Israelites.

Archaeological discoveries in Palestine help us reconstruct the history of the conquest, and they support the view that the conquest took a much longer time than the "standard" account in Joshua indicates. Excavations at several towns in Palestine show they were destroyed in the latter part of the thirteenth century B.C.; these include Bethel, Lachish, Debir, and Hazor. Other towns were not destroyed until succeeding centuries. The first wave of conquest took place in the thirteenth century B.C., especially in the central highland region of Canaan, which was not thickly populated at this time. In the succeeding centuries the Hebrews gradually extended their power over the territory to the south and the north, and last of all conquered the strong Canaanite cities along the plain of Jezreel and the coastal plain. The conquest was not complete until the time of David, who brought large areas into the empire he ruled.

The conquest was not entirely by force of arms. Joshua 9 tells how the incoming Hebrews made a covenant with the people of Gibeon, and spared their lives; they may have made similar agreements with other peoples, and thus conquered them by diplomacy rather than by military measures. There were times when the Hebrews fought with one another, and they undoubtedly lost some battles to the Canaanites. Their final success resulted in part from the divisions among the Canaanite city-states and the attempt of the Philistines to gain a foothold in Canaan at the same time; it resulted also from the vigor of the Hebrews, and the sense of unity given them by their common worship of Yahweh. The whole period of the conquest and settlement lasted nearly three hundred years (from about 1250 B.C. to the time of David, who ruled 1000-960 B.C.).

Sometime in this period the Israelites formed a sacral federation of twelve tribes, with a central sanctuary for the worship of Yahweh by all the tribes, which was located at Shiloh (and perhaps successively at other places). To this sacral, or religious, tribal organization some scholars give a name which is derived from Greek, "amphictyony." The bond which united the separate tribes was their common worship of Yahweh, and each tribe probably had responsibility for the worship at the shrine for one month out of the year. Worship was carried on, of course, at other local sanctuaries, but at the central shrine sacrifices were offered by all the tribes.

When they came into Canaan, the Hebrews adopted some of the practices and even beliefs of the Canaanites. When they settled as farmers, they began to offer more frequent animal sacrifices, and they took over some of the rites and ceremonies used by the Canaanites, since their own worship in the desert had been very simple. They took over the seasonal festivals of the Canaanites, giving them the names of the Feast of Unleavened Bread (united with their Passover), the Feast of Weeks (which subsequently came to be known as Pentecost), and the fall harvest Feast of Tabernacles. Some of the Hebrews deserted Yahweh to worship Baal, and some of them simply added Baal worship to their Yahweh worship. Eventually the leaders in Hebrew religion came to believe that Yahweh could provide all of the benefits for which the Canaanites worshiped Baal (such as control of the weather and the gift of fertility), and that he was a deity sufficient for all their needs.

A distinctive feature of the Israelite worship in this period, according to some scholars, was an annual festival of covenant renewal at the central sanctuary. This type of ceremony is not described in detail, but is suggested by passages such as Joshua 8:30-35; 24; Deuteronomy 11:26-32; 26:1-11; and 27. In this festival, there was a recital of the mighty acts of Yahweh on behalf of his people, such as the exodus from Egypt and the conquest of the land of Canaan; a reading of the Law, such as the Ten Commandments; and a renewal of the covenant through a reaffirmation by the people of their intention to obey Yahweh's commands. In this type of worship, emphasis was laid upon a recognition of what Yahweh had done for Israel, and upon Israel's response to him by obedience to his law.

A very important religious object in the period of conquest and settlement was the ark. Whatever else the ark may have been, it was a symbol to the Israelites of the presence with them of Yahweh as a god of war. Its full name was "the ark of Yahweh of hosts enthroned on the cherubim" (1 Samuel 4:4; 2 Samuel 6:2). In this phrase "hosts" meant originally the hosts of Israel's armies, not the heavenly hosts. When the Israelites went out to battle, they took the ark with them and said: "Arise, O LORD, and let thy enemies be scattered;

and let them that hate thee flee before thee." When it returned to camp with them, they said: "Return, O LORD, to the ten thousand thousands of Israel." (Numbers 10:35-36.) On one occasion the Philistines captured the ark and inflicted a severe defeat upon the Hebrews, but the presence of the ark caused so much affliction among the Philistines that they returned it to the Israelites (1 Samuel 4:10—7:2). The ark was at Shiloh when the central sanctuary was there (1 Samuel 3:3), and it was eventually installed in the temple built by Solomon in Jerusalem.

We do not know just what the ark looked like. The most probable conjecture is that it was a portable throne for the invisible Yahweh. The throne was the "mercy seat" of Exodus 25:17, 21; it was supported by cherubim, figures that were partly human and partly animal (probably winged, human-headed lions) carved on the sides of the ark.

The leaders of Israel in the period of settlement in Canaan are known as "judges." Their careers are described in the book with the same name. The name "judge" is somewhat unfortunate, for it may suggest to us a man who sits on a bench and decides cases at law. The Hebrew judges did much more than that. They were men who had been filled with the spirit of Yahweh, and thus empowered to carry out mighty exploits in his name. Often they led the Israelites in successful battle against an enemy and then ruled over them for a period of time. Deciding cases at law may have been one of their functions, but it was not their main function. Sometimes they were leaders of only one tribe, but some were leaders of groups of tribes or the whole federation. Some were men of much higher stature than others. Samson, for example, performed famous deeds of individual valor against the Philistines, but never won a real victory over them and was not a ruler of Israel.

The United Monarchy

The loose tribal organization formed by the Israelites had to give way to a stronger type of union under a kingship, largely because of the pressure from the Philistines, who were threatening to take over the land of Canaan and subjugate Israel. The Philistines were a people of Indo-European origin who entered Palestine at approximately the same time as the Hebrews who had made the exodus from Egypt. They were part of a great movement of Sea Peoples from the Aegean islands and coastlands who swept down into Syria-Palestine and attempted to invade Egypt, but without success. The Philistines had a higher material culture than the Hebrews, with a monopoly on the manufacture of iron weapons, and their union in a confederation of five city-states was stronger than the Israelites sacral federation.

The two books of Samuel (originally one book in Hebrew) constitute an unusually valuable source of information concerning the establishment of the monarchy and the reigns of Saul and David, and the reign of Solomon is covered in 1 Kings 2—11. These books come to us from the hands of the Deuteronomic editor. First and Second Samuel contain two strands of narrative, the earlier of which is much more authentic than the latter. The early strand indicates that the kingdom resulted from the initiative of Yahweh in providing Israel with a king (1 Samuel 9:15-17; 10:1-2), whereas the later strand says that the anointing of a king meant the rejection of Yahweh (1 Samuel 8:7; 10:19). Discounting these and other inconsistencies between the two strands, we can get an excellent picture of this period.

Saul won his position in much the same manner as the older judges had. When Israelites east of the Jordan were threatened by the Ammonites, "the spirit of God came mightily upon Saul" (1 Samuel 11:6), and he rallied the Hebrews and led them in victory against the Ammonites. Thereafter he was acclaimed king at the sanctuary in Gilgal. Samuel, a highly regarded prophet-judge, inspired Saul and at first supported him in his reign.

Saul was a disappointment to Samuel and his fellow Israelites. He was a man of large stature, but he was primarily a military chieftain, with little administrative skill. He won victories over Ammonites and Amalekites, and led in battle against the Philistines, but won over the latter no decisive victories. He ruled a small territory from his capital of Gibeah, a few miles north of Jerusalem.

Saul was impulsive and superstitious, and during his reign seems to have become emotionally and mentally unstable. The Old Testament says that the spirit of Yahweh departed from him, "and an evil spirit from Yahweh tormented him" (1 Samuel 16:14). He tried to murder David and his own son Jonathan; he broke with Samuel; and toward the end of his life he consulted one of the witches whom he himself had sought to outlaw. The sense of rejection by Yahweh through his representative Samuel and the rivalry with David doubtless contributed to his breakdown.

David was a man of far superior talents who was the real founder of the Israelite monarchy. Under him Israel became a true nation, and in fact a small empire. No Hebrew king ruled over more territory than David, and no one made a more lasting impression upon the history and traditions of the nation. He was a well-rounded man, a musician and poet, a diplomat as well as a military general, with ability to inspire loyalty from many kinds of persons. If he had glaring personal faults (exhibited in his committing adultery with Bathsheba and contriving the murder of her husband), they serve to show he was a flesh-and-blood human being rather than a plaster saint.

David won his kingdom in part by diplomacy and in part by military force. While he was an outlaw from Saul's court he became a vassal of the Philistine ruler, Achish of Gath. He ingratiated himself with the leaders of Judah, who anointed him king in Hebron at the death of Saul. Upon the death of Saul's son two years later, David was anointed king over Israel. One of his first acts was to capture Jerusalem from the Jebusites (a Canaanite group that had held it before this time), and make it his capital. He settled scores with the Philistines, probably by making a treaty of mutual nonaggression with them after showing them his military strength, and they were henceforth confined to southwestern Palestine. He decisively defeated the remaining Canaanites, and made subservient to him the surrounding nations of Edom, Moab, Ammon, and Damascus. He organized his kingdom along the lines used in Egypt, with a standing army, a priesthood, and various cabinet officials.

David was a loyal devotee of Yahweh throughout his life. Even during his outlaw days he "consulted Yahweh" as to what course he should take, and after he became king, he served on occasion as a priest to make sacrifices to Yahweh. His most important contribution to religion was to bring up to Jerusalem the ark of Yahweh and install it in a tent sanctuary. After the Philistines returned the ark to the Hebrews, it was allowed to remain at Kirjath-jearim during the reign of Saul, who paid no attention to it. By his action David promoted the worship of Yahweh, made Jerusalem a religious center, and established ties with the older traditions which had been built around the ark.

David took steps to organize the priesthood, with Abiathar and Zadok as the principal priests. In his reign there arose a new type of prophet. Saul himself had been an ecstatic prophet, indulging in an abnormal type of behavior described in 1 Samuel 10:5-13. In the time of David there were prophets who delivered to the king "the word of the LORD" with great ethical significance. The outstanding example is Nathan the prophet, who rebuked King David in the name of Yahweh for his sin with Bathsheba; it is very significant that David accepted the rebuke and repented of his sin (2 Samuel 12: 1-25).

Israelite tradition attributed to David the authorship of many of the Psalms. This tradition rests upon the fact that David was a musician who played the lyre at Saul's court (1 Samuel 16:23), and that he did write the poems lamenting the deaths of Saul and Jonathan (2 Samuel 1:17-27), and of Abner (2 Samuel 3:33-34). Unfortunately we have no way of determining whether David actually composed any of the poems in the Psalter.

David's son, King Solomon, was a very different type of ruler. He was born in the royal palace in Jerusalem, the second son of David and Bathsheba. He was no soldier, and did not need to be. The task of Solomon was to organize the kingdom he inherited from his father, build up commerce and industry, and form commercial and political relationships with other nations. Solomon succeeded in raising his kingdom to an apex of material prosperity and increasing its prestige among the nations of his time, but he did so at the cost of the oppression of his people and even the loss of some territory.

Solomon strengthened the national organization by adding to the royal cabinet and dividing the land into twelve administrative districts for purposes of taxation. He exploited the iron and copper mines in the region of the Dead Sea, and made a refinery and factory at Ezion-Geber, which became also the base for his fleet of trading ships. He carried on trade with many countries, including Ophir—roughly the same as modern Somaliland on the east coast of Africa plus some of the southwestern coast of Arabia. The purpose of the visit of the Arabian Queen of Sheba was to make agreements concerning trade relations and caravan routes. Solomon carried on an extensive trade in horses and chariots, buying chariots in Egypt and horses in Cilicia (Asia Minor), and selling them to the kings of Aramean and Hittite city-states north of Israel. He made a marriage alliance with Egypt and no doubt other countries; in this manner Solomon secured most of the wives in his large harem.

The temple in Jerusalem was Solomon's most significant contribution to the religion of Israel. Because there was no Hebrew tradition for the erection of buildings such as Solomon wished this one to be, he made a treaty with the Phoenician king of Tyre to provide him with skilled workmen, architects, and cedar wood. Since the Phoenicians were essentially Canaanites, we may say that the basic architecture and much of the symbolism were borrowed from the Canaanites. As such it was offensive to many of the strictest worshipers of Yahweh, who objected to such foreign influence and believed that a tent sanctuary was most appropriate for their deity. At first the Jerusalem temple was a royal chapel, intended primarily for the worship of the king and his household. It gradually attained prestige and importance, and in the reign of King Josiah was made the exclusive, central place of worship for the whole nation.

Solomon placed in the Holy of Holies of his temple the ark of Yahweh, which symbolized the deity's residence there. The inmost room was dark, without windows, and the idea that Yahweh dwelled in that place is most clearly stated in the poem uttered by the king at the time of the dedication of the temple, as it is preserved in 1 Kings 8:12-13;

"The LORD has set the sun in the heavens.
but has said that he would dwell in thick darkness.

I have built thee an exalted house,
a place for thee to dwell in for ever."

Solomon became famous for his wisdom, and a large part
of the Book of Proverbs, the Song of Solomon, and Ecclesiastes were attributed to him. Thus he was considered the
father or patron of "wisdom literature." While it is certain
that he did not compose all of this literature, he may have
encouraged the collection and composition of proverbial sayings and other literature of this general category. The account
in 1 Kings describes him as unusually wise and shrewd in
deciding difficult cases at law (3:16-28), and says he uttered
three thousand proverbs and a thousand and five songs (4:32).
Since wisdom literature flourished especially in Egypt, and
Solomon had close ties with that country, it may be that he
was influenced by the Egyptians in this area.

As a patron of culture Solomon may also have encouraged
the writing of the first national epic of Israel, which we have
seen was composed by the Yahwist, or J (see above p. 48).
Conditions were ripe in Solomon's time for the writing of such
a work, for there was material prosperity and a strong national
consciousness. The Yahwist collected the various traditions
of his people from many sources, both written and oral, and
wrote an epic which began with the account of
Yahweh's creation of man in the Garden of Eden, and man's
first sin that led to his expulsion from the garden (Genesis
2:4b—3:24), and continued down to the death of Moses. If
we may assign to this writer the early materials in Joshua-
Judges and the early strand of narrative in 1 and 2 Samuel,
then he carried the story down to the beginning of Solomon's
reign. This was absolutely the first *history* ever written in the
literature of the world. The Yahwist wrote a narrative that
was magnificent in its sweep, in classical Hebrew prose, and
depicted Yahweh as the deity who created the world and

guided man's destiny from the beginning down to the time of his making for himself a covenant people through whom he might bless all mankind.

The Divided Monarchy

The nation was split in two upon the death of Solomon. The split must be attributed in large part to the oppressive policies of Solomon, who had made his subjects work at forced labor on his massive building enterprises and other projects, and contribute heavily from their agricultural products. His son Rehoboam acted stupidly in promising the Israelites only heavier burdens.

Thereafter Palestine was divided into two kingdoms: Judah in the south and Israel (sometimes called Ephraim, from the name of a large tribe) in the north. Israel continued to exist as an independent kingdom for almost exactly two hundred years, until 721 B.C., when Samaria was captured by King Sargon and Israel was made into a province of the Assyrian empire. Judah retained its independence for nearly a century and a half longer, until Jerusalem was captured by King Nebuchadnezzar and Judah was made a province of the Chaldean (or Neo-Babylonian) empire (587 B.C.). Judah lasted longer because its land was smaller, more isolated, and thus less attractive to foreign invaders; and because the Davidic dynasty in Judah was stronger and more stable than the government of Israel. The northern kingdom was always more subject to foreign influences in its religion than Judah, and Canaanite Baalism was stronger there, though Judah frequently strayed from pure Yahwism.

We do not have space here to trace in detail the history of the two nations in this long period of time. The Old Testament gives us the names of the kings that ruled the two nations, but some of them are little more than names; for only a few do we have much information. The Deuteronomic editor of 1 and 2 Kings was more interested in religious history than in political and social history, and gives special attention to kings who made religious reforms. We can supplement his information from other sources, such as the annals of Assyrian kings and archaelogical discoveries in Palestine.

During this era, the Hebrew kingdoms came into frequent conflict with other world powers. In the reigns of David and Solomon several Aramean kingdoms had been established to the north and northeast, most notably the kingdom of Syria around Damascus. This kingdom carried on intermittent warfare with the Hebrews until its own destruction in the eighth century.

The great world power for most of the period was the Assyrian empire. That empire enjoyed its greatest prominence between the accession to the throne of Tiglath-pileser III in 745 B.C., and the fall of Nineveh, its capital, in 612 B.C. Thereafter, the dominant world power was the Chaldean (or Neo-Babylonian) empire, whose best-known king was Nebuchadnezzar. The Assyrians brought about the fall of the northern kingdom, and an Assyrian king invaded Judah and besieged Jerusalem in 701 B.C. He would have captured the city if King Hezekiah had not surrendered to him. One reason that Judah lasted longer than Israel was that the Judaean kings at critical times paid tribute to Assyria and saved their nation from destruction.

Egypt was relatively weak throughout this era. From time to time, however, the Hebrew kings sought to play power politics by allying themselves with Egypt against the empire which ruled in Mesopotamia. It was as a result of such attempts that both Samaria and Jerusalem fell and the Hebrew kingdoms lost their existence as independent nations.

The outstanding individuals in the religion of this long period were the Hebrew prophets. Since they were spokesmen for Yahweh to their own people, we can see mirrored in their messages many important aspects of Hebrew life.

Elijah lived in the reign of Ahab in the middle of the ninth century B.C. In a crucial period, when Queen Jezebel was an active evangelist for the religion of her deities, the Phoenician god Baal and goddess Ashera, Elijah appeared as a fiery and courageous champion of Yahweh. He called upon his people to choose between Yahweh and Baal, and insisted that Yahweh was sufficient for all their needs, including those for which some of them worshiped Baal. His younger contemporary and successor, Elisha, was less important. He was a popular miracle worker, and head of a group of prophets known as "sons of the prophets."

A century later, Amos prophesied at Bethel and other places in the northern kingdom, though he was a native of Tekoa in Judah. He was a shepherd and dresser of sycamore trees who felt the call of Yahweh to prophesy to his people Israel. Amos saw people living in prosperity and ease, and practicing a religion that put emphasis on punctilious offering of sacrifices and other outward rites rather than on moral character. He saw the poor oppressed by the wealthy, and the innocent made the victims of injustice in courts of law. Amos cried out in the name of Yahweh for a religion that would emphasize righteousness and justice in everyday living, and he recognized that Yahweh was concerned with other nations as well as Israel.

Hosea came a little later than Amos. Little is known of his personal life, except of his marriage. His wife, Gomer, proved unfaithful to him and Hosea at first determined to divorce her; but then, in obedience to the command of Yahweh, he decided that he would continue to love her and be her husband. Through his own experience he learned that God had love and compassion for Israel, in spite of Israel's infidelity to him. He called on Israel to love Yahweh in return.

Isaiah was the first great prophet of Judah. He spent his whole life in Jerusalem, prophesying from 742 to around 700 B.C., not only speaking publicly to the people but advising kings of Judah when they consulted him. Isaiah spoke out against the pride of the nation, which put trust in foreign alliances and military measures for safety, and challenged the Judaeans to have faith in Yahweh.

A younger contemporary of Isaiah was Micah, who lived in a village in southwestern Palestine. He represented the rural peasantry, and considered the cities as centers of gross iniquity. He had the courage to prophesy that the day would come when even Jerusalem and its temple would be in ruins.

In the latter part of the seventh century Judah experienced a radical revolution under King Josiah (621 B.C.). A book of the law was found in the temple, and made the basis of far-reaching reforms in the national religious life. All sacrificial worship was confined to the temple in Jerusalem, and all the local sanctuaries were abolished; the temple ritual was purified of foreign influences, especially those imported from Assyria; and attempts were made to incorporate prophetic ideals of justice and charity in the laws of the land. We have seen that this book of the law was very probably the Book of Deuteronomy (or a large portion of it, such as chapters 5—28). Unfortunately, the Deuteronomic reforms were not long-lasting, for the successors of Josiah gave no strong support to their continuance.

Jeremiah was the prophet during Judah's decline and fall. He preached against his nation's false reliance on the temple and its services when the people did not experience moral reformation, and said that their sin was due to "the stubbornness of the evil heart." He took the unpopular position of advocating submission to Babylonia's yoke, for he said Yahweh had given the sovereignty to Babylonia. Jeremiah suffered grievously for his prophecies, at one time being placed in an abandoned cistern with the expectation that he would die of suffocation and starvation. Toward the end of his life he spoke of the time when Yahweh would make with the nation a new covenant, in which he would write the law on men's hearts so that all men would know God directly and experience his forgiveness (Jeremiah 31:31-34).

The prophet Ezekiel lived in Babylonia just before and after the fall of Jerusalem. He prophesied against the pagan practices of Israel in their worship and predicted the fall of the city; after its fall he looked forward to a time of restoration and renewal, and his book presents detailed blueprints of the restored land and temple.

The Babylonian Exile

Babylonian armies had to invade Palestine twice to put down revolts against their authority. The first time, the Judaean king Jehoiachin surrendered the city of Jerusalem, and the Babylonians took him and many of the leading Jews into exile (598 B.C.). The second time the city of Jerusalem held out under siege for a year and a half, and finally was captured (587 B.C.). This time the Babylonians devastated much of the land of Judah and its capital, deported many Jews to Babylonia, and ended the political independence of Judah. They installed a governor in charge of the land, Gedaliah, a member of an old Jewish family.[1]

The fall of Jerusalem and the termination of political independence naturally had great significance for the life and faith of the Jews. The temple and royal palace were in ruins; many people must have thought that Marduk, god of Babylon, had now defeated Yahweh. The people left in Palestine are

---

[1] We speak of the people of Palestine of this and following periods as "Jews." The name is derived from "Judaeans," inhabitants of Judah. For the preexilic period, the people in general are called "Hebrews" or "Israelites." The last-named term is sometimes employed specifically for the inhabitants of the northern kingdom, Israel, to distinguish them from the Judaeans of the south. The religion of the Jews in the postexilic age is often called "Judaism," to distinguish it from the older Israelite or Hebrew religion.

described as "some of the poorest of the land" who remained as vinedressers and plowmen (2 Kings 25:12). The leading citizens were taken into exile in Babylonia. They were not, to be sure, placed in prison or in concentration camps, but rather settled in several cities and given considerable control over their own affairs. The Babylonians were not cruel oppressors over them. But they were in a foreign land. The feelings of many of them are expressed in Psalm 137. They lamented that they could not "sing Yahweh's song in a foreign land," and vowed never to forget Jerusalem. They pronounced a curse on Babylon for destroying their beloved city, saying: "Happy shall he be who takes your little ones and dashes them against the rock!"

As the Jews recovered from the blow that had fallen, a good deal of literature was produced in Palestine and Babylonia. The series of poems in the Book of Lamentations were written, to express the sorrow of the people and their feeling that Yahweh had deserted Zion; yet they also could say:

"The steadfast love of the LORD never ceases, . . .
The LORD is good to those who wait for him" (3:22, 25).

Sometime during the exile or soon thereafter the books of history discussed above (pp. 50-51) were completed by the Deuteronomic historian, bringing the story down to the time that King Jehoiachin was released from prison in Babylon and allowed to dine regularly at the king's table. The Priestly writers (P) composed their work in this century (possibly in Babylonia) adding it to the J and E histories. They sought to preserve the priestly traditions concerning Israel's past, and to set down in writing the laws and regulations concerning worship which had been developed from ancient times in the Jerusalem temple.

The greatest writing of this time comes from an anonymous prophet whom we call the Second Isaiah, or Deutero-Isaiah, because his message is preserved in the latter part of the Book of Isaiah, chapters 40—55. (Some interpreters also attribute to him Isaiah 56—66, but those chapters are probably from later prophets, some of whom were his disciples.) Second Isaiah was one of the greatest prophets and most creative thinkers in ancient Israel. In his message is to be found the highest conception of Yahweh's nature and work before New Testament days.

Second Isaiah believed that it was Yahweh who had decreed the destruction of Jerusalem and the exile of the Jews, as a consequence of their repeated sins against him. But now Yahweh had a message of comfort: his people had paid double for their sins, and Yahweh was about to come to redeem them. The instrument of Yahweh's will was Cyrus, a Persian who had begun his career as head of the little kingdom of Anshan and had embarked upon a successful career of world conquest. Second Isaiah could even speak of Cyrus as Yahweh's "anointed" (45:1)—that is, appointed to carry out his purpose. The Jews would soon be released from captivity in Babylonia and be allowed to return in triumph to Zion. The latter part of Second Isaiah's work (chapters 49—55) may come from the time after Cyrus actually conquered Babylon (539 B.C.) and decreed that the Jews might return.

Second Isaiah proclaimed that Yahweh was not simply the God of the Jews, but the one and only God of the whole world, the God both of nature and of history. Yahweh had created the universe, and had guided the destinies of the peoples, including Israel. The time would come, he said, when all nations would bow before this God.

This prophet created the remarkable figure of the Suffering Servant of Yahweh, depicted especially in four poems, 42:1-4; 49:1-6; 50:4-9; 52:13—53:12. Interpreters differ widely on the question of the identification of this figure. It is clear that in some passages Israel is the Servant (41:8; 49:3);

but in some other passages, most notably chapter 53, the Servant may be an individual of the future. Whoever the Servant may be, Second Isaiah sought by means of this figure to convince men that suffering which is willingly borne may be vicariously redemptive for others: God can work through the suffering of his Servant for the salvation of mankind.

The Persian and Hellenistic Periods

Cyrus fulfilled in limited measure the expectations of Second Isaiah. In October, 539 B.C., one of his generals entered Babylon without a battle, for the policies of the last Chaldean king, Nabonidus, had aroused much disaffection among his subjects. Cyrus soon issued a decree permitting the Jews to return to Jerusalem and ordering the rebuilding of their temple (Ezra 1:2-4; 6:3-5). This was in accord with the policies of Cyrus known from his own records. He was a tolerant ruler, encouraging captive peoples to go back to their native lands, and to return various gods to their proper shrines.

Some of the Jews took advantage of this opportunity, but there was no general exodus from Babylonia to Palestine. Many of the exiles had settled down and adjusted to life in Babylonia, and some had even prospered; they did not really wish to return to Zion and endure all the hardships they would encounter. A small group did return under the leadership of Sheshbazzar, called "the prince of Judah" (Ezra 1:8). They took back to Jerusalem the temple objects which had been stolen by Nebuchadnezzar, but made little or no progress in rebuilding the temple for nearly two decades.

In 520 B.C. there was a great upsurge of interest, promoted by the prophets Haggai and Zechariah, and led by Zerubbabel, governor of Judah, and the high priest Joshua. The two prophets encouraged the Jews to rebuild the temple, promising that Yahweh would bless them in the undertaking. It appears that they also promoted a movement for Jewish political independence, with Zerubbabel as a messianic ruler; chaotic conditions in the Persian empire that attended the accession of the new Persian king, Darius, seemed to present them with a favorable opportunity for such a revolt. It did not succeed; probably the Persians learned of it and removed Zerubbabel. Work on the temple proceeded, and after four years the restored temple was dedicated.

However, the rebuilding of the place of worship did not bring the expected prosperity. Around the year 500 B.C. the prophet Malachi appeared to give renewed encouragement to the Jews. His book shows that the people had become discouraged and were failing to bring the required sacrifices and full tithes, the priesthood was corrupt, and many people were becoming cynical. Malachi called on them to be faithful in their religious observances and await the coming of their Lord.

Within the next century two very important leaders came from Babylonia to infuse new life in the residents of Judah: Ezra and Nehemiah. The books bearing their names have been edited by the Chronicler, and there is some confusion in the order of the events which they record. All things considered, it seems most likely that Nehemiah preceded Ezra; the former first came to Jerusalem in 444 B.C., and the latter in 397 B.C.

Nehemiah was a layman who had been cupbearer to the Persian king, Artaxerxes I, who appointed him governor of Judah. Nehemiah's great work was to lead the people in restoring the wall of Jerusalem. This not only gave them needed military protection, but raised the prestige of Jerusalem and the spirits of the Jews. Nehemiah was a layman who proved to be a very effective leader in the face of strong opposition from some of the people of Jerusalem and from Samaritans in the north.

Ezra was a priest and a scribe skilled in the law of Moses. He enforced a policy of strict racial purity, breaking up the marriage of many of the Jews with foreign women. His outstanding work was to introduce a book, called "the book of the law of Moses," the reading of which is described in Nehemiah 8. This must have been an important work, for its reading led to a great observance of the Feast of Tabernacles and to religious reforms. We do not know for certain what this book was; some interpreters think it was the strand of the Pentateuch we have called P, while others think it was the finished Pentateuch. Whatever it was, we can be sure that around this time the Pentateuch did reach virtually its present form, and that many of the viewpoints promoted in the Priestly writing became dominant in Jewish life. Emphasis was laid on observance of the Law, the temple ritual became very elaborate, Sabbath observance was stressed, and a policy of racial exclusiveness was pursued.

Two little books of the Old Testament apparently were written about the time of Ezra and Nehemiah, to counteract the nationalistic tendencies which they promoted: the Books of Ruth and Jonah. The former is a classic short story, claiming to come from the time of the judges. Its purpose was to show, in an indirect way, that not all foreigners were objectionable, for even king David had Moabite blood, inherited from his great-grandmother Ruth. The Book of Jonah is different from all other prophetic books: it is a story *about* a prophet, not a collection of prophetic messages, and Jonah was a recalcitrant prophet who ran away from his prophetic task, and sulked when his mission was successful. The message of this little book is that God's mercy encompasses even the wicked city of Nineveh, and is expressed toward foreign peoples when they turn to him in repentance. In this story the foreigners are depicted in a far more favorable light than the prophet Jonah.

The Book of Job, a literary classic, may have reached its final form in the Persian period. It contains same ancient materials, and is a composite work. It deals with one of the most difficult of all religious problems: why does God allow the innocent to suffer? Job was a righteous and upright man, but he suffered miserably. He did not claim perfection, but could not see that his sin justified the depth of suffering he experienced. The book clearly rejects the orthodox view that suffering is punishment for sin, and suggests several alternative solutions. The principal one is that given in chapters 38-42: Job is granted a vision of God as the Creator and Sustainer of the universe, and with this vision he is satisfied, for in such a God he has learned to have faith, trusting that his ways are just and right.

The Book of Esther has its setting in the Persian empire, but may have been written later, even as late as the second century B.C. This is a strange book for the Bible: it does not once mention the name of God, it is filled with cruelties, and not a single noble character appears on its pages. It is a thoroughly secular book, presenting the legendary basis for the Jewish observance of the feast of Purim. While it may rest on some historical incident, it contains fictional embellishments, and the historicity cannot be confirmed from any source.

The Persian rule of the Jews in Palestine lasted from 538 to the conquest of the land by Alexander the Great, 332 B.C. The Persian empire was given a strong organization by Darius, but the Persians were tolerant in religious matters. The Jews enjoyed a great deal of local autonomy under their priests, and were left to pursue their own affairs so long as they paid taxes and did not revolt. Aramaic, the official language of the Persian empire, gradually replaced Hebrew as the spoken language of everyday life.

The age of Hellenistic domination of the Jews began when Alexander took over Judah in his career of world conquest. There had been some Greek influence in the land before this time, and it naturally became much stronger when the Jews passed under Hellenistic rule. After the death of Alexander at the age of thirty-three, his generals fell to quarreling among themselves for control of the empire. Ptolemy secured control of Palestine, along with Egypt. The Jews continued through the third century B.C. under Ptolemaic rule. They enjoyed a large measure of control of their own affairs, with the power of the priests increasing. Greek was the international language of the Hellenistic world, and the Jews could not help being influenced by Greek ways and Greek thought.

The Book of Ecclesiastes was composed in this time. The author was a very skeptical teacher who doubted many of the orthodox views of his age. He did not doubt God's existence, but questioned whether God's ways are governed by justice so that the righteous and wise are rewarded and the wicked and foolish are punished. It is difficult to trace direct Greek influence in his thinking, but he must have been influenced by the general air of Greek freedom. (The book has received editorial additions which were intended to make it appear more orthodox than the original edition actually was.)

Two of the longer books of the Old Testament may have reached their present form in the Hellenistic age. One of these was the Psalter, which the Jews used in their worship in the Second Temple as a hymnal and prayer book. The Psalter was built up over a long period of time, and is a union of several collections of psalms, some of which may go back to the time of David. Some may indeed be Hebrew adaptations of very early Canaanite hymns. It reached the form in which we now have it in the Hellenistic age or soon thereafter.

The Book of Proverbs also is the result of a long process of growth, which may have begun in Solomon's time. The oldest collection is the central part of the book, 10:1—22:16, and the latest part is the introduction, chapters 1-9. The Proverbs represent the accumulated wisdom of the sages of Israel who sought to teach their fellow men how to live successfully and happily. The religious element is not prominent in the book, though of course Yahweh was thought of as continually rewarding the wise and punishing the foolish. The book is largely man-centered, and presents the results of many centuries of men's experiences.

In the third century the Jewish community in Alexandria, Egypt, grew rapidly, and Greek became the spoken language. Because many Jews lost the ability to read Hebrew, a translation into Greek was begun so that the Alexandrian Jews might be able to read their Scriptures. Legend has it that this project, which led to the version known as the Septuagint, began about 250 B.C. The translation was not complete until nearly two centuries later.

The Maccabean Revolt

During the postexilic ages we have just been surveying, the people of Judah had usually been left free to pursue their own religion undisturbed, and none of the rulers to whom they had been subject sought actively to convert them to their religion or forbid them to follow their own beliefs and customs. In the second century B.C. this policy changed radically.

Shortly after the beginning of the second century, political control of Palestine changed hands when Antiochus III defeated Ptolemy V. The Jews were now under the Seleucids. For a time the old policy continued, but a great change was made by Antiochus IV, known as Epiphanes, "God manifest." In the year 167 B.C. he sent an army to Jerusalem which plundered the city and despoiled the temple. The king issued decrees forbidding the Jews to follow their religious customs— the offering of sacrifices, Sabbath observance, circumcision, and so on. They were ordered to sacrifice pork, and to worship the Greek god Zeus, whose cult was introduced into the Jerusalem temple. Antiochus himself claimed to be divine. While some Jews were quite ready to accept these measures, it was not long before a strong revolt broke out. It was led by the priest Mattathias and his sons, one of whom had the name Judas Maccabee, "the Hammer." They refused to follow the king's edicts, and organized guerrilla forces to fight against the Seleucids. By December of 164 B.C. they had regained control of the temple, which was rededicated to the worship of Yahweh; this act is still commemorated by the Jews in the feast of Hanukkah (near Christmas). In part because of their own vigor and in part because of the weaknesses and corruptions in the Seleucid empire, the followers of the Maccabeans (also called Hasmoneans) were increasingly successful, and before long they had complete political control of Palestine. John Hyrcanus (134-104 B.C.) was the first to take the title of king, and he ruled over a very large territory. Jewish independence continued until the Roman conquest of Jerusalem in 63 B.C.

The Book of Daniel was composed in the early part of the Maccabean revolt, between the desolation of the temple by Antiochus and its rededication. This book professes to recount events in the time of the Babylonian exile, when the seer Daniel is supposed to have lived. The real setting, however, is the time of Antiochus Epiphanes, who is represented by the figures of Nebuchadnezzar and Belshazzar, the "little horn" of 8:9, and other symbols. Daniel is an apocalypse, the only complete book of this type in the Old Testament. The word apocalypse means "revelation," and the book professes to contain revelations of the future received by Daniel the seer. Its purpose was to give encouragement to the supporters of the Maccabean revolt, holding out to them the hope that, if they would remain true to their religion, the kingdom of God would finally supersede all the kingdoms of this earth (7:27), for God controls the nations of the world and their history.

This is an appropriate note for the end of our survey of the Old Testament history.

III

the faith of the old testament

THE OLD TESTAMENT IS CONSIDERED AS SCRIP-
ture by both Jews and Christians. For the Jew it *is* his Bible.
Many Jews believe that the Talmud gives the fulfillment and
correct interpretation of the Old Testament. For the Christian,
the Old Testament is only a part of his Bible; he finds in the
New Testament its fulfillment and the key to its correct understanding. Many Christians look upon the Old Testament as
only a long introduction to the New, and consider many parts
of the Old Testament to be wholly outworn and irrelevant
to Christian life and belief. It is true, of course, that some parts
of the Old Testament are primitive and cannot be accepted
by the Christian today, and that some parts of it—such as the
long sections dealing with sacrificial ritual—are irrelevant to
his life. But the Old Testament is not merely an introduction
to the New; it is a significant part of the Christian Bible in
its own right. When Christians have neglected it, their religion
has been impoverished.

As we survey in this chapter the faith of the Old Testament,
we shall be concerned primarily with those items that are still
relevant for the Christian, or necessary to his understanding

of the New. The Old Testament contains an account of man's increasing understanding of God, and of his own place in relationship to God and the world. This understanding did not proceed in evolutionary fashion, always going upward, but if there was in it genuine progress, there are some things that men once believed or did that have now been outgrown or become outmoded. We shall not dwell unduly upon these, but attempt to set forth the faith of the Old Testament largely in terms that are still valid and significant.

There are two facts that are basic to the understanding of the Old Testament, or two keys that will help us see what is most important in it.

The first is that the Old Testament seeks constantly to set forth *the sovereignty of God*. The faith of the Old Testament is not man-centered, but God-centered. It proclaims the belief that God is the sovereign Lord both of nature and of history, and that man finds his right relationship to God when he recognizes him as Creator, Sustainer, and Redeemer. When man fails to acknowledge God as such, he falls into sin and failure.

The second key is *the concept of the covenant* which God made between himself and Israel. In our survey of the history in the last chapter, we saw that the covenant was made in the time of Moses. It was an agreement by which Yahweh became the God of the Israelite tribes, and they undertook to be the obedient people of Yahweh. This covenant notion pervades much of the subsequent history, even when the word itself is not used. The idea was abused and misunderstood in many quarters. The time came when Jeremiah spoke of the making of a new covenant between Yahweh and Israel (Jeremiah 31:31-34).

The concept of the covenant binds together the two Testaments, Old and New. The Hebrew term for covenant was translated by the Greeks with a word that is often rendered in the New Testament as "testament." The new covenant is specifically referred to several times in the New Testament, and the early Christians thought of themselves as the people of the new covenant. We shall attempt to see the significance of this idea in future pages, but we should always avoid using the idea of the two covenants as a way to separate the Old and New Testaments; it is rather a concept that binds them together.

Yahweh, the Covenant God of Israel

The God who revealed himself in the Old Testament through the history of Israel, and the words and lives of chosen individuals, is the same God who revealed himself in the New Testament, above all in the life of Jesus Christ. The nature of God did not change between the Old and New Testaments; he did not change from being a wrathful God who sought only justice to being a loving, merciful father. There are, to be sure, some sub-Christian understandings of God's nature in the Old Testament; these were mistaken, and did not correctly represent God. Jesus Christ came to fulfill and complete —not to contradict—the revelation of God which had been given primarily through the people among whom Jesus was born, was educated, lived, and was crucified.

We have been speaking of the God of the Old Testament under the name "Yahweh." It is well to pause here to explain that name, and to show why we use that form instead of "Jehovah."

The Hebrews wrote the name of their God as YHWH. This was his personal name. It is called the Divine Name or the Tetragrammaton, because it is made up of four letters. In the early days, we must point out, the Hebrews wrote their language with *consonants* only. Of course they had to pronounce *vowels* in order to speak, but the vowels were transmitted orally and not originally written down.

In the course of time the Hebrews ceased to pronounce the Divine Name, YHWH. Just what their reasons were we do not know: perhaps they considered the name too sacred to pronounce, or they feared its abuse and misuse (as in magical rites), or they came to think that giving their deity a personal name implied too much about the existence of other gods. So, instead of pronouncing the personal Divine Name, the Hebrews simply used the general word "Lord," which in Hebrew is *'adonay*. Eventually, in writing their Scripture they devised a scheme for indicating to the reader that, when he came across the Divine Name, he should not pronounce it in its ancient fashion, but rather say "Lord": they wrote the vowel signs of *'adonay* with the consonants YHWH. In the Middle Ages, when Latin was in general use, Christian scholars misunderstood this scheme, and they thought the Divine Name should be pronounced and transcribed just as it was written—that is, Yehowah, or Jehovah, since in Latin J was pronounced Y, and V was pronounced W. (Look at the Hebrew word *'adonay,* and you will see that the second and third vowels are *o* and *a;* the first vowel shifted by a regular phonetic process from *a* to *e,* so that you get Jehov*a*h.)

The word "Jehovah" never existed among the ancient Jews. It is a hybrid name, made up of the consonants of one word and the vowels of another. But how *did* the Hebrews in most ancient times actually pronounce the Divine Name? Our best information suggests that they pronounced it "Yahweh." Its proper pronunciation was preserved in certain priestly circles, and a few early Christian fathers said that they had learned it was pronounced in approximately that manner. In modern times the American Standard Version used the form Jehovah, but the Revised Standard Version reverts to the older King James Version's practice of translating this Divine Name, in most places, as LORD. Thus, in the Revised Standard Version, when you see LORD (or, in a few places GOD), you can know that the Divine Name is used in the Hebrew.

Yahweh was the covenant God of Israel. Though this deity may have been worshiped by a small group of people before the making of the covenant of Sinai, such as members of Moses' own family and clan or the Midianites from whom he secured a wife, it was at Sinai that Yahweh became Israel's God. As a covenant God, Yahweh was not a natural deity or a nature God. He was not a God whom Israel had worshiped from time immemorial, but one who had in a moment in history chosen Israel and been chosen by Israel. Nor was he a personification of some element or force in nature, as many of the pagan gods of antiquity were, personifying the sun or the moon or the force of the storm or the like.

Yahweh was the God of a people, for the covenant was made with the people of Israel. Moses was the mediator of the covenant at Sinai, but the covenant was not with him. Later the Hebrews came to believe that Yahweh made a covenant especially with King David, but that was because he was king of Israel, and the covenant was with him and his dynasty, not simply with David as an individual. Nevertheless, we must point out that Yahweh often had dealings with individuals, and the religion of Israel was not simply a national religion. He dealt with Moses, with judges, with many separate prophets, with the kings, and with many other individuals. While in the early stages of Israel's religion its collective or community aspect was emphasized, individualism was not entirely lacking. From the time of Jeremiah and Ezekiel on, when the nation was broken up, much greater stress was placed on the relationship between the individual and God. Jeremiah taught that the Israelite could find Yahweh even in the foreign land of Babylonia, away from his homeland and his beloved temple, if he sought him with his whole heart (29:13).

The making of the covenant shows that Yahweh was a gracious God. The covenant was not a contract made between equals; rather, Yahweh took the initiative and offered the covenant to Israel, and Israel accepted the offer. Thus, the covenant illustrates the fact that from early times Yahweh was a God of grace.

Though the covenant was offered by Yahweh to Israel, the covenant always involved a very significant element of mutuality and reciprocity. A key sentence of the covenant relationship was: "You shall be my people, and I will be your God." God made a promise to Israel, but at the same time he demanded from them the obedience which a people should render their God. Israel received blessings from God, but Yahweh expected that they would give in return their worship and service. It would be a mistake to look upon the covenant as a bargain or a contract, but the mutual element should not be overlooked. The prophets were continually warning Israel that they must not expect to receive blessings from God without obeying him in return. The people were too often inclined to look upon the covenant as a one-sided arrangement, and the prophets had to remind them of its two-sided nature. They often implied that Yahweh might break the covenant and cast off Israel, if the Israelites persisted in misunderstanding its nature.

Yahweh was to Israel the sovereign Lord of history. He guided the events through which the Hebrews lived, and used those events for their salvation. The Israelites saw the hand of God especially in certain mighty acts of their history: the guiding of the wandering patriarchs, the exodus from Egypt, the safe leading through the wilderness, the conquest of the land of promise, and the establishment of the dynasty of David. But these were not the only acts of God in Israel's history; they could see his hand also in the exile into Babylonia, the return from exile (which was a new exodus), and all the other events through which they lived. The Yahwist in his history traced the activity of Yahweh in the early events. The Deuteronomist emphasized the fact that the exodus from Egypt was an act of redemption. It was the exodus from Egypt and the crossing of the Red Sea which the Israelites came to consider as the mightiest act of Yahweh's redemption. It was an incontrovertible *fact* of their past, and it was an obvious freeing of a people from the bondage of slavery.

The prophets taught the Israelites to see the hand of God in the events through which they lived, showing them that Yahweh could even use pagan kings to perform his will. In the days of Isaiah, the Assyrians threatened to destroy Judah, but that prophet said that the Assyrian king was the rod of Yahweh's anger, a tool in his hand with which he would punish the people of Judah for their sin; yet, the same God could turn his anger against Assyria if she became proud and boastful (10:5-19). Jeremiah said that the Babylonian king, Nebuchadnezzar, was the servant of Yahweh, into whose hands Yahweh had given the rule of Judah and various other lands (27:6). Second Isaiah went to the extent of saying that Cyrus was "anointed" by Yahweh as his agent (45:1): Cyrus would prepare the way for the return of the exiles to Zion, and thus carry out the will of Yahweh, though Cyrus was not a worshiper of Yahweh. Second Isaiah said that Yahweh "brings princes to nought, and makes the rulers of the earth as nothing." (40:23) Thus the prophets taught Israel that Yahweh controls history, not only guiding the destiny of Israel but also using the rulers of other nations to the end that God's rule might eventually extend over all the earth and his sovereignty be recognized by all peoples (Isaiah 45:22-23).

The Israelites believed that their God was also the Creator of the earth, the Maker of the world in which they lived and the Sustainer of nature. The Old Testament opens with a magnificent account of the creation of the universe, the earth, and man, in an orderly and systematic manner through the spoken word of God. This chapter is a relatively late product, coming from the Priestly writing, but the idea that Yahweh was Creator was an early idea. The Yahwist described the creation of man and the beasts (2:4-24), and his account may have originally opened with an account of the earth's creation. In Genesis 14:19-20, the king of Jerusalem blesses Abraham by "God Most High, maker of heaven and earth." Job 38-41 describes in unforgettable poetry how the Lord "laid the foundations of the earth . . . when the morning stars sang together, and all the sons of God shouted for joy," and how the Lord sustains all the processes of the natural world in ways that are beyond the understanding of man. Second Isaiah describes over and over in highly poetic terms the creation by Yahweh, and makes it abundantly clear that the God of Creation and the God of History are one and the same.

The account of creation in Genesis 1 repeatedly says that God looked upon his handiwork and found it to be good. And finally "God saw everything that he had made, and behold, it was very good" (Genesis 1:31). This is an important aspect of the Old Testament faith. There were people in the ancient world who believed that the world of matter is inherently evil and must be completely overcome. The Israelite believed that the world of matter, which had been created by the sovereign word of God, was good and not evil; it might be corrupted, and it might need redemption, but it was not by nature evil or the source of evil. Furthermore, he believed that the same God who had created the world in an orderly manner would sustain it. The Hebrews did not have the modern conception of "natural law," but in some respects they approached it. They believed that Yahweh exercised direct control over the world and its processes; he could even make it rain upon one city and withhold rain from another (Amos 4:7). Through his direct control he might use the forces of nature to chasten man. Yet, generally Yahweh's control was exercised in an orderly and dependable manner. Second Isaiah insisted that the God who formed the earth "did not create it a chaos, he formed it to be inhabited" (45:18).

The God who created the earth and who controls history is known primarily by what he does. The Old Testament has little interest in speculation regarding the being or essence of God; the Hebrews knew the nature of God by what he did. Two aspects of his nature call for special attention: Yahweh is righteous; and Yahweh is a God of love.

When the Israelite affirmed that Yahweh is a righteous God, he meant three things.

First, he meant that Yahweh acts in a manner that is fair, equitable, and right. Abraham said to Yahweh before the destruction of Sodom and Gomorrah: "Shall not the Judge of all the earth do right?" (Genesis 18:25) Yahweh as the Judge does that which is right, rewarding the obedient and faithful and punishing the disobedient and sinful. His own actions are not arbitrary and whimsical; he is trustworthy and dependable. There are, to be sure, passages in the Old Testament in which Yahweh is represented as acting in a manner that appears to us as arbitrary and unjust. For example, Exodus 4:24-26 says that, when Moses was in the wilderness, Yahweh met him at a lodging place and sought to kill him. His wife performed an act of circumcision on their son, and this strangely averted Yahweh's anger. This appears primitive and unworthy to us. We can scarcely believe that this represents the true God at all; it is a piece of undigested pagan mythology that attracts attention to itself by its very inconsistency with most of the Old Testament view of Yahweh's nature. Isaiah expressed the characteristic view when he said:

> ... the LORD of hosts is exalted in justice,
> and the Holy God shows himself holy
> in righteousness" (5:16).

Many of the gods and goddesses of the ancient world, especially those of Mesopotamia, were arbitrary and unpredictable. On the contrary, Yahweh was trustworthy and faithful, even though the best thinkers of Old Testament times never believed they could fully understand the ways of God.

In the second place, the righteous God demands righteousness of those who are in covenant with him. The righteous God is properly worshiped and served by means of righteousness in action. In a long passage, Amos declares that Yahweh rejects the elaborate feasts, the noisome assemblies, the piled-up sacrifices, and the ritual music of the Hebrew worship; the true desire of Yahweh is expressed in the demand:

> But let justice roll down like waters,
> and righteousness like an everflowing stream.
>
> —Amos 5:24

For Amos, righteousness meant fairness and equity in the courts of law, honesty in business dealings, generous treatment of the poor by the wealthy, and so on. We shall return to this topic when we speak below of the ethics of the Old Testament.

The righteousness of God has a third meaning that is deeper than both of the above. The Hebrew word that is most often translated as "righteousness" (*tsédek,* or *tsedakah*) is sometimes better translated as "deliverance, salvation, saving act" or the like. This can be seen most clearly in passages in Second Isaiah in which the usual word for "righteousness" is used as a synonym for salvation. In the following quotation from Isaiah 51:5, 6 it is rendered "deliverance":

"My *deliverance* draws near speedily,
  my salvation has gone forth, . . .
. . . my salvation will be for ever,
  and my *deliverance* will never be ended."

In a very significant passage in Micah 6:5, the plural of this word is rendered as "saving acts," as follows:

"O my people, remember what Balak king of Moab devised,
  and what Balaam the son of Beor answered him,
and what happened from Shittim to Gilgal,
  that you may know *the saving acts* of the LORD."

It is not difficult to see how the Israelite conception of the righteousness of God came to have such an active meaning. Yahweh's righteousness is not an abstract, passive quality of his nature, not simply his rightness. He *is* right, he *demands* the right, but his nature is such that he reaches out to man to *produce* the right, and thus to create righteousness among men. Edmond Jacob has well said that the righteousness of Yahweh "is not of the type of the blindfolded maiden holding a balance in her hand," but Yahweh "extends one arm to the wretch stretched out on the ground whilst the other pushes away the one who causes the misfortunes."[1] The God of the Old Testament is not a Being concerned only with maintaining his own holiness and righteousness, but a person who is concerned with man and his fortunes, extending his power to bring about among men the conditions he desires.

This leads us naturally to discuss the other outstanding feature of Yahweh's nature: he is a God of love. There can be no question at all that the Old Testament maintains over and over that God is a loving God, not—as he is often de-

---

[1] *Theology of the Old Testament* (New York: Harper & Row, Publishers, Inc., 1958), p. 99.

picted—a stern and wrathful deity always seeking only cold justice and vengeance.

Yahweh's love for Israel stands out most clearly, perhaps, in the message of the prophet Hosea. He compares Yahweh with the father of a child, and shows the tenderness of his love for Israel:

> When Israel was a child, I loved him,
> and out of Egypt I called my son. (11:1)

Hosea goes on to describe how Yahweh nurtured and brought up his child, treating him "with the bands of love"; but Israel was continually faithless, and Yahweh considered casting the nation away. But then he cried out:

> How can I give you up, O Ephraim!
> How can I hand you over, O Israel! . . .
> My heart recoils within me,
> my compassion grows warm and tender.
> I will not execute my fierce anger,
> I will not again destroy Ephraim. (11:8-9)

Hosea saw in his marital experience with Gomer a parallel to the love of Yahweh for Israel: he was told that he should continue to love her in spite of her infidelity, "even as the LORD loves the people of Israel, though they turn to other gods." (3:1)

There are many other specific passages that could be cited, but we wish to call attention particularly to one word in the Old Testament which is used many times to express the love of God for Israel. It is the short Hebrew word, *hésed*. This word cannot be rendered by any single English word with satisfaction. English versions have often rendered it as "loving-kindness" or "mercy." Careful studies have shown that this word is frequently used in the Old Testament of various human and human-divine relationships when there is a covenant existing between two parties, either expressed or implied. It may be used of the relationship of father and son, of king and subject, of friends, of host and guest, and so on. Thus, *hésed* is that attitude and set of actions proper between two parties standing in a covenant relationship. Between equals it may be a relationship of loyalty and kindness; between inferior and superior it may be devotion, faithfulness, and the like. In a religious sense the Old Testament uses this of the proper relationship between God and Israel: each is expected to show *hésed* to the other. On man's side that calls for loyalty, faithfulness, devotion, and love; on God's side, it is "steadfast love," as the Revised Standard Version frequently translates it. In Psalm 136 the refrain occurs as every second line: "for his steadfast love endures for ever." Exodus 34:6-7 contains a long declaration about Yahweh that is repeated several times with minor variations in Numbers 14:18; Psalms 86:15; 103:8; 145:8; Joel 2:13; Jonah 4:2; Nehemiah 9:17:

"The LORD, the LORD, a God merciful and gracious, slow to anger, and abounding in *steadfast love* and faithfulness, keeping *steadfast love* for thousands, forgiving iniquity and transgression and sin, but who will by no means clear the guilty, visiting the iniquity of the fathers upon the children and the children's children, to the third and fourth generation."

God's love is "steadfast" in that it is both strong and enduring. The last-quoted statement contains both the promise that Yahweh forgives iniquity and the threat that he punishes the wicked. This is not inconsistent with his love. There is no fundamental antagonism between God's love and his justice, for his love would not be genuine if it continually and forever permitted disobedience. The notion, however, that Yahweh visited the sins of the fathers upon the children was later overcome by the Hebrews (see Ezekiel 18).

Our discussion of the nature of Yahweh may be misleading if it gives the impression that we can give a neat and clear-cut definition and description of the God of the Old Testament. We cannot perceive his nature fully unless we can see on the pages of the Old Testament the wrestlings with God of men such as Hosea and Jeremiah and Job. No prophet of the Old Testament was more faithful to his mission than Jeremiah, and no prophet was so conscious of the sustaining presence of Yahweh in all his trials. Yet, Jeremiah experienced the compulsive, almost "demonic" power of God that led him to accuse Yahweh of deceiving him (15:18; 20:7). The men of Israel knew that they could trust their God, but they knew also that he might manifest himself in unexpected and unpredictable ways, and that they could never wholly comprehend him with their human minds. Job was led to cry out (26:14):

"Lo, these are but the outskirts of his ways;
and how small a whisper do we hear of him!
But the thunder of his power who can understand?"

Israel, the Covenant People

The covenant was made with the people of Israel, not with a race or a nation or with any individual. Israel was the "people of Yahweh," bound to him and to one another by the ties of a covenant.

The early sources concerning the people of Israel indicate that they were made up of quite varied elements, and were far from being a homogeneous or "pure" race. The covenant at Sinai was probably made by the group that had come out of the land of Egypt and some of the desert clans or tribes. After the entrance into the land of Canaan, they apparently accepted into the covenant some groups that had not gone down into Egypt but had settled permanently in Canaan; this is probably what is meant by the ceremony at Shechem described in Joshua 24. The one thing these groups had in common was their worship of Yahweh, and that was what held them together.

Israel was therefore a people chosen or elected by Yahweh. Many modern men do not like the idea of a "chosen people," for it suggests to them false pride in race or nationality, or a sense of superiority over others. It is important, therefore, to see what the Old Testament really means by designating Israel as a "chosen people."

Why was Israel chosen? The Old Testament makes it abundantly clear that Israel was not chosen because of her merit or her inherent superiority to other nations. Israel was chosen because of the love of God. Deuteronomy 7:6-8 declares: "You are a people holy to the LORD your God; the LORD your God has chosen you to be a people for his own possession, out of all the peoples that are on the face of the earth. It was not because you were more in number than any other people that the LORD set his love upon you and chose you, for you were the fewest of all peoples; but it is because the LORD loves you, and is keeping the oath which he swore to your fathers. . . ." (See also Deuteronomy 9:4-6.) Israel was not chosen because of her goodness or greatness, but her greatness arose from the fact that she was chosen by Yahweh.

The purpose of the election of Israel was not that Israel might boast in her position or enjoy special privileges, but that Israel might serve the Lord. There were no doubt many people among the Israelites who believed that the covenant election gave them superior privileges and blessings, and that Yahweh would continue to bless them in spite of their attitude toward him. Some may have gone so far as to think that Yahweh's very existence was bound up with the existence of the chosen people. To such as these Amos uttered a message of fundamental import:

"You only have I known
    of all the families of the earth;
therefore I will punish you
    for all your iniquities." (3:2)

Amos agrees with those who said that Yahweh had really chosen Israel, but he insisted that the choice was for service and for the fulfillment of obligations; if Israel did not live up to her obligations to God, then the punishment of Israel would be all the greater. The principle is the same as that expressed in Luke 12:48: "Every one to whom much is given, of him will much be required."

The mission of Israel as the chosen people is involved in Second Isaiah's figure of the Suffering Servant of the Lord. This figure is difficult to interpret, and it may be that no single interpretation does full justice to it. Any interpretation must recognize that in certain passages Israel is identified as the servant: Isaiah 41:8; 44:1, 2; 45:4; 48:20; 49:3. One of the facets of the message of Second Isaiah was his appeal to Israel to *be the servant of Yahweh.* He could see that the Israelites in exile were discouraged and despondent; they felt forsaken by their God. He summoned them to be what Yahweh intended for them to be: Yahweh's servant and his witnesses (43:10, 12). As such they were to witness to the religion of Yahweh and enable other nations to recognize him as God. They were to give witness to God by being the faithful and obedient people of Yahweh. Second Isaiah says that other nations will come to Israel and say:

" 'God is with you only, and there is no other,
no god besides him.' " (45:14)

Perhaps Second Isaiah's appeal was really made to a chosen circle within the people in exile rather than to the whole group.

The notion that the mission of Israel could not be carried out by the whole nation or people, but rather by a faithful minority, is expressed in the idea of a remnant, which is found first in Isaiah. That prophet named one of his sons "Shear-yashub," signifying "A remnant shall return"—perhaps with the meaning that a remnant would return to Yahweh in repentance. In his message he spoke several times of a remnant that would be preserved in spite of disaster to the nation, and when he gathered around him a group of disciples, he may have been taking steps to insure the survival of such a remnant. In later times the idea of a remnant was presented in various ways; sometimes there was the view that a remnant of Israel would conquer the other nations (Micah 5:7-9), but this was a nationalistic conception that did not accord with earlier views of the election of Israel.

When we see that the best interpreters in the Old Testament said that Israel was chosen because of God's gracious love, rather than because of merit, and that the election was for service, not for pride and self-satisfaction, we can see that this was one of the noblest doctrines of the Old Testament. It is a historical fact that Israel *was* a witness to the true God; our Christian faith arose out of the Hebrew-Jewish faith, and if there had not been faithful witnesses to carry it on from generation to generation, the Christian religion as we know it could not have arisen. Often Christians have depicted the history of Israel as being a long, unrelieved record of infidelity and rebellion against God. Perhaps the reading of the prophets can give some justification for such a gloomy view. But prophetic sermons are not accurate surveys of the faith and morals of a whole people. There were the prophets and their disciples; there were the psalmists and sages; there were all of those who produced and transmitted the Scriptures. Surely God provided a faithful minority—a righteous remnant—through which his message was handed on, even if the people as a whole were not loyal to their mission.

The Nature and Destiny of Man

The question of the nature of man can be broken down into three separate questions: What is man in his interior makeup?

What is he in relationship to God? What is he in relationship to the world which God has created?

As for the first question, the Old Testament view is that man is a unity of matter and spirit. The combination of these two make him a "soul." This is expressed in the account of man's creation in Genesis 2:7: "The LORD God formed man of the dust of the ground, and breathed into his nostrils the breath of life; and man became a living soul." (KJV) The Hebrew word here translated "soul" is *néfesh,* but it does not mean soul in the sense in which we ordinarily understand that term today, as the spiritual or invisible part of man. By *néfesh* the Old Testament most characteristically means the total self, the person, man as a whole. *Néfesh* is not what one *has* as a part of himself, but what he *is* as a totality.

Man is thus an animated body, not an incarnated soul. The difference between these two conceptions is important. The latter is characteristic of the Greeks, who believed that man is composed of an immortal, pure soul housed in a mortal, corrupt body. The Hebrews did not think that the material part of man, which they designated as body or flesh or dust, is in itself evil or corrupt. It is weak and fallible, subject to corruption, but not naturally evil. The psalmist could speak of the flesh as longing for God, as the soul does:

> O God, thou art my God, I seek thee,
>   my soul *(néfesh)* thirsts for thee;
> my flesh faints for thee,
>   as in a dry and weary land where no water is.
>   —Psalm 63:1

Ezekiel spoke of the "heart of flesh" as a synonym of the new heart, the opposite of the "heart of stone" (Ezekiel 36:26). The material part of man is a creation of God, and God has mercy upon man because he remembers that he is dust (Psalm 103:14). The spirit or breath comes from God, as the account in Genesis 2:7 indicates, and it is spirit that man shares with God, who is spiritual in his nature.

When we turn to think of man in his relationship to God and to the rest of the creation of God, we turn most naturally to the account of the creation of the world and man in the first chapter of Genesis. There man is represented as the crown and climax of God's creative activity, made in the image of God. "So God created man in his own image, in the image of God he created him; male and female he created them" (Genesis 1:27).

There has been much discussion as to the meaning of the phrase, "the image of God," and many theological disputes have centered around it. Some interpreters have thought it means that man was made in the physical image of God, or that his upright posture makes him like God and sets him off from the animals. This interpretation is highly improbable. The first chapter of Genesis is from the Priestly writer, who wrote relatively late in Hebrew history and had a very exalted conception of God. It is not at all likely that he really thought of Yahweh as existing in physical form, though it is true that many Old Testament writers often employ figurative language and speak of God's hand or arm or mouth, or the like.

In its immediate setting, the making of man in God's image probably meant that man was created to have dominion over the animals in his world. Immediately after the account of creation in Genesis 1:27, we read that God blessed man and said, "Be fruitful and multiply, and fill the earth and subdue it; and have dominion over the fish of the sea and over the birds of the air and over every living thing that moves upon the earth." Man, created in the image of God, was expected to exercise dominion over the other living things on earth, and to subdue the earth, just as God exercised rule over man. One of the best commentaries on the idea of the image of God is given in Psalm 8. Immediately after asking, "What is man that thou art mindful of him?" the psalmist answers:

> . . . thou hast made him little less than God [or, angels],
>   and dost crown him with glory and honor.
> Thou hast given him dominion over the works of thy
>   hands;
>   thou has put all things under his feet. . . .

Man is given dominion over the other works of God's hands, but is not given self-dominion. As a creature of God, he is expected to give God dominion over himself. Yet, being in the image of God, man enjoys a relationship that is not one of servile cringing before a master, but one of fellowship in obedience. Man does not have within himself "a spark of the divine," but he has a heavenward door by which he may enjoy fellowship with the God who made him, if he recognizes that God is his Creator. He is expected to rule over the animals, but as a being made in God's image not to sink to the level of the animals.

Yet man continually sins in the sight of God, in whose image he was made. The third chapter of Genesis tells the story of man's first sin and his consequent expulsion from the Garden of Eden. This profound and revealing story should be taken as a symbol of the sin of every man, showing how man sins and the consequences of his failure to obey God. Yahweh placed Adam and Eve in the Garden to till it, and gave them much freedom, but forbade them to eat of the tree of the knowledge of good and evil. They knew God's command, and they were free to obey or disobey. They disobeyed, in part because they succumbed to external temptation (symbolized by the serpent) and in part because they were not willing to accept their role as creatures of God, but wished to be "like God," usurping for themselves that which was forbidden them. The most immediate consequence of their rebellion was alienation from the God who had made them: they hid themselves from the presence of God. Then, as they talked with God, Adam and Eve each tried to evade responsibility for the decisions they had made, attempting to pass the burden of responsibility to the other or to the serpent. There are doubtless many details of this story that are puzzling to us, but it emphasizes several basic aspects of the Old Testament way of looking at man and his sin. Though man is a creature of God and under his sovereignty, God does not treat him as a puppet, but has given him freedom of choice— to obey or to disobey. Sin is disobedience to God, disharmony with his will. It raises a barrier between man and God, breaking the fellowship which God desires to exist between them. All sin is sin against God, as the psalmist says in 51:4:

> Against thee, thee only, have I sinned,
>   and done that which is evil in thy sight.

The Old Testament does not present a doctrine of original sin or of man's total depravity, as these were worked out by Christian theologians, though it does give some basis for those doctrines. The account of man's first sin and expulsion from the Garden is not referred to in later books of the Old Testament, and it is not said that man inherits from Adam his guilt or his sinfulness. Man sins because of his selfishness and pride, the stubbornness of his heart, his desire to rule himself rather than accept God's rule. The Old Testament puts much emphasis on the deadening effect of custom and habit, the unwillingness of men to break out of their accustomed ways to follow God's way. Jeremiah said to the people of his day:

> Can the Ethiopian change his skin
>   or the leopard his spots?
> Then also you can do good
>   who are accustomed to do evil. (13:23)

God punishes man's sin. The prophets and others said much about this; they could not believe that a moral and righteous God would allow man to sin and sin indefinitely without punishment. But in the Old Testament God's punishment of Israel or of individual men is often presented as discipline or chastening, designed not to destroy but rather to teach men and bring them back to God. The prophets complained that Israel refused to learn from God's chastening, but persisted in their rebellion against him.

The Old Testament has a promise of salvation from sin. The primary requirement for God's forgiveness is that man repent. The Old Testament expresses its view of repentance with two separate words: one means literally to "change one's mind, or purpose," and the other means to "turn" away from sin and toward God. Repentance that is genuine and effective involves acknowledgement and confession of sin, repudiation of the ways of wrongdoing and rebellion, and active turning in both spirit and action to the way of obedience. The prophets often called for repentance, and among them none was more insistent than Jeremiah. Here is the way he phrases his summons to repentance in 4:1-4:

"If you return, O Israel, says the LORD,
    to me you should return.
If you remove your abominations from my presence,
    and do not waver,
and if you swear, 'As the LORD lives,'
    in truth, in justice, and in uprightness,
then nations shall bless themselves in him,
    and in him shall they glory."

    ·   ·   ·   ·   ·   ·   ·   ·   ·   ·   ·   ·

"Break up your fallow ground,
    and sow not among thorns.

Circumcise yourselves to the LORD,
remove the foreskin of your hearts,
O men of Judah and inhabitants of Jerusalem."

The Book of Psalms offers some examples of unusually fine prayers of penitence, in which the psalmists confess sin and pray for forgiveness; see Psalms 32, 38, 51, 130, and 143. In Psalm 51:10 the suppliant prays for "a clean heart" and "a new and right spirit," and restoration of the sinner to fellowship with God.

But does not the Old Testament say that sacrifice is necessary to atone for sin, or to obtain God's forgiveness? The ancient ritual of the Hebrews did include a great many offerings, both of animals and of agricultural products. Some were offered to secure atonement or expiation from sin, but not all were for this purpose. Some were for other purposes, such as the thank-offerings, which were designed to express gratitude. But the Old Testament never says that a sacrifice can bring about forgiveness or salvation merely by the performance of an external rite. Where sacrifice was offered for sin, the sinner was expected to confess his sin and be penitent, and in some cases of offense against a fellow man, the law demanded restitution. The great prophets did not ask the people to bring sacrifice, but simply to turn to God in repentance. In Proverbs 21:27 we read:

The sacrifice of the wicked is an abomination;
how much more when he brings it with evil intent.

The Priestly legislation provided sacrifices for sins that were committed "unwittingly"—that is, through inadvertence or ignorance. It did not provide sacrifices for those that were committed "with a high hand"—that is, defiantly and insolently in the face of all warnings and in full knowledge of what one was doing (Numbers 15:27-31; Leviticus 4:2 etc.). Yet the Old Testament shows repeatedly that forgiveness was open for flagrant sinners who turned to God in repentance (see the example of David, 2 Samuel 12:12-14). Ezekiel said that Yahweh has no pleasure in the death of the wicked, but rather desires that the wicked turn from his way, in repentance, and live (Ezekiel 18:23, 32).

As for the ultimate destiny of man, the Old Testament has little hope of a blessed life for man after death. It does present a view of "immortality" in the sense that it depicts the survival of men after death, but that survival is not generally presented as being in either "heaven" or "hell" in the New Testament sense. For most of the Old Testament, survival was pictured as being in a place called Sheol. This was not a place of punishment, nor a place of reward for the righteous, but an unattractive place to which the Hebrews believed all men would go upon death. The various descriptions of Sheol are not wholly consistent. It was usually thought to be a great underground region, perhaps a city with walls and gates, a place of darkness, a land from which no man would return. It was sometimes called the Pit, or Abaddon, or Destruction. Some passages of Scripture suggest that Yahweh's rule did not extend to Sheol (Psalms 6:5; 30:9; 88:4-5), while others suggest that his power did extend into that region beyond death (Amos 9:2; Deuteronomy 32:22; Psalm 139:7-10). It was not a region to which man could look forward with pleasure; only Job could describe its existence as welcome because he was so miserable on this earth (3:11-19). Sheol was the great leveler, for the great and small, the rich and the poor, would all be alike there. Its inhabitants are called "shades," by which probably was meant persons in a weakened state rather than disembodied spirits. There are occasional suggestions of distinctions in Sheol (Isaiah 14:4-20; Ezekiel 32:21-31), with the lowest places reserved for the greatest enemies of Israel. In general Israel's belief in Sheol was similar to that of the belief of the Greeks in Hades and Babylonian belief in Aralu.

In late Old Testament times the belief arose in a resurrection from the dead; this is clearly attested in only two passages, Daniel 12:2 and Isaiah 26:19. Daniel was written in the early Maccabean age, and Isaiah 24-27 probably in the Hellenistic age. The Daniel passage does not depict a universal resurrection, but only of "many," to life again on this earth. The Isaiah verse speaks of a resurrection of the righteous. The Hebrews believed in the resurrection of the body and the total self. We must recall that for them man is a unity of body and spirit. Resurrection of the body is not the same as "immortality of the soul," when the soul is thought of as the spiritual, invisible element of man. There are a few passages that use the figure of resurrection to symbolize the revival of the nation (Ezekiel 37:1-14; Hosea 6:2) but these do not concern individual resurrection.

There are hints of other kinds of "immortality" in the Old Testament. Ecclesiastes 12:7 speaks of death as a time when the two parts of which man is made will dissolve, so that "the dust returns to the earth as it was, and the spirit returns to God who gave it." Psalm 104:29 is similar.

Two persons in the Old Testament are reported to have escaped death by being translated directly to heaven: Enoch (Genesis 5:24) and Elijah (2 Kings 2:11). It is quite possible that this hope for translation directly to heaven, to be in fellowship with God, is expressed in certain of the Psalms, particularly 16:8-11; 49:15; and 73:23-24. The interpretation of those Psalms is difficult, but the word "receive" or "take" is used in the last two as in the account of Enoch, and the emphasis in any event is upon continuation of fellowship with God.

The Old Testament thus presents no clear and consistent hope for the individual after death. More characteristic of the faith of the Old Testament is the national hope for a Golden Age in the future that is often called the "Messianic age." The Israelites believed, as we have seen, that Yahweh is the sovereign LORD of history. Now, history is not just the past and the present; it embraces the future. So, if Yahweh was to be the LORD of *all* history, the Israelites believed that the future—their future—would belong to him, and he would exercise his sovereignty in that future. They did not believe that history consists of a series of cycles, repeated endlessly, but that history has a goal and a consummation. That goal is the realization of God's sovereignty.

The English word Messiah is taken directly from a Hebrew word that means "anointed"; the word Christ has the same meaning, derived directly from the Greek *Christos*. In ancient Israel kings and priests were regularly anointed, and on rare occasions prophets. Once even the pagan king Cyrus is referred to as Yahweh's anointed (Isaiah 45:1). Anointing with oil signified that the one who received it was a representative and agent of God, infused in some manner with a portion of his power.

It is a curious fact that the word "Messiah" is never used in the Old Testament specifically of the coming savior of the people, though by the time of Jesus it had become virtually a technical term for the expected savior and redeemer. The Old Testament does sometimes refer to a coming figure who is to be the agent of God in the coming Golden Age, but the Israelites insisted that the coming Age is to be brought about by God himself; it is to be *his* kingdom. So the Old Testament usually calls God himself the Savior or Redeemer. Furthermore, the Hebrews had more interest in the conditions of the messianic age (if we may use that term loosely to apply to the coming Golden Age) than in the nature of the messianic figure.

We do not find in the Old Testament a clear and uniform expectation regarding the coming messianic age, any more than we find uniformity in the hope for life after death. Certain factors are constant, but many of the details vary. The most constant factors are the activity and presence of God and the reign of his will, and the prevalence of conditions of righteousness, prosperity, and peace.

Sometimes the future age comes without the advent of a messianic figure, but Yahweh himself is depicted as coming directly to earth. For example, Isaiah 2:2-4 and Micah 4:1-4 look forward to a time when all the nations will come to the temple in Zion to learn God's law, Yahweh himself will judge the nations, and the peoples will "beat their swords into plowshares, and their spears into pruning hooks." Amos spoke of the coming day of Yahweh as a time of darkness and gloom, and of judgment for Israel; he did not speak of a Messiah. When a messianic figure occurs in these expectations, he is usually a king of the dynasty of David, or one who will rule like David; see Isaiah 9:7; 11:1; Jeremiah 23:5; Ezekiel 34:23-24; Micah 5:2. Sometimes no reference is made to the Davidic ancestry of the coming king, as in Zechariah 9:9, where the emphasis is laid on his humility.

In the hopes for the future, it is sometimes said that Israel will rule over other nations, and there is even gloating over the defeat of her enemies, as in Micah 4:13; 7:10; Isaiah 61:5-7. At other times, the messianic hope becomes truly universalistic, with the expectation that all nations will come to recognize the sovereignty of Yahweh, and, though Israel's witness to the faith in Yahweh is recognized, Israel is not depicted as a conquering people. This is the view found in the work of Second Isaiah (see 45:22-25). The messianic age is depicted as a time when there will be peace, when even the previously wild animals are tame, as they had been in the Garden of Eden (Isaiah 11:6), and when there are plentiful

harvests giving food for all (Amos 9:13; Joel 3:18). Once
it is described as a time when Yahweh will pour out his spirit
on "all flesh," so that many will prophesy, and have dreams
and visions (Joel 2:28). Isaiah 25:6 speaks of a great banquet
to be served by Yahweh, to which all peoples will come.
Ezekiel says that Yahweh will give Israel a new heart and a
new spirit (36:26), as Jeremiah promised the making of a new
covenant in which the law would be written on man's heart
(31:31-34).

In the period before the Babylonian exile, when the monarchy was still in existence, the Hebrews usually expected that
the ideal kingdom would be set up on this earth, with the
ideal king coming to the throne after the devastations of war
and other calamities were over. In the period after the exile,
the hopes for the future became more transcendent and supernatural; often it was said that there would come great cosmic
disturbances, after which a new heaven and new earth would
be created. History came to be more sharply divided between
"this age" and "the age to come." These tendencies were
intensified in the apocalyptic literature, such as Daniel and
much of the literature written between the two Testaments.

Two figures that are described in the Old Testament require
brief comment here. One is the figure of the Suffering Servant
of the LORD in Second Isaiah. We have seen that the Servant
is sometimes identified with Israel, but have suggested that
this identification may not be applicable in every case. The
fourth Servant poem, Isaiah 52:13—53:12, seems to go beyond
the others in picturing the Servant as an individual, and here
the idea of vicarious suffering is prominent. It is quite possible
that in this poem, if not in the others, Second Isaiah had in
mind a future individual. Perhaps he did not have in mind
specifically a Messiah, for in 40:10-11 he speaks of Yahweh
himself coming to rule Israel, without a mediator. There is
no clear evidence in the Old Testament, or in other Jewish

literature before the time of Christ, that the Suffering Servant was considered by the Jews to be a messianic savior.

The other figure is that of "one like a son of man" in Daniel 7:13-14, who receives the dominion and kingdom from Yahweh, the Ancient of Days. Some scholars believe that this is not a messianic figure, but a representative of the "saints of the Most High" who, in Daniel 7:18, are described as receiving the kingdom. In any event, the Son of man was interpreted as a messianic figure in intertestamental literature composed not long after the Book of Daniel.

Israelite hopes for the future Golden Age, or messianic era, thus were not uniform, but contained considerable variety. Some were strongly nationalistic, others were universalistic; some emphasized spiritual conditions of the new age, whereas others emphasized material conditions. In all there was a fundamental faith that God would, in his way and in his time, bring to fulfillment the promises and the ideals set before his covenant people.

What Does the Lord Require?

Micah 6:1-8 gives an excellent summary of the Israelite faith in Yahweh as the classical prophets understood it. In verse 6 the prophet asks,

"With what shall I come before the LORD?"
He asks whether he should come with burnt offerings, with thousands of rams or ten thousands of rivers of oil, or even with the sacrifice of his first-born son. Then he receives the answer:

"He has showed you, O man, what is good;
 and what does the LORD require of you
but to do justice, and to love kindness,
 and to walk humbly with your God?"

Here we have a succinct definition of "what is good," or of Old Testament ethics: it is *what the Lord requires of man.* As a covenant God, Yahweh had the right to make demands of his covenant people. In the description of the ceremony by which the covenant was ratified, in Exodus 24:1-11, we are told that Moses read to the people the "book of the covenant," and they responded: "All that the LORD has spoken we will do, and we will be obedient." The laws of Yahweh are thus the terms of the covenant which Israel undertook to obey; they are what Yahweh required of Israel.

In the Old Testament there are various ways of interpreting in specific detail what Yahweh requires of Israel. The prophets of the preexilic period speak of the requirement in terms such as justice, righteousness, steadfast love, faith in God, humility, repentance, knowledge of God, and the like. A famous statement, in addition to Micah 6:8, is that of Hosea 6:6:

For I desire steadfast love and not sacrifice,
the knowledge of God, rather than burnt offerings.

As we read the prophets, we can see that specifically they thought Yahweh required that men practice impartiality in courts of law, avoiding bribery and giving the same justice to the rich and the poor; that merchants be fair and honest in their dealings with customers; that the wealthy and powerful refrain from oppressing the poor and weak; that Israelites show compassion upon the unfortunate members of society, such as widows and orphans; that the Hebrews refrain from worshiping foreign gods or adopting degrading customs associated with some forms of foreign worship; that they renounce nationalistic ambitions; and that they seek to follow the will of Yahweh in all phases of life. Many passages in these prophets denounce the elaborate ceremonies carried on by the Israelites in their worship. Some passages suggest that the prophets thought such ceremonies were useless, and no part of Yahweh's real requirement (see especially Amos 5:25 and Jeremiah 7:22). Others suggest that the ritual should be purified of its pagan elements and be given a connection with the moral life of the people. The prophets considered the worship as it was actually carried out by the people only an offense to Yahweh, whose primary requirements could be stated in terms of right rather than rite, in everyday living rather than in the activities that take place within the temple. The prophetic point of view was expressed by the psalmist:

> The sacrifice acceptable to God is a broken spirit;
> a broken and contrite heart, O God, thou wilt
> not despise.—Psalm 51:17

The requirements of Yahweh were set forth by others in the various codes of law or bodies of legislation embodied in the Pentateuch. Scholars have isolated seven codes of law, or sets of regulations, within the Pentateuch, roughly in chronological order as follows: (1) the Ten Commandments, or Ethical Decalogue, Exodus 20:1-17; Deuteronomy 5:6-21; (2) the Ritual Decalogue, Exodus 34:17-28; (3) the Twelve Curses, Deuteronomy 27:15-26; (4) the Covenant Code, Exodus 21-23; (5) the Deuteronomic Code, Deuteronomy 12—26; (6) the Holiness Code, Leviticus 17—26; and (7) the Priestly Code, Leviticus, with some legal materials in the other books. These have various forms, and most of them include both ethical and ceremonial regulations. Many are what we would term civil laws, regulating such matters as slavery, family life, court procedure, military affairs, and so on. Many are more specifically "religious," setting forth laws concerning festivals, Sabbath observance, food prohibitions, sacrifice, the priesthood, and so on. The Israelites would hardly have made the distinctions which we make within these laws, for they considered Yahweh to be the source of all law, and a notion such as "separation of church and state" would have been meaningless to them in the preexilic period. The king was the high priest, in theory if not always in practice; we have definite record of some of the kings officiating as priests. Thus, religion and affairs of the state were very closely bound together. The various laws within these codes developed over a long period of time. Some are inconsistent with others, and some are probably too idealistic ever to have been put into practice. Some are scarcely in harmony with ideals proclaimed by the prophets.

A third place in which we may find the requirements of Yahweh set forth in detail is in Proverbs. This book can be described as a handbook of practical ethics. It presents in axiomatic, proverbial form the accumulated wisdom of many generations, gathered and edited by the sages of Israel. As early as the time of Jeremiah (18:18), and probably much earlier, the "wise men" constituted a recognized class in Israel, whose mission was to give "counsel," especially to the youth. The Book of Proverbs is a distillation of their principles and advice.

The wise men did not, like the prophets, prefix their sayings with, "Thus saith the Lord." Their wisdom was based primarily upon experience, and was designed to help people to be successful and prosperous. A specific religious element is not prominent in the Proverbs. Nevertheless, the wise men certainly believed that they were teaching the requirements of God, and that those who followed their counsel would be pleasing in the sight of Yahweh.

The ethical standards of the Book of Proverbs are generally utilitarian; they do not in general represent the noblest, self-denying standards set forth in some other parts of the Bible. Such standards are not, however, to be despised for ordinary living. The wise men of the Book of Proverbs emphasize such virtues as industry, honesty, marital fidelity, obedience of parents by children, proper discipline of children, ability to listen to advice, humility, avoidance of gossip and loose talk, kindness to animals, patience, and returning good for evil. He who lives by such virtues is wise; he who does not is a fool. In general the rewards of the wise man are long life, a good reputation, a tranquil mind, and often material prosperity. Some of the proverbs represent wealth as the reward of wisdom, and consider poverty to be a curse. But many of the proverbs decry wealth that is gotten dishonestly.

The religion of the Old Testament has often been stigmatized as *arid legalism*. Christians have sometimes charged that the Israelites thought too much about obedience to law, and obeyed the law only out of dread of the punishment that their stern God might inflict upon them for disobedience. Or, they have charged that the Israelites failed to make a distinction between the grave moral offenses and trivial ceremonial offenses, setting both upon the same plane. Or, they have said that the Jews stifled the sense of freedom and joy which faith in God should promote, by hedging life about with too many petty prohibitions.

We must readily admit that a religion like that of the Old Testament, which involves belief in a God who has a will for the total life of man, can sink into an arid legalism. The very idea of a covenant could be debased into the notion of a bargain between man and God, with men thinking that they should give something to God in order that he might give something to them. In the latest period of Old Testament history, Judaism became especially subject to the corruption of legalism, when there was a great accumulation of regulations to be observed, and when the stricter Jews sought to isolate themselves from the impurities of the pagan religions around them. We must not forget, however, that Christianity has at times and in certain of its manifestations been legalistic in an objectionable sense. We hope that enough has already been said in this chapter about the faith of the Old Testament to counteract the charge of arid legalism, and to show that the faith of Israel at its best was not legalistic. Men did not obey God out of a sense of trembling terror, but out of a feeling of gratitude for what God had done for Israel, and from a desire to please the God who loved them. This was expressed most forcefully by Jeremiah (9:23-24):

> Thus says the LORD: "Let not the wise man glory in his wisdom, let not the mighty man glory in his might, let not the rich man glory in his riches; but let him who glories glory in this, that he understands and knows me, that I am the LORD who practice kindness [*hésed*], justice, and righteousness in the earth; for in these things I delight, says the LORD."

The Israelite who understood his faith knew that his God was characterized by steadfast love, justice, and righteousness, and that his own life would be pleasing to God if it was informed by the same qualities. This did not require the over-meticulous keeping of trivial regulations, but it did involve the belief that God has a will for the total life of individual men and of his people, and that they could leave God out of any phase of life only at their own peril.

Furthermore, there is evidence within the Old Testament that many who held the faith of the Old Testament did not find the law to be a burden, but rather to be a source of constant joy and delight. The longest of the Psalms, the 119th, has this as its constant theme, with every verse speaking joyfully and thankfully of God's law or word or statute. The theme of joy in life under the law is found also in Psalm 19:7-14. This psalmist said of the ordinances of the LORD (vs. 10):

> More to be desired are they than gold,
>   even much fine gold;
> sweeter also than honey
>   and drippings of the honeycomb.

IV

the apocrypha

YOU HAVE PROBABLY SEEN A PULPIT BIBLE OR an old family Bible that contains a group of books printed between the Old and New Testaments. These are called "the Apocrypha." You may have been intrigued by these books, and wondered what is in them and what standing they should have in your Bible. Maybe you have heard that most of them are found in Catholic Bibles, where they are printed along with the books of the Old Testament in such a way as to suggest that they are fully authoritative.

In popular usage the word "apocryphal" often means spurious, legendary, or not authentic. This meaning is not really appropriate to the books under discussion. The word "apocrypha" means, according to its origin, books that were "hidden away." In its earliest use it was applied to books that were of a mysterious nature and thus were "hidden" except from those who were initiated. Later it was applied to books that were "hidden," or withdrawn from ordinary use, because they were heretical or were not considered to be fully authoritative.

We ought to define the Apocrypha strictly as those books, or additions to Old Testament books, which are found in the

121

Latin Vulgate but not in the Hebrew Bible. According to this definition the following books comprise the Apocrypha: I and II Maccabees, Ecclesiasticus (or Sirach), The Wisdom of Solomon, Judith, Tobit, I and II Esdras, Baruch and The Letter of Jeremiah, The Prayer of Manasseh, Additions to Esther, and Additions to Daniel.

All of these books are contained in the Greek Septuagint, except II Esdras, but some editions of the Septuagint also contain books known as III and IV Maccabees. These books were written in the period between about 200 B.C. and A.D. 100, a very crucial time which saw the beginning of Christianity. Various types of literature are contained in the Apocrypha, as in the Old Testament canon itself. Some are historical narratives (I-II Maccabees, I Esdras); some are wisdom books similar to Proverbs or Ecclesiastes (Ecclesiasticus, Wisdom of Solomon); some are books of historical fiction (Tobit, Judith); and one is an apocalyptic work, II Esdras.

In a later chapter we shall discuss the formation of the canon of the Old Testament, and seek to show why our Protestant Old Testament has only thirty-nine books. We shall see that the canon was not definitely fixed until the end of the first century A.D., when the rabbis of the Academy of Jamnia decided that certain books should be considered authoritative, but eliminated others. The Jews usually referred to the latter group as "outside" books, including the Apocrypha.

Jews have since that time had a Bible of only thirty-nine books; they have never considered the Apocrypha as scripture, though in modern times many Jewish scholars have recognized that they are of value in studying the history of their religion. Among Christians, however, there have been differences of opinion. Today there is a clear-cut division between Roman Catholics and Protestants regarding the Apocrypha, but in the course of history both groups have entertained varying attitudes toward these books.

Since some of these books were written before the Christian era, they were known to New Testament writers, and exercised influence upon the New Testament itself. In the first four or five hundred years of Christian history, many leaders of the church referred to or quoted some books of the Apocrypha as if they were Scripture. Yet, some leaders were aware that they were not in the Jewish Bible, and displayed uneasiness over treating them as Scripture. For example, Jerome, who translated the Vulgate, knew they were not in the Hebrew text; he said that the Apocrypha might be read for edification, but should not be read in order to confirm church doctrines. Nevertheless he did include them in his Vulgate, and this tended to give them authority and make them generally known. However, another great Catholic leader at the same time, Augustine, generally accepted the books of the Apocrypha as fully authoritative.

In the course of the centuries, through the influence of the Latin Vulgate, Roman Catholics came more and more to regard the Apocrypha as Scripture, departing from Jerome's attitude. In the Council of Trent, 1546, the Roman Catholic church declared all of the books of the Apocrypha (except I-II Esdras and the Prayer of Manasseh) to be sacred and canonical. The three excepted books are often printed as an appendix to the New Testament. Therefore, for a Roman Catholic the books of the Apocrypha, with these exceptions, are as much a part of his Bible as Genesis, Isaiah, or Luke.

The Roman Catholic attitude was partly a reaction against the view of these books taken by the early Protestant Reformers. When Martin Luther published his German translation of the Bible, he placed the Apocrypha together between the Old and New Testament, with the explanation: "These books are not held equal to the sacred Scriptures, and yet are useful and good for reading." As a scholar he knew they were not in the Hebrew Bible, and as a Reformer he did not approve some of the doctrines that Roman Catholics derived from them. A somewhat similar attitude was adopted by the Church of England, which is officially the view of the Episcopal Church in the United States. Concerning the Apocrypha, Article Six of the Thirty-Nine Articles (adopted by the Church of England in 1562) says: "the other books (as Jerome saith) the Church doth read for example of life and instruction of manners; but yet doth it not apply them to establish any doctrine."

Protestant churches of the Calvinistic type, however, follow the attitude expressed in the Westminster Confession, which says clearly that the Apocrypha are not inspired and not part of the Canon of Scripture, and thus are to be used simply as "human writings."

Most Protestant churches of modern time merely ignore the Apocrypha, and there is no worldwide Protestant council which can pronounce on their authority today. The practical effect is that in most Protestant churches the Old Testament has the same books as the Jewish Bible, and the Roman Catholic church has a longer Old Testament.

In the chapter below on the canon we shall raise the question as to our attitude toward the Apocrypha: can they be considered as being in any sense authoritative or religiously valuable for our use today? We may here anticipate our discussion by saying that, whatever view we may take of their *authority*, we should not fail to recognize that they have great value in any study of developments within Judaism of the period in which they were written, and thus they form a most important part of the background of the New Testament.

Anyone who wishes to read the books of the Apocrypha can secure a Revised Standard Version of them that is published separately, or a translation by E. J. Goodspeed. It is possible also to secure editions of the Revised Standard Version which contain the Apocrypha along with the Old and New

Testaments; and Goodspeed's translation is included in *The
Complete Bible: An American Translation,* published by the
University of Chicago Press.

The Old Testament Apocrypha

In this section we shall describe briefly each of the books of
the Apocrypha, indicating the contents of each, the probable
date of composition, and its significance for the reader today.

First Maccabees is a narrative which gives the history of the
Jews from the accession of Antiochus IV Epiphanes (175 B.C.)
to the death of Simon (134 B.C.), forty stirring and generally
victorious years in the life of the Jewish nation. The name
"Maccabee" is derived from a title or nickname given to one
of the first leaders of this period, Judas. He was called Judas
Maccabee (or Maccabeus), probably meaning "The Hammer." The name came to be applied to all of the leaders
of his family, though the name Hasmonean is more accurate
(derived from an ancestor of Judas).

This book is a trustworthy and straightforward account of
the events of this forty-year period. It tells how Antiochus IV,
the Seleucid ruler, sought to wipe out the Jewish religion and
make the Jewish people live and worship as Greeks. This
provoked a rebellion which was led by a priest named Mattathias and his five sons. Three of the sons were successively
military leaders who gradually won more and more independence—Judas, Jonathan, and Simon. Under Judas the Jews
won sufficient freedom to rededicate their temple in Jerusalem;
under Simon they secured political independence and were
able to make him their high priest and governor.

The author of I Maccabees was a Palestinian Jew writing
in Hebrew about 100 B.C. He composed his narrative from a
strong sense of national pride in the victories of his people,
and saw the guiding hand of God in all of their successes.
He does not make the religious element prominent, however,

and is reticent about naming God, usually employing the synonym "Heaven." His account is much more trustworthy as history than that which is found in II Maccabees, and it is indeed our principal source of information for what happened in the years which it covers. Anyone can read it as a reliable record of a period which not only was a glorious one in Jewish history, but also a time when important developments were taking place in their religion. We can see, for example, the beginnings of the division of the Jews into the two main parties of the Sadducees and Pharisees.

Martin Luther said of I Maccabees that it was not unworthy to be reckoned among the books of Holy Scripture, and the poet Coleridge said that the story of the Maccabees was inspiring enough to be inspired.

Second Maccabees covers the first fifteen years of the history related in I Maccabees, but its author told the history from a viewpoint far different from that of I Maccabees. It is a book of religious instruction, designed to show the great superiority of the Jewish religion over that of the pagans, rather than a sober and straightforward historical narrative.

Second Maccabees claims to be a summary of a larger work composed in five volumes by Jason of Cyrene. Nothing definite is known about Jason, but we may surmise that he was a very devout Jew living in Alexandria around 100 B.C.; the author who summarized his work in II Maccabees probably lived sometime within the following century.

This book opens with two letters written by the Jews of Judah to their brethren in Jerusalem, admonishing them to observe the feasts of Tabernacles and of Hanukkah, the latter celebrating the purification and rededication of the temple in the early part of the Maccabean Age. Then the history begins a little before the accession of Antiochus Epiphanes, relating how his immediate predecessor tried to rob the Jerusalem temple, but was frustrated by the sudden appearance of a heavenly rider on a horse. The book goes on to tell of the intrigues of certain Jews to get the high priesthood, and of the defection of some to the Greek religion and Greek way of life. Then follows the account of the attempt of Antiochus Epiphanes to wipe out Judaism and compel the Jews to worship as Greeks. Chapters 6 and 7 relate the famous stories of the martyrdom of Eleazar the scribe, and of the mother and her seven sons, all of whom gladly went to a horrible death rather than eat pork. The remainder of the book, chapters 8—15, tells of the outbreak and progress of the Maccabean revolt, down to the defeat of the Syrian general Nicanor in 160 B.C.

Second Maccabees adds little to our knowledge of events in the Maccabean period, but has great value as an illustration of how one writer, representing the Pharisaic point of view, interpreted the events of the time. The author was deeply convinced that God controls in detail the history of the Jews, working directly and miraculously to defeat their enemies, and at the same time punishing Israel to discipline them for their sins. There are several accounts of dreams and of the appearance of angels and heavenly riders, and the like. The author is so unhistorical as to make the Seleucid king Antiochus Epiphanes experience a deathbed repentance and vow to become a Jew.

Second Maccabees shows clearly that many Jews expected resurrection of the flesh for the righteous, but apparently not of the wicked, who would suffer annihilation or eternal death. The martyrs who observed the Law could face death calmly because they looked forward to a future resurrection. One can find here examples of intercession by deceased saints on behalf of the living (15:12-16), and of the offering of prayers and sacrifices by the living on behalf of the dead (12:43-45).

We should read II Maccabees not so much as a work of history as a book which reflects important religious beliefs of the time when it was composed, the century before the coming of Christ. The beliefs it reflects are those of the Pharisees rather than the Sadducees. The modern reader will see here the basis for certain Catholic doctrines not held by Protestants such as the existence of Purgatory, and readily understand why the Protestant Reformers did not approve of this book but gladly placed it among the Apocrypha rather than in Scripture.

Ecclesiasticus is one of the most worthwhile and important books in the Apocrypha. It came closer to being accepted into the canon of the Old Testament than any of the others, and had a wide influence in both Judaism and Christianity. Unfortunately this work is known by several titles which cause confusion. Its ancient title in Greek manuscripts was "The Wisdom of Jesus the Son of Sirach," but in the Latin Vulgate it was called "Ecclesiasticus." The former title indicates that the author's name was Jesus son of Sirach, the name "Jesus" being the Greek equivalent of Hebrew "Joshua." The title of the book (or the author's name) is sometimes given as Ben Sira or Sirach. The Vulgate title, "Ecclesiasticus," indicates that it was "The Church Book," the most important (or longest) of the books which were read in church but were not fully canonical. In the present volume we have usually called it simply "Sirach" as a short, convenient title which cannot be confused with the Old Testament book of Ecclesiastes.

This book can be rather precisely dated, and it is the only apocryphal book whose author is known. The grandson of the author made a translation of it from Hebrew into Greek, and wrote a Prologue to explain what he had done. He came to Egypt in 132 B.C. and made his translation soon thereafter. His grandfather must have written around 180 B.C.

Jesus the son of Sirach was a Jewish teacher and scholar who apparently conducted an academy in Jerusalem, where he taught young men from the upper classes in what was then known as "wisdom." His book may be a transcript of his classroom lectures. In 38:24—39:11 he describes the ideal "scribe," and we can see in it a portrait of the author himself. He learned wisdom from study of the Scriptures, experience, and observation, and sought to inculcate in his pupils those qualities which would make them successful in life and truly religious. The author had traveled widely, probably on diplomatic missions for his people (34:9-12; 39:4).

Sirach is so loosely organized that it is impossible here to give an outline of its contents. Much of it consists of brief maxims, but some parts are longer essays; in form and style it is much like the Book of Proverbs. It deals with such diverse matters as table etiquette, the treatment of children by parents, the relationships between husband and wife, the dangers of loose women, diet, making sacrifice, giving alms, and so on. The long section in chapters 44 to 50 which begins "Let us now praise famous men," is the best-known passage in all of the Apocrypha, being read sometimes at funerals or memorial services.

Sirach reflects the traditional or orthodox Judaism of the time when it was written, before the rise of the Pharisaic and Sadducean parties. The book teaches that Wisdom is eternal (24:9), and identifies the Law of Moses with Wisdom (24:23-25). It encourages the practicing of the ritual of the temple, but says clearly that the sacrifices of the lawless are not acceptable to God, who is pleased only with the offerings of the righteous man (34:18—35:11). It has no doctrine of resurrection, nor of rewards and punishments in a future life. The author shows great distrust of women (25:16-26; 26:10-12; 42:9-14), and writes like a man who is unhappily married and has headstrong daughters.

Sirach influenced some parts of the New Testament. The Book of James particularly shows similarities in both wording and contents. The teachings of Jesus sometimes remind one of Sirach, both in form and in their content. Compare for example, Jesus' parable of the rich fool (Luke 12:16-20) with Sirach 11:18-19. A prominent New Testament scholar has said it is quite possible that "Jesus of Nazareth may have read and recollected phrases in the Wisdom of Jesus the son of Sirach."[1]

The Wisdom of Solomon belongs to the same general category of "wisdom literature" as Sirach, but it differs markedly from it in some respects. It is a clearly organized religious treatise directed to both Gentiles and Jews, designed to show the nature and great value of Wisdom, rather than a collection of maxims on various subjects. Its author was a Hellenistic Jew writing in Greek, probably in the city of Alexandria in Egypt, rather than a Jerusalem sage writing in Hebrew. In this book the personification of Wisdom reaches its climax, and certain beliefs that had profound influence on Christianity are set forth for the first time.

The Wisdom of Solomon can be divided into three well-defined sections: (1) chapters 1—5 exhort Jews to seek Wisdom because it brings salvation to the righteous Jews and condemnation to those who disregard it; (2) chapters 6—9, addressed primarily to pagan rulers, explain what Wisdom is and how it can be attained; and (3) chapters 10—19 show how, in the history of Israel, Wisdom has saved the Israelites and punished their adversaries, the Egyptians and others. This author wanted to show both that Judaism was superior to pagan religion, and that Judaism could be reconciled with the best Hellenistic philosophy of his time.

The author impersonates King Solomon, as did the author of the Old Testament Book of Ecclesiastes. Actually he was

---

[1]Bruce M. Metzger, *An Introduction to the Apocrypha* (New York: Oxford University Press, 1957), p. 169.

in all likelihood a Hellenistic Jew who had a good philosophical education, living in Alexandria in the first century B.C.

Wisdom is very highly personified in this book, being spoken of as a woman, as in the Book of Proverbs. She was "the fashioner of all things" (7:22). A long description in 7:22—8:1 attributes to her twenty-one qualities, including intelligence, holiness, beneficence, and omnipotence. She is "a breath of the power of God . . . a pure emanation of the glory of the Almighty . . . a reflection of eternal light . . . an image of [God's] goodness." Wisdom is divine, and the author almost says that Wisdom is equal to God.

In a number of important teachings this book accords better with the Greek thought of the time than with characteristically Hebraic ideas of the Old Testament. The following four points should be noted:

(1) Man consists of an immortal, pre-existent soul and a perishable body. The author says, "a good soul fell to my lot . . . [but] a perishable body weighs down the soul, and this earthy tent burdens the thoughtful mind" (8:19; 9:15). Here he talks much more like Plato and his followers, than Moses and the prophets.

(2) In his doctrine of the future life he speaks of the immortality of the soul rather than the resurrection of the body. The eternal soul leaves the corruptible body. Rather than saying that man receives his rewards and punishments in this life, he says that man is rewarded in the future life. One's moral character on earth determines his future destiny. "The souls of the righteous are in the hands of God" in heavenly bliss (3:1-9), but the ungodly will be punished, by annihilation or by eternal torment (1:13-16; 4:18-20). This author says that death came into the world by the envy of the devil (2:24), thus for the first time identifying the serpent of the garden of Eden with the devil.

(3) God created the world out of formless matter (11:17). His description of creation reminds many scholars of Plato's description in the *Timaeus*, rather than Genesis.

(4) In his description of Wisdom pseudo-Solomon sounds as if he knew of the Hellenistic idea of the *logos* (sometimes translated as "Word"), which was an impersonal mediator between God and the created world. Phrases such as "pure emanation of the glory of the Almighty" and "image of his goodness" sound much more Greek than Jewish.

The Wisdom of Solomon undoubtedly influenced early Christian writers, especially Paul and the author of Hebrews. Paul's thought is in some places so close to that of Wisdom that a Roman Catholic scholar, Msgr. Ronald Knox, once suggested that perhaps Paul wrote the book before he became a Christian. This is not likely to be true, but "there can be little doubt that the Apostle had at one time made a close study of this Apocryphal book."[2] For example, Paul's statement in Romans 1:20-22 that man can know the power of God through observing his creation, but has foolishly turned away to the worship of idols, has a close parallel in *Wisdom*, chapter 13. Also, Paul's unusual figure of God as a Potter making vessels both for wrath and for mercy sounds very much like *Wisdom* 15:7. A verse quoted above, 9:15, expresses a thought similar to 2 Corinthians 5:1-4.

In the early Christian church this book was valued for its predictions of Christ. The verse, "Blessed is the wood by which righteousness comes" (14:7), which was used of the ark of Noah, was interpreted as referring to the crucifixion of Jesus on the cross. Throughout Christian history some of the ideas of the Wisdom of Solomon have been used when attempts have been made to combine Hebrew and Greek teachings.

Judith is a story which tells how a heroic Jewish woman

---

[2]*Ibid.*, p. 163.

saved her people in a time of grave national crisis through her bravery and cunning. It was written in the middle of the second century B.C. when the Jews were engaged in the Maccabean struggle against the Greeks.

The story which it relates is as follows: Nebuchadnezzar, ruler of the Assyrians, defeated the Medes, and then turned against the nations of western Asia that had refused to join him in the conflict. After he had defeated some of them, the rest surrendered, except the people of Judea. They refused to submit, trusting in their God to save them, Nebuchadnezzar besieged their city of Bethulia, and when he cut off their water supply, the Jews were reduced almost to starvation. As they were just about to surrender, Judith came forward to ask that they give her time to carry out a plan she had for their salvation.

Judith—whose name means "the Jewess"—was a wealthy widow who was very beautiful and also very religious, observing scrupulously the Law of Moses. She besought her fellow Jews not to put God to the test, but remember that "God is not like man, to be threatened, nor like a human being, to be won over by pleading" (8:16). After a long prayer to God, she set out to the camp of Holofernes, the general of the Assyrian armies, taking along a bag filled with "kosher" food. She gained access to the tent of Holofernes by claiming that she could show him how to defeat his enemy without losing a man. She told Holofernes that the Jews were about to sin against their God by eating forbidden food, and, when their God turned against them, the Assyrians could easily defeat them. For three days Judith remained with the Assyrians, returning each night to her own town to take her ritual bath and to renew her food supply.

On the fourth day Holofernes prepared a great banquet for Judith, inviting his slaves, and intending to violate her. At the height of the banquet all the guests left, and Judith was alone with Holofernes. As he lay in a drunken stupor, she took his sword and cut off his head. She placed his head in her food bag and went back to her own people. With the loss of their general, the Assyrians were put into a panic and the Jews easily slaughtered them. Judith was a great heroine to her people, and she lived to the age of 105 without ever remarrying.

This story is very obviously fiction, not history. It is filled with historical inaccuracies and incredible details. For example, Nebuchadnezzar is described as ruling over the Assyrians in the great city of Nineveh; the Jews have returned from their captivity and rebuilt their temple. In reality Nebuchadnezzar was ruler over the Babylonians, and the Assyrian city of Nineveh had already fallen when he became king; it was Nebuchadnezzar himself who took the Jews captive to Babylonia, and they returned to their land and rebuilt their temple many years after his death. Judith is a legendary or wholly fictitious figure, and the story was told in order to admonish the Jews to remain loyal to their faith, which was conceived in an ultra-orthodox manner, and to resist their enemies.

The modern Christian reader of this book may admire it as an interesting and well-written short story, but he probably will not consider it an edifying one. Though the style is sometimes too florid and occasionally turgid, the author describes his leading characters well and makes artful use of suspense. Judith is represented as brave and patriotic, but she deliberately uses deceit and flagrantly employs her feminine charms to entice Holofernes into a situation where she can assassinate him. The story glorifies war and exalts the Jewish nation. To be fair to the book, however, one must remember that it was written in a time when the Jews were engaged in a struggle for their religion and their national existence. It is hardly more nationalistic, or even more fictional, than the Book of Esther.

The great value in Judith is that it reflects a type of religion that was prominent in this period, an early form of Pharisaism that put great emphasis on observance of the Law of Moses, especially with regard to personal purity and strict keeping of the rules regarding food. Even when Judith is enjoying the banquet with Holofernes, she drinks only the wine she had brought with her, and the food prepared by her maid, consisting of parched grain, a cake of dried fruit, and fine bread.

Tobit is another fictional story. It does not have as interesting a plot as Judith, but contains good character portrayal. It tells the story of a very righteous Jew who suffers many afflictions, but is cared for by God and ends his life with rewards and honor. It was written about 180 B.C., before the outbreak of the Maccabean revolt.

Tobit was a Jew of Galilee in the eighth century B.C. He was taken captive to Nineveh by Shalmaneser. He kept the Law very scrupulously and was very charitable to the poor, but he had all his property confiscated, became blind, and had a bitter quarrel with his wife. He was so miserable that he prayed for death to come to him.

In faraway Media a kinswoman of Tobit named Sarah was suffering misfortune also. She was married to seven husbands, but in each case the husband died before the marriage could be consummated; they were all killed by a demon named Asmodeus, who was in love with Sarah. At this point Tobit sent his son, Tobias, to Media to recover ten talents of silver that Tobit had deposited there in his better days. Tobias succeeded in doing this and also in marrying Sarah. He was able to frighten away the demon who had murdered her previous husbands, by making a smoke of the heart and liver of a fish. The happy couple returned to Tobit in Nineveh, and Tobias cured his father's blindness by rubbing on his eyes the gall of the fish.

Tobit advised his son to leave Nineveh, for it was to be destroyed, as prophesied by Jonah. Both men grew old with honor, and Tobias lived to see the destruction of Nineveh.

This story is clearly fictional; no part of it can be proved to be historical. It is most valuable, however, as a portrayal of the type of personal religion which was highly prized by many Jews at the time it was written. Tobit keeps the Law of Moses carefully, and even goes beyond it to observe the oral law which was developing to a strictness beyond that of the written one. He observes the dietary laws even in a foreign land; he fasts often, and properly keeps the feasts. He prays often, and the prayers in the book are probably typical of the prayers of Judaism at this time. Above all, he is generous in alms-giving and performs many acts of charity. The book says that "almsgiving delivers from death, and it will purge away every sin. Those who perform deeds of charity and of righteousness will have fulness of life" (12:9). In his speech to his son, Tobit utters the Golden Rule in a negative form: "What you hate, do not do to any one" (4:15). One of the basic teachings of the book is that God in his providential care looks after the righteous. Though he may allow them to be afflicted, he rewards them in the end. Tobit may remind us in some respects of Job, but he never questions the doctrine of divine retribution as Job did.

One of the very interesting features of this book is its emphasis on magic, and on the activity of angels and demons. It was an evil demon, Asmodeus, who killed the first seven husbands of Sarah, and Tobias got the better of him by magical means taught him by the angel, Raphael. That angel appeared in human form as the man Azarias, to accompany Tobias on his journey to Media and make him prosper. Tobit's blindness was cured by a form of magic. Raphael is described as "one of the seven holy angels who present the prayers of the saints and enter into the presence of the glory of the Holy One" (12:15).

The book of Tobit was very popular in ancient times among the Jews. Throughout Christian history it has been used in various ways in connections with marriages and marriage ceremonies. For example, among the Old Order Amish in the United States, it has often been made the basis of the wedding sermon, though it is not recognized as Scripture. Martin Luther said that Tobit is "a truly beautiful, wholesome and profitable fiction, the work of a gifted poet. . . . A book useful and good for us Christians to read."

First Esdras is an unusual apocryphal book in that most of it is substantially identical with a long section of the Old Testament: 2 Chronicles 35:1—36:23, the whole of Ezra, and Nehemiah 7:73—8:12. Thus it tells the history of the Jews from the celebration of the Passover in the time of King Josiah (621 B.C.) to the reading of the Law under Ezra (about 400 B.C.). The only lengthy addition is contained in I Esdras 3:1—5:6, which tells the story of the contest of three youths who were personal guardsmen of the Persian king, Darius. That part of I Esdras which is identical with the Old Testament was apparently translated into Greek from the Hebrew-Aramaic text, virtually the same as our standard text in the Hebrew Bible. Considerable confusion is caused by the fact that the book we are calling I Esdras is sometimes referred to as "Greek Ezra," and in the Vulgate it is called III Esdras and printed after the New Testament.

The story of the three youths is interpolated into the older history, and we can here confine our attention to it. The story is as follows: During the time that the work on the Jerusalem temple was suspended, in the second year of King Darius, three young members of the king's bodyguard proposed, after a great banquet, that they enter into a contest to see which one could state "what one thing is strongest." They thought that the king would then bestow honor and riches on the one whose statement seemed to him wisest. Each wrote his statement and sealed it, and the three were put under the pillow of the king. One wrote that wine is strongest; the second wrote that the king is strongest; and the third wrote, "Women are strongest, but truth is victor over all things." The king then gave each youth an opportunity to defend his statement. They spoke in turn about the strength of wine, the great power of the king, and the greatness of women; but the third said that "truth endures and is strong for ever, and lives and prevails for ever and ever" (4:38). The third youth won. As his reward he requested that the king give orders to rebuild Jerusalem, to return there the vessels that had been taken away, and to complete the temple. King Darius complied with his request, and soon many Jews were on their way back to Jerusalem to carry out his orders.

This tale of three youths is probably of Persian origin, and the author of this book has made excellent use of it. The verdict that "Great is Truth, and mighty above all things," as the King James Version renders 4:41, has become proverbial, and was interpreted by some early Christian theologians as prophesying the coming of Christ.

Second Esdras is an entirely different kind of work. It is not history, as one might expect, but an apocalypse, belonging to that type of literature we know best in the Old Testament in the Book of Daniel and in the New Testament in Revelation. The English "apocalypse" is derived from a Greek word meaning "revelation." A book of this type is filled largely with revelations concerning the future, which is often depicted through the use of various symbols.

The heart of II Esdras is contained in chapters 3—14, a Jewish work written in Aramaic toward the end of the first century A.D. To this two chapters have been prefixed, and two chapters added, by Christian authors in the two following centuries. This apocryphal book is thus of mixed Jewish and Christian origin, and contains some of the latest material in the Apocrypha. We pointed out above that it is not considered as Scripture by the Roman Catholics, but is usually printed *after* the New Testament; Catholics call this book IV Esdras.

In chapters 3—14 Ezra, the Old Testament priest and scribe, is the recipient of seven visions. In these he seeks an answer to the questions: How can a God who is both just and almighty permit his own chosen people to suffer so much at the hands of their enemies, and how can he allow the unrighteous to prosper more than the righteous? One of the answers he receives from an angel is that it is impossible for man to understand the ways of God. When Ezra then asks why man was given intelligence, if he cannot understand such matters, he is told that he must wait to see the coming of the new age, when God will issue rewards and punishments. He will send his Messiah, who will rule for 400 years. After that will come the resurrection and judgment, when the wicked will be consigned to a hell of torment and the saved will go to a paradise of delight. Only a few will be saved, the great majority of men being punished for their sins. In the course of the visions, many details concerning the future are presented. The fourth beast of Daniel, chapter 7, is represented in II Esdras 11—12 as an eagle with twelve wings and three heads, and the interpretation explains this as the Roman Empire that is to be overthrown by the coming Messiah.

The Christian preface to the Ezra apocalypse indicates that God will reject the Jewish people because of their sins, and give his name to other nations (1:24-37).

The modern reader of this book will find in it much that is bizarre and unattractive; it is a difficult work to appreciate and understand. It is valuable, however, as showing how the Jewish people reacted to their sufferings after the fall of Jerusalem to the Romans in A.D. 70, and in illustrating many similarities between Jewish and Christian expectations for the future. Because it wrestles with the problem of the relationship between the justice and the love of God, the book deals with one of the most important and most difficult of all religious questions.

Baruch and *The Letter of Jeremiah* are joined together in the Latin Vulgate; in the King James Version the latter is printed as chapter 6 of *Baruch*. The two books are, however, quite different in their nature and purpose, and come from different authors. Their only connection is the fact that Baruch was the secretary and companion of the Old Testament prophet Jeremiah. Both may be considered as additions to the Book of Jeremiah, made long after that prophet died.

Baruch claims to contain the book which Baruch wrote in Babylon after the Chaldeans captured and burned Jerusalem, and took away many exiles. It says that he read the book in the hearing of the exiled king Jeconiah (Jehoiachin) and many others in Babylon. When they heard it they wept, fasted, and prayed to the Lord, and took up a collection to send to their fellow Jews left in Jerusalem. They requested that they pray for the life of Nebuchadnezzar, the king of Babylon, and his son Belshazzar, and that they read the book as their confession of sin in the house of the LORD on the days of the feasts and appointed seasons.

The contents of the book are only in part appropriate to the description in this introductory section. Baruch 1:15—3:8 is a long confession of sin in prose, more suitable to Jews in exile than those in Jerusalem. The rest of the book is poetry, largely addressed to Israel. Baruch 3:9—4:4 praises wisdom or knowledge, and 4:5—5:9 addresses words of comfort and hope to Jerusalem, largely in the spirit of Second Isaiah.

The book of Baruch may have been written by two or three different writers, probably in the second century or early in the first century B.C. The last section could have been written as late as the first century A.D., after the fall of Jerusalem to the Romans. The book had more influence in early Christian circles than in Judaism. Several early Christian writers saw especially in 3:36-37 a prediction of the coming of Christ as the incarnation of God:

> He [God] found the whole way to knowledge,
>   and gave her to Jacob his servant
>   and to Israel whom he loved.
> Afterward she appeared upon earth and lived among
>   men.

The brief *Letter of Jeremiah* professes to be the letter which Jeremiah wrote to the captives in Babylonia, as described in Jeremiah 29:1-3. It is not actually a letter so much as a sermon on the folly of idolatry. It warns the Jews against the worship of the Babylonian gods, because they are completely useless and lifeless. Over and over the book says of them, "they are not gods." Even the Chaldeans themselves sometimes dishonor them (vs. 40). The tone of this polemic against idolatry is very much like that which is found in Second Isaiah and in Jeremiah 10:1-16.

The Letter of Jeremiah cannot be dated with accuracy. It certainly was not penned by the prophet himself; it was probably written in the second or third century B.C. The early Christians sometimes used it in their struggles against pagan idolatry in the Roman Empire.

The Prayer of Manasseh professes to be the prayer uttered by the Judean king, Manasseh, when he was in prison in Babylon, where he had been taken by the Assyrian king (2 Chronicles 33:11-13). It is a noble, well-constructed prayer consisting of three parts: (1) an invocation addressed to the LORD as creator and as the one who gives repentance and forgiveness to sinners; (2) a confession of sin and supplication for pardon; and (3) a closing doxology. This prayer teaches the mercy of God and the efficacy of repentance, when made even by one who had been as deeply wicked as Manasseh. The LORD is the author both of the repentance of the sinner and of his forgiveness. This prayer was not an original part of 2 Chronicles, but was composed in the first or second century B.C. In the Protestant Apocrypha it is printed as a separate book, though it consists of only 15 verses; in Catholic Bibles it is usually printed at the end of the New Testament.

The Additions to Esther have had a curious history that has caused confusion to readers. They are found in the Greek Septuagint distributed in various places where they are appropriate. When Jerome made his translation of the Bible into Latin, he first translated the Hebrew text of the book, and then collected all of the additions which were in the Greek, and put them at the end of the book. The King James Version also put them at the end of the canonical book, entitling them "The Rest of the Chapters of the Book of Esther which are found neither in the Hebrew nor in the Chaldee." These additions constitute 107 verses. The modern reader can make sense of them only if he reads them at the appropriate points of the story of Esther as they are contained in the Septuagint. It is customary to number them with letters A to F, and they may be summarized as follows:

A precedes the opening of the book in its canonical form, and contains a dream of Mordecai in which he saw two great dragons, ready to fight. When the Jews cried to God for help, there arose a tiny spring that became a great river. When Mordecai awoke, he overheard two eunuchs planning to assassinate the Persian king, and he reported it to the king. He was rewarded with a position at the royal court.

B should follow Esther 3:13; it purports to be the edict which the king sent to the provincial governors commanding the massacre of the Jews.

C and D follow the fourth chapter of Esther. C contains the prayers of Mordecai and Esther calling upon their God for help. D is an expansion of Esther 5:1-2 telling how Esther approached the king on his throne and was received by him.

E follows after 8:12 and claims to be the text of the royal edict which revoked the former one (B), ordering the governors to permit the Jews to follow their own laws and customs.

F should come after the closing verse of the canonical Esther. It supplies the interpretation of Mordecai's dream of Addition A. The two dragons represented Mordecai and Haman, and the tiny spring which became a great river represented Esther. It explains that God "made two lots, one for the people of God and one for all the nations." These events are thus to be celebrated in the Feast of Purim (meaning "lots"). A postscript says that one Dositheus and his son brought to Egypt the Letter of Purim which had been translated by Lysimachus a resident of Jerusalem. This last has been interpreted by some scholars as applying to the whole Greek version of Esther.

The motivation of these additions to the Old Testament Book of Esther is not difficult to discover. The Old Testament Book does not even once refer to God, and seems to go out of its way to avoid being religious, making no mention even of prayer. It is a very secular and nationalistic book. These additions were designed to supply the religious element that was lacking, and to give further authentication to the book by adding the text of the royal decrees which affected the Jews. Unfortunately there are a few contradictions between these additions and the canonical book, such as the date when Mordecai discovered the plot against the king, and the nationality of Haman. Also, the mutual hostility between Jews and Gentiles in the Additions is deeper than in the canonical book. The hostility here becomes a divinely ordained conflict between the two groups. (A few scholars, some of them eminent, have interpreted these Additions in exactly the opposite manner: the Greek form of the Book of Esther represents its original Semitic form, and the Old Testament form is an abbreviation of it. When the Feast of Purim became a hilarious celebration, all the religious references in the book were deliberately removed.)

These Additions to the Book of Esther may help the modern reader understand why in early Christian times some Jewish rabbis and Christian leaders could declare that this was not a sacred book, and why Protestants like Martin Luther have said it should not be in the Bible. It is somewhat more palatable in its longer form, but in that form God is made to bless Jewish nationalism and to be the author of Jewish-Gentile hostility.

The Additions to Daniel are found in various positions in the ancient versions of that book. In the Latin Vulgate, the Prayer of Azariah and the Song of the Three Young Men are placed within chapter 3, after verse 23. The story of Susanna and the Elders is at the end of the book, numbered chapter 13, and the story of Bel and the Dragon is numbered as chapter 14. In Protestant editions of the Apocrypha these are usually printed as three separate books.

The third chapter of Daniel relates how the three companions of Daniel were cast into a fiery furnace when they refused to bow down to the image set up by Nebuchadnezzar. The Prayer of Azariah continues the story after verse 23. The three young men walked about in the flames singing hymns to God. Then follows a long prayer by one of the three, Azariah. It is in substance a confession of the sin of his people and a plea for their deliverance. He prays: "with a contrite heart and a humble spirit may we be accepted, as though it were with burnt offerings of rams and bulls." This prayer is not really appropriate to the situation; it must have been from some collection of prayers inserted by an editor who thought it fitting that the companions should pray for their people rather than themselves. The latter part of this Addition is a long hymn of praise in which all of God's creatures, both animate and inanimate, are summoned to bless the LORD. It is similar in sentiment to Psalm 148, and in form to Psalm 136. This hymn has found its way into the Roman service of the mass, and the Anglican service of morning prayer (as an alternative to the Te Deum).

The story of Susanna is pure fiction. It is an early detective story, illustrating the themes of the innocent falsely accused and of the clever young judge. Susanna was the wife of Joakim, a Jew living in Babylon. She was very beautiful and also very religious. Two elders who served as judges fell in love with her, and one day they surprised her as she was taking a bath in her garden. They proposed that she lie with them, on the threat that if she did not do so they would say they had apprehended her in embrace with a young man. She refused, saying that she would not sin in the sight of the LORD. On their accusation she was condemned to die, but as she was being led away to execution, Daniel protested she had not been given a fair trial. He was then given the opportunity to examine the two elders separately, and they could not agree in naming the kind of tree under which they had found the couple. So they were put to death, and Susanna was spared.

This story has several obvious morals, but it is not certain that it was told for a didactic purpose. It came to be very popular in Christian literature and art; many artists have depicted the scene of Susanna being accosted by the two elders.

The two stories of Bel and the Dragon were intended to heap ridicule upon heathen idolatry. Bel was a Babylonian idol worshiped by King Cyrus, but Daniel would not revere him because he was not a living God. Cyrus protested that he was a living God, for he consumed so much food: every day he was given twelve bushels of flour, forty sheep, and fifty gallons of wine. In a test, Daniel proved that the food and wine were consumed by the priests who had a trapdoor beneath the table on which the offerings were placed. Daniel had his servants sift ashes on the floor, and the priests left footprints that betrayed them, in spite of the fact that the door to the temple remained sealed. So the king put the priests to death, and Daniel destroyed Bel and its temple.

The great Dragon was another idol worshiped by the Babylonians, but Daniel claimed he could slay it without sword or club. He prepared a mixture of pitch, fat, and hair; when this was fed to the Dragon, it burst open. The Babylonians then accused their king of becoming a Jew, and he handed Daniel over to them to be thrown into the lions' den. But Daniel was miraculously preserved from harm. The prophet Habakkuk of Judea brought him food, when that prophet was transported to Babylon by an angel, who lifted him up by the hair of his head. Daniel was rescued by the king, and the men who plotted against him were thrown into the den to be devoured.

These Additions to Daniel were made sometime after the original book was completed; they must date from the latter part of the second century, or from the first century B.C.

The Pseudepigrapha

In the period between the third century B.C. and the second century A.D., the Jews wrote many books. Some of them became a part of the Old Testament, such as Daniel, Ecclesiastes, and Esther. Others constituted the Apocrypha that we have just discussed. Still others are now generally known by the name of Pseudepigrapha. These might be called books of the third grade, if we designate the Old Testament books as first grade and the Apocrypha as second grade. Some of the Pseudepigrapha are long and tedious, and some received Christian additions, but they are all valuable as illustrating developments

in Judaism for the period, and some afford important insight
into New Testament teachings. Many are apocalyptic in nature,
and set forth the messianic expectations which the Jews held
at this important time.

The word "pseudepigraph" means literally a work that is
composed in the name of, or is ascribed to, someone other than
the actual author—usually an ancient writer or hero who is well-
known. There are in fact books of both the Old and New Testaments that fit this description—such as Ecclesiastes, Daniel,
and the Book of Hebrews. Most of the books that we are here
technically calling Pseudepigrapha were written in the name of,
or describe the doings of, ancient biblical characters such as
Enoch, Moses, Solomon, Baruch, Ezra, or Isaiah. Since these
books are so numerous, and often so long, we cannot discuss
them in full here. The following will give the reader a little
information about some of the more important books of the
group.[3]

The Book of Enoch is a very long work of 108 chapters
written by various writers over a period of a century beginning
about 160 B.C. Enoch is the early figure of whom Genesis says:
"Enoch walked with God; and he was not, for God took him"
(5:24). Much of this long collection of materials is a description of Enoch's conducted tour of the heavens and the under-
world. He learns the secrets of astronomy, is told about the
course of history, sees the fallen angels, the devil, and the
Messiah and foresees various events that are to take place at
the end of this age.

The book is of special value because of the various titles
and descriptions it gives of the Messiah, thus depicting the
messianic expectations of the Jews in this era. The title "Son

---

[3]Many of them are collected in the second volume of the large work edited by R. H.
Charles under the title, *The Apocrypha and Pseudepigrapha of the Old Testament* (Oxford:
Clarendon Press, 1913). There is no general agreement among scholars as to precisely what
books belong in this classification. The confusion is made greater by the fact that Roman
Catholic scholars often refer to these books as "apocrypha," since the books which
Protestants usually call Apocrypha are recognized by Roman Catholics as Scripture.

of man" is given to the Messiah for the first time, when the figure of Daniel 7:13 is interpreted messianically (Enoch 46:2-4).

The little Epistle of Jude in the New Testament quotes Enoch 1:9. In many respects the Enoch materials influenced the New Testament more than any other book of the Pseudepigrapha, and more than most of the Apocrypha.

The Testament of the Twelve Patriarchs is a different type of book, being especially valuable as reflecting Jewish ethical teachings in the second century before Christ. It represents each of the sons of Jacob as giving to his descendants his parting advice, just before he is to die. He dwells on his own sins and the misfortunes that resulted from them, and recommends the opposite virtues. Most of the patriarchs make predictions for the future age in addition to giving wise advice.

This book considers sin to be universal, resulting from the combination in each man of two inclinations given him by God—the good inclination and the evil inclination. The individual sins that are most condemned are hatred, lying, envy, lust, and covetousness; the corresponding virtues are patience, truthfulness, love, purity, and generosity. At two points in particular this book seems to anticipate the New Testament. For the first time the love of God and of one's neighbor are combined, as in the Testament of Issachar 5:2: "Love the Lord and your neighbor; have compassion on the poor and weak." The teaching on forgiveness of one's enemies is very high: "Love ye one another from the heart; and if a man sin against thee, speak peaceably to him, and in thy soul hold not guile; and if he repent and confess, forgive him. . . . And if he be shameless and persist in his wrong-doing, even so forgive him from the heart, and leave to God the avenging" (Testament of Gad 6:3-7). In its original form this work looked forward to the coming of a priestly Messiah from the line of Levi.

The Book of Jubilees is a paraphrase and expansion of the Book of Genesis and the first twelve chapters of Exodus, probably written in the second century B.C. The author omits some unsavory details of the patriarchal stories in Genesis, such as Abraham's white lie concerning his wife Sarah, and he attributes to Satan (whom he calls Mastema) certain actions which the biblical books ascribed to God, such as the testing of Abraham by the sacrifice of Isaac, and the attempt to kill Moses related in Exodus 4:24. This book glorifies the Law as eternal, and strongly insists that the Jews must be pure and avoid taking over any elements of paganism from the Gentiles.

The Psalms of Solomon consist of 18 poems modeled after the Psalms in the Old Testament. They are ascribed to Solomon, though he is not mentioned in any of them, and some have titles and musical notations similar to those of the Psalter. This collection of poems can be rather closely dated in the middle of the first century B.C., for there are allusions to the overthrow of the Hasmonean dynasty and capture of Jerusalem that very likely refer to the capture of that city by the Roman Pompey in 63 B.C.; his death in Egypt fifteen years later is apparently referred to in 2:30.

The Psalms of Solomon speak constantly of the contrast between the righteous and the ungodly. The ungodly are described as proud and insolent because of their wealth, disrespectful of God and his sanctuary, addicted to sexual impurity, hypocritical and so on. The righteous, on the other hand, are those who obey God's Law, trust in him, and await his bringing in of his kingdom through a Messiah of the line of David. These two groups are often interpreted as the Sadducees and the Pharisees, and it is likely the poems were written by members of the Pharisaic party. The 17th Psalm describes the coming of the Messiah from the line of David to be a righteous king, ruling over a holy people and giving them victory over their enemies.

The Dead Sea Scrolls

The documents that are popularly called the Dead Sea Scrolls have received a great deal of publicity. The original group was accidentally discovered in 1947 in a cave near the northwestern corner of the Dead Sea, south of the city of Jericho. Subsequently widespread search was made for other documents in the same general area. Scientific excavations have been carried on in some of the caves, and also at a site called Khirbet Qumran which was the headquarters of the sect that preserved the scrolls. A great many documents and fragments of documents have been discovered, or purchased from natives, and it will be many years before all of them are studied and published by scholars. A more accurate designation of the materials would be Qumran documents, after the name of the area in which they were found, Wadi Qumran. Some documents, mostly of a somewhat later date, were found in another region, Wadi Murabbaat, south of Qumran.

The materials included in this large group constitute complete copies or fragments of books of the Bible (all except the Book of Esther being represented), commentaries on Biblical books (of which the commentary on Habakkuk is the most nearly complete), books of the Apocrypha and Pseudepigrapha, and books which were previously unknown. The name Dead Sea Scrolls is sometimes given specifically to the original group of seven documents. These were: an almost complete copy of the Book of Isaiah, made in about 100 B.C.; a fragmentary copy of the last third of the Book of Isaiah, made a century or more later; a commentary on the Book of Habakkuk; and four works previously unknown. The first-named copy of Isaiah is the oldest virtually complete manuscript of any part of the Bible now known. The commentary on Habakkuk (like the other commentaries discovered) is not a commentary in the modern sense of the word; it quotes the biblical text and then seeks to show how the words of the prophet are applicable to the author's own time and the events of his age or the immediate future.

The sect that preserved these scrolls is considered by many scholars to be the sect known to Josephus, Philo, and some other ancient writers as Essenes. The designation is in general appropriate to them. They were a strict group of Jews, who had gone out into the desert to "prepare the way of the Lord" by studying the Law, copying and preserving their books. They followed an ascetic type of life which involved communal ownership of property, communal meals, and ritual purity. They were awaiting the coming of a prophet and two Messiahs, one from the line of Aaron and one from the line of David, and the final day of judgment.

The previously unknown books of this sect may appropriately be classed with the Pseudepigrapha that we have discussed. In fact, some of the Pseudepigrapha may have been composed by Essenes, and copies of some of them were preserved at Qumran. We shall describe briefly the four books as examples of the literature of this important sect that flourished in the first two centuries B.C. and in the first century A.D. down to the capture of Jerusalem by the Romans.

The Manual of Discipline describes many beliefs and practices of the Qumran community. At the outset it says that those who wish to become members must love all the children of light and hate all the children of darkness, and must bring into the community all of their mind, their strength, and their wealth. It goes on to describe the ceremony by which the new members were initiated into the covenant of the community, and the ceremony of the annual renewal of the covenant. Then, an important section describes some of the basic beliefs. Everything that exists was created by the God of knowledge. God created man to rule the world, and made two spirits—a spirit of truth and light, and a spirit of perversity and darkness.

These two spirits struggle together in man's heart until God's final visitation, when he will destroy darkness and perversity, and truth will emerge triumphant.

A long section sets forth the various detailed rules by which the members must live, and by which they must conduct themselves in their meetings, and the penalties for breaking the rules. The Manual closes with praise of God, promising obedience to him, and declaring that man is saved by the righteousness of God.

The Hymns of Praise are a collection of psalms or hymns, similar to the Old Testament Psalter and to the Psalms of Solomon. They are sometimes called the Thanksgiving Hymns, because many of the individual psalms begin, "I thank thee, O Lord, that thou hast. . . ." But not all express thanksgiving; some express lamentation or trust or other sentiments. They stress the all-embracing providence of God, and the contrasts between the men who have been chosen by God and are loyal to him, and the sons of darkness or of Belial. God is praised for rescuing his chosen ones from many afflictions. These hymns were very probably used in the ritual ceremonies of the Qumran Essenes.

The War Scroll describes the war, or series of battles, between the sons of light and the sons of darkness. The former are the tribes of Levi, Judah, and Benjamin; the latter are various foreign nations and those who have violated the covenant. The scroll goes into great detail to describe the battle array, the requirements for military service, the battle standards and their inscriptions, the blowing of the trumpets, the priestly prayers, and so on. This scroll has been a puzzle to interpreters. In some respects it seems to be concerned with real military conflicts. In other respects it is highly unrealistic. The armies are represented as fighting for a space of forty years, but both sides observe the sabbatical years (once every seven years). The sons of light gradually defeat their enemies one by one, but there is a final battle in which they are aided by the angels and a conclusive victory over evil is won. The best interpretation seems to be that this is an Essene version of the final "Battle of Armageddon" at the end of the age, such as we are familiar with in the New Testament Book of Revelation.

The Genesis Apocryphon is a work in the Aramaic language (all of the above being in Hebrew), which is similar to the Book of Jubilees discussed above; it paraphrases and expands upon narratives in the Book of Genesis. This scroll was so poorly preserved, and so dry and brittle when it was discovered, that it could not be unrolled until scholars had worked out a method of doing so without having it go to pieces entirely. Only a few chapters have been published, and it seems that much of the scroll is too damaged to be read with satisfaction. As an example of its contents, we may point out that in the part which corresponds to the twelfth chapter of Genesis, which tells of Abraham and Sarah going down into Egypt, the beauty of Sarah is described in much detail. One great value of this scroll is that it is one of the very few documents we now have available written in the language which was spoken in Palestine in the time of Jesus, and very near to if not actually during his lifetime.

The Dead Sea Scrolls have already proved very useful in illuminating the background of Jewish life and faith against which Christianity arose. As more and more of the documents are published, they will throw more light upon various phases of biblical study.

The New Testament Apocrypha

There are no apocryphal books of the New Testament in the same strict sense that there are Apocrypha to the Old Testament. We have seen that the Old Testament Apocrypha are accepted as canonical by certain branches of the Christian church, but not by others. We shall see in a later chapter, when we discuss the formation of the New Testament canon, that certain books of the New Testament were accepted more readily than others, and that some books appeared on a few early lists that were not in the end included in the New Testament. Also, the Book of Revelation has not been accepted as completely canonical by the Eastern Orthodox Churches.

There are, however, certain books that are called New Testament apocrypha in the broad sense. They are similar to the books in the canon; some were considered for the canon, but most of them were not. In fact, many in this group have been produced since the New Testament canon was closed. The New Testament apocrypha are, therefore, rejected books and books written in imitation of the authoritative New Testament works. They were composed mostly between the second and eighth centuries A.D. Some are known only by reference in ancient writers, and some are in fragmentary form; only a few have been preserved in full.

Among the books that were produced in early Christian times and were considered as authoritative in certain Christian circles—sometimes heretical circles—were the Gospel of Peter and the Gospel of the Hebrews; the Acts of Paul; the Letter of Barnabas and the Letter of Clement of Rome to the Corinthians; the Revelation of Peter, and an apocalyptic book called The Shepherd of Hermas. Of some of these we may say that they "almost made the New Testament canon," but were finally rejected for one reason or another.

The other apocryphal books are legion in number. An unusually large number of Gospels were produced, in spite of the fact that the church decided very early that there should be only four Gospels. There were books of this kind attributed to Bartholomew, James, Matthias, Philip, and others. These often expand areas in the life of Jesus which are only briefly touched on in the canonical Gospels, particularly the childhood of Jesus and the events after the crucifixion. There were Acts ascribed to Andrew, Barnabas, Peter, Pilate and others. A few epistles were produced, such as 3 Corinthians, the Epistle of the Apostles, the Epistles of Paul and Seneca, and so on. There were Apocalypses of James, Paul, Stephen, Thomas, and the Virgin. The Apocalypse of Paul professes to tell what he experienced when he was "caught up to the third heaven" (2 Corinthians 12:2).

We may illustrate in a little detail the contents of these books from the so-called "infancy Gospels" and from the recently discovered Gospel of Thomas.

One of the infancy Gospels tells about several miracles performed by Jesus when he was a child. He was playing in a brook one Sabbath day and making some sparrows out of clay. When this was reported to Joseph, he rebuked Jesus for doing this on the Sabbath. At this Jesus clapped his hands together, and the sparrows took to flight and went away chirping. On another occasion a child ran and dashed against the shoulder of Jesus, whereupon Jesus pronounced a curse upon him and he immediately died. When the parents complained to Joseph, Jesus smote them with blindness. On another occasion he is represented as raising up a child who died after falling from an upper story of a house where he had been playing with Jesus and other boys.[4]

A recently discovered apocryphal book is the Gospel of Thomas in the Coptic language. This was found in southern Egypt near the time of the discovery of the Dead Sea Scrolls in Palestine. It was in a collection of forty-nine treatises written in the Coptic language which was discovered by a peasant in a large earthen jar. This work has now been published in full,

---

[4]See M. R. James, ed., *The Apocryphal New Testament* (Oxford: Clarendon Press, 1953), pp. 49-50. This is an excellent collection of apocryphal books of the New Testament, containing translations of many, and a collection of references to others that are known only by name or in very fragmentary form.

and has been translated and studied by scholars.[5] This Gospel
of Thomas was probably written in Greek in the second or
third century, for many of the sayings in it were found earlier
on Greek papyri discovered in Egypt at Oxyrhynchus.

Though this is called a "gospel," it does not have the same
form as the New Testament Gospels. It is almost exclusively
a collection of the sayings of Jesus, with no action and no
events recorded. The preface to it says, "These are the secret
words which Jesus the Living spoke and Didymus Judas
Thomas wrote. And He said: He who will find the interpretation of these words will not taste death." Some of the sayings
are just the same as those recorded in the canonical Gospels;
some are like the canonical Gospels, with more or less modi-
fication; but others are quite different from the sayings of Jesus
in the New Testament. They represent Jesus in a much more
mystical form; he is a propounder of secret teachings which
only a limited number of people can understand. The following selection from this gospel will illustrate both the similarity
to the New Testament and the difference from it.

Jesus said:

> I am the light
>   which is over everything.
> I am the All;
>   (from me) the All has gone forth,
>   and to me the All has returned.
> Split wood: I am there.
> Lift up the stone, and you will find me there.[6]

The latter part of this saying was found on a Greek papyrus
from Oxyrhynchus, and has been widely quoted. It should be
obvious that this gospel was from a sect which had a different

---

[5] A good translation and full discussion are given in R. M. Grant and D. N. Freedman, *The Secret Sayings of Jesus* (London: Fontana Books, 1960).
[6] *Ibid.*, p. 167; cf. p. 45.

conception of Jesus from the main stream of Christianity; probably it was made up of Christian Gnostics.

These apocryphal books of the New Testament add very little, if anything, to our authentic knowledge concerning the life of Christ and the history of the early Christian church. Many of them are plainly spurious and legendary (such as the infancy gospels). They are of value, however, as reflecting the ideas and beliefs that were held by some Christians at various stages of history when they were written.

V

new testament
history and literature

THE NEW TESTAMENT IS MUCH SHORTER THAN the Old, consisting of twenty-seven books, and the New Testament period of history covers only a century and a half. Yet, the New Testament is of crucial importance for the Christian faith, for in this brief period events of climactic and enduring significance took place.

In the present chapter we shall survey the history and literature of the New Testament, and in the following chapter its message.

The Roman Rule

The latest books of the Old Testament and some of the Apocrypha were written in the Hasmonean (or Maccabean) Age (164 to 63 B.C.). The Hasmoneans succeeded in establishing their rule over a large territory, but their reign did not last long. Some Jews lost interest in political independence after religious freedom was won. A few of the Hasmonean rulers were corrupt, and toward the end of the period there was much internal friction. It was not difficult, therefore, for the Romans to conquer Palestine. In 63 B.C. the Roman general,

Pompey, captured Jerusalem, and Judea became a part of the Roman empire. Palestine was to remain under Roman rule throughout the whole of the New Testament era.

In many ways the Roman conquest was a genuine liberation, and was hailed by some Jews as such. The Romans introduced order and organization where there had been much disorder and some corruption. The Romans had a genius for government, and were usually not oppressive masters. They were generally tolerant toward local customs, including religious practices, and allowed considerable authority to local courts to settle difficulties according to local laws. In Jerusalem the Sanhedrin, composed of seventy members presided over by the high priest, had a great deal of authority over the Jews, though they apparently could not impose the sentence of death.

The Roman governors in Palestine had various titles at various times, and the division of the country changed from time to time. The task of the governor was to see that order prevailed, that taxes were paid, that travel was safe, and that Roman citizens could be tried by Roman law. Of course, the governors differed in their ability and character, but most of them were hated by the Jews simply because they represented a foreign power.

The first strong governor was Herod the Great, who was "king of the Jews" from 37 B.C. until 4 B.C. He was responsible for the slaughter of the innocent children toward the end of his reign, as reported in Matthew 2:16. The Jews despised Herod the Great because he was an agent of Rome, and also because he was an Idumaean, not a Jew. Idumaea was the territory south of Judea which had been settled by the Edomites at the time of the Babylonian capture of Jerusalem in the sixth century, and the antagonism between Idumaeans and Jews was deep. Yet, Herod was in reality an able and efficient ruler. He rebuilt the temple of Jerusalem, enlarging and beautifying it so that the saying arose in ancient times,

"Whoever has not seen the temple of Herod, has seen nothing beautiful."

When Herod died, his kingdom was divided into three parts among three of his sons. Judea, Samaria, and Idumaea fell to Archelaus, but he proved to be a despotic and very unpopular ruler, and his territory was placed under procurators after A.D. 6. Galilee and a district across the Jordan called Perea were administered by Antipas, who remained in office until A.D. 39. Antipas was thus the governor of that part of the land in which Jesus grew up. Antipas is usually referred to in the Gospels as Herod the tetrarch, though once as King Herod (Mark 6:14). It was he who imprisoned and executed John the Baptist after John rebuked him for marrying his sister-in-law Herodias (Matthew 14:1-12), and he participated in the trial of Jesus, according to Luke 23:7-12. Jesus once called Antipas "that fox" (Luke 13:32).

The third son of Herod the Great, Philip, inherited the region north and east of Galilee; when Jesus was at Caesarea Philippi, he was in Philip's capital city. He was popular with his subjects, and governed until his death in A.D. 34.

We have seen that after A.D. 6 Judea was governed by procurators. A procurator was responsible solely to the emperor in Rome, and held his position only so long as his administration was satisfactory to the emperor. Little is known about several of the procurators, and we need mention only one— Pontius Pilate, the fifth procurator from A.D. 26 to 36. Pilate probably was a reasonably good and fair-minded procurator; he certainly was far better than some of his successors. The fact that he remained in office for a period of ten years speaks in his favor, but little authentic information concerning his governorship is available.

One of the worst and most unpopular of the Roman emperors, Gaius Caligula, came to the throne in A.D. 37. He appointed his close friend Agrippa, grandson of Herod the

Great, as tetrarch over the territory north and east of Galilee; subsequently, Agrippa was given rule over the other parts of Palestine, so that for three years (A.D. 41-44) he was king of the Jews, governing approximately the same territory as Herod the Great. Agrippa made generous gifts to the temple and observed Jewish laws; his subjects remembered that his grandmother was a Hasmonean. Agrippa, however, was responsible for the first Roman persecution of Christians; he put to death James the brother of John, and imprisoned Peter (Acts 12:1-2). Perhaps one of his motives was to please the Jews.

Agrippa's successors had the title of procurator, and ruled over most of Palestine. Some of them were very harsh in their treatment of their subjects, and Jewish unrest grew rapidly during the time that the Christian movement was becoming more and more successful, especially outside of Palestine.

The Jewish military revolt against Rome broke out in A.D. 66. Four years later it was quelled when Titus conquered Jerusalem and burned the temple. Rome now adopted a very harsh attitude toward the land. The center of Judaism was moved from Jerusalem to the town of Jamnia, near the Mediterranean coast. The Jewish Christians fled from Jerusalem to Pella in Transjordan. The fall of Jerusalem and the cessation of sacrifice in the temple marked a turning point in the religion of Judaism, and had profound influence upon the spread of Christianity.

Little is known of the details of the history of the Jews in Palestine in the next few decades. The Romans banned the practice of circumcision, a rite which had been of central significance in Judaism. The emperor Hadrian (A.D. 117-138) decided to rebuild Jerusalem and erect there a temple to Jupiter. A second and final revolt of the Jews broke out, A.D. 132-135. It was led by an obscure figure called Bar Cocheba, who claimed to be the promised Messiah, with the blessing of a great spiritual leader, Rabbi Akiba. Letters of Bar Cocheba have recently been found near the Dead Sea. This revolt was put down as the earlier one had been, and this time the Romans rebuilt Jerusalem as a Roman city, Aelia Capitolina, and forbade any Jew to enter its gates, on pain of death. At this point we may end our survey of the Roman rule of Palestine; some of the Roman officials will have to be mentioned as later we discuss the rise of the Christian church.

A great many Jews lived outside Palestine in other parts of the Roman empire. These were the Jews of the dispersion, known technically as the Diaspora. They had been migrating from Palestine for various reasons since the fall of Samaria in the eighth century, and by this time there were probably four or five million Jews in the Roman empire, of whom not more than a fifth lived in Palestine. Alexandria in Egypt had a far larger Jewish population than Jerusalem.

It was difficult for those Jews to observe their religion, and some of them became assimilated. But the Jews were generally treated well by the Roman authorities and given special privileges. They were not compelled to worship the Roman gods or the Roman emperor; instead they were allowed to pray for the emperor in their synagogues. On the Sabbath no Jew could be summoned to court or be compelled to work. They could keep their dietary laws; in many cities they established their own markets. Every Jew above the age of 20 was expected to pay half a shekel annually to the temple in Jerusalem, and no hindrance was placed against this custom. Occasionally there were shameful anti-Jewish pogroms, but on the other hand many Gentiles were attracted by the monotheism and high ethical standards of Judaism.

Every reader of the New Testament should keep in mind that Christianity arose in a small, Eastern province of the Roman empire. Palestine was a little colony of Rome. The Jews and the early Christians were living under a foreign power, and were not their own political masters. Jesus was tempted to take up the sword against Rome, but steadfastly refused to do so. He would not take the path of violent revolution, though one of his disciples had the title of Zealot. Jesus died by crucifixion, which was a Roman rather than a Jewish mode of capital punishment.

The Apostle Paul was a Roman citizen, and near the end of his life made an appeal to be heard by Caesar. His attitude toward the Roman government may explain many of his statements, such as Romans 13:1-7, in which he admonishes Christians to "be subject to the governing authorities."

Religious Developments in Judaism

Important religious developments took place in Judaism in the period embracing the two centuries before Christ and the first century of the Christian era. Judaism was undergoing change, and there were many cross currents. It was by no means a dead or dying faith, nor an arid legalism, as it has often been pictured. We do scant justice to Christianity if we say that it triumphed over a religion that was only a dry legalism. Christianity arose in a time of ferment for the Jewish faith and triumphed over a religion that for many was dynamic and life-giving.

In the last chapter dealing with the Apocrypha, we mentioned in passing some of the developments that occurred in this period. Some of the more important we may summarize as follows.

The Law assumed more and more importance in the Jewish faith. The word "Law," which translates Hebrew *Torah*, meant several things. Sometimes it meant the Pentateuch; at other times it meant the whole of the Scripture; at other times it meant a specific set of commands, such as the Ten Commandments. In its fullest sense *Torah* meant all that the Jews believed God had revealed to them on Mount Sinai. They came to believe that the Law was eternal, and that it could be identified with Wisdom. Their faith was that God had revealed the Law to them, and that the Law revealed to them God and his will.

On the other hand, some of the books of the Apocrypha sought to make Judaism appealing to the Greeks, and beliefs were set forth that were more in accord with Greek ideas than with the Old Testament. The Wisdom of Solomon is a good example; here the characteristic doctrine of personal survival is immortality of the soul, not resurrection of the body.

A very important development in Judaism was in the realm of that type of thought which we call apocalyptic. In the Old Testament the Book of Daniel is an apocalypse. Among the books discussed in the last chapter, apocalyptic ideas are especially prevalent in II Esdras, Enoch, the Qumran books, and many of the Pseudepigrapha. Apocalyptic thought concerns itself with expectations and hopes for the future, for the ending of this present age and the beginning of a new age. Often it includes the hope of the appearance of a Messiah. In Jewish apocalyptic thought there was no orthodox, generally accepted doctrine concerning the new age and the Messiah, but several different types of expectation were prevalent, as we have seen.[1] In the Qumran sect there was hope for the coming of a prophet and then of two Messiahs, one a lay Messiah from the line of David, and one a priestly Messiah from the line of Aaron. It does not appear that the Jews expected the Messiah to be a man who by suffering would bring salvation to the nation. After the fall of Jerusalem A.D. 70 and the increasing spread of Christianity, apocalyptic thought became less and less popular in Judaism.

Another development in Judaism was a great increase in the belief in angels and in demons. This can be seen in Daniel,

---

[1] See pp. 112-15.

and then in later books such as Tobit and Enoch. The angels were thought of as intermediaries between God and man, bringing God's presence closer to men; demons were evil spirits, who often caused disease. Developments in this area of belief may have been much influenced by Persian religion.

Judaism continued to be a religion with very high ethical standards. The Jews read the prophets as well as the Pentateuch. In a book such as the Testament of the Twelve Patriarchs very high ethical ideals are stated, including a form of the Golden Rule and the injunction to forgive one's enemies.

Several important parties developed in Judaism, and we shall be better able to understand references to them in the New Testament if we describe here the principal parties and groups.

The Pharisees originated in the Hasmonean period, being first mentioned by name in the second century B.C. Their name means "Separatists," but it is not known from whom or what they sought to separate themselves—from the priests, from uncleanness, or from the common people. They called themselves by a term meaning "Associates." The Pharisees have often been grossly misunderstood, especially from New Testament references. We readily think of them simply as hypocrites. In reality they were the progressives of their day who were very much concerned with making religion a vital part of everyday life. In a sense they were liberals and modernists, for they adopted ideas which were new in their day, such as belief in angels and resurrection from the dead. Above all they believed in what was called the oral law. This was the body of tradition that grew up, in oral rather than in written form, for the purpose of applying the Law to everyday life. They did not think of this as being additional to the Law, but only as interpretation and application of the Law, which worked out its implications. Even the oral law, they could say, was revealed at Sinai. For example, the written law forbade work on the Sabbath, but did not define work. The oral law set out in detail what constituted work and what did not.

The Pharisees were laymen, usually of the middle class, and had great influence on the people. It was their type of religion that survived the fall of Jerusalem, and that eventually was incorporated in the Talmud and other rabbinic writings.

There can be no doubt that some Pharisees were hypocritical, and deserved the censure heaped on them in the Gospels. Yet, their principle of applying religion to all of life was basically correct, and many of their teachings were very helpful. They made the mistake of thinking that the whole of life can be regulated by detailed regulations.

As we think of the relationship between Jesus and the Pharisees, we must remember that Luke reports that he several times ate in the homes of Pharisees (7:36; 11:37; 14:1), and that it was Pharisees who warned him that Herod Antipas intended to kill him (13:31).

The Sadducees were a second important party. They differed from the Pharisees in denying the validity of the oral law. They accepted only the Pentateuch, and denied the new doctrines of resurrection and of angelology. The Sadducees were the priestly aristocracy, conservative in outlook, and usually inclined to come to terms with the Roman authorities. The high priest was appointed by the Romans. The priests came from this party but not all Sadducees were priests. Some of them were the landed, wealthy aristocracy, and the temple had great wealth. The Sadducees did not have great influence with the people, and when the temple sacrifices ceased A.D. 70, they virtually passed out of existence.

Another party was the Essenes. They are never named in the New Testament, but we have seen that the Qumran sect which preserved the Dead Sea Scrolls probably were Essenes (see p. 151). They were an ascetic group who withdrew from ordinary life to live in monastic communities, in which they practiced community of goods. Josephus says that the Essenes had "a reputation for cultivating peculiar sanctity." They practiced frequent lustrations, and emphasized personal purity of life.

The Zealots constituted another important group, but hardly a separate party. They were the men who wished to take up arms against Rome and reestablish Jewish independence. They became increasingly influential as time went on, and were leaders in the Jewish revolt of A.D. 66-70. Simon the Zealot is listed among the disciples of Jesus in Luke 6:15.

The Scribes were not a separate party, but many of them were Pharisees. They were lawyers or teachers of the Law; perhaps the best term for us to use of them is scholars. They knew the Law, and were able to decide minute questions arising from it.

The masses of the people were called "the people of the land" (Hebrew 'ammê hā-'āretz). The word does not always mean poor people; some of the wealthy belonged to this group. They were people who did not have the learning, the inclination, or the leisure to keep the Law in the Pharisaic sense. Many of them, of course, were poor and felt they could not offer up the required tithes and take the time to observe the Law strictly. It is likely that many of Jesus' disciples came from this group, and he made a strong appeal to them.

In addition to the temple in Jerusalem, there was a very important religious institution of the Jews that deserves special discussion: the synagogue.

The synagogue perhaps originated in a very informal manner when Jews in the Babylonian exile began to assemble in the homes of some of their number for discussion, study, and worship. By the first century A.D. there were numerous synagogues in Palestine and all over the Roman world wherever Jews lived in any number. Many Jews never saw the temple. The synagogue was the center of their religious life. It was not a place for sacrifice, but for congregational worship and religious instruction. In it the Jews assembled on the Sabbath and on two other days of the week to worship God and study their Scripture. Their services of worship consisted essentially of prayer, reading the Scriptures in a regular cycle (both Pentateuch and Prophets), and exposition of the Scriptures. Since most Jews could not understand Hebrew, there was usually an oral translation of the Scripture into the vernacular language—Aramaic in Palestine, probably Greek in synagogues of the Diaspora (or the Greek translation itself was read).

There was no priesthood or ordained ministry in the synagogues. Any competent person might be called upon to read the Scripture and to expound it, as Jesus was at Nazareth (Luke 4:16-30). Each had a ruler of the synagogue, who generally maintained order, arranged the services, and the like.

The synagogue was a very important institution in the rise of Christianity. Jesus and his disciples attended its services, and their religious life and nurture owed much more to it than to the temple. Furthermore, Paul and other early missionaries often preached in the synagogues. The organization and worship of the Christian church were modeled more after those of the synagogue than of the temple.

The Four Gospels

The Gospels were written later than the letters of Paul—most of them, if not all of them. It would be logical from one point of view to survey Paul's letters first, but since the Gospels record the life of Jesus, which preceded the ministry of Paul, it is preferable to give a brief introduction to the Gospels before we survey the life of Jesus and then the career of Paul.

What is a Gospel? It is not a biography or history in the modern sense of the word. It does not cover the whole of the life and teachings of Jesus, but omits many things about which we would like to have information. It does not intend to be an objective and scientific history of the life of Jesus and his early disciples.

The word gospel means "good news." It translates the Greek word *evangélion,* from which we derive evangel, evangelical, evangelist, and similar words. An evangelist was one who preached or wrote about the good news. Thus a Gospel is an account of the good news of what God has done for man by sending his Son for man's salvation. It contains a narrative of the life of Jesus, with little or no emphasis on his childhood, a record of many of his teachings and actions (especially his miracles), and a long account of the events surrounding his passion and resurrection. The purpose of a Gospel is well stated in John 20:31: "these are written that you may believe that Jesus is the Christ, the Son of God, and that believing you may have life in his name." A Gospel was intended to convert men to belief in Jesus as the Christ and Savior, to instruct those who already believed, and to give aid in the administration of the life of the continuing Christian community.

The first three Gospels are usually called the Synoptic Gospels, to distinguish them from John. They have a common framework or narrative, and often agree in subject matter and even vocabulary. They are synoptic in that they "see alike" the Gospel story. Of the 661 verses in Mark, Matthew has about 600 in substance or actual wording, and Luke has about 350. Altogether, only 31 verses of Mark fail to appear also in Matthew and Luke. On the other hand, Matthew and Luke have between 200 and 250 verses in common that are not found in Mark, consisting chiefly of sayings of Jesus. These facts are usually explained by a simple theory. Mark's was the earliest Gospel, and both Matthew and Luke made use of it. They also made use of another source commonly called Q, the initial letter of the German *Quelle,* meaning "Source."

This was something like a "little gospel," consisting mostly of Jesus' sayings, with very little narrative. Scholars attempt to reconstruct Q by putting together the materials which Matthew and Luke have in common, but did not get from Mark.

Matthew and Luke each used additional materials which they derived neither from Mark nor from Q. Whether these were earlier gospels, or whether they were simply collections of material (partly oral and partly written), we do not know.

The Book of John stands apart from the Synoptic Gospels because it follows a different narrative framework, and presents in some respects a different interpretation of the life of Jesus.

A period of thirty or forty years separates the lifetime of Jesus from the date of Mark. Why did the Christians wait so long to write down the story of the good news? What was happening in the Christian community in this period?

One of the principal reasons they waited so long was that the early followers of Jesus expected he would soon return from heaven to which he had ascended. They believed that he would return to them on clouds of glory, and much of their life centered around hope of that event, which is called the *parousia*. Under such circumstances, why should they write books?

Another fact is that many of the early Christians came from the lower classes of society, and were nonliterary people. Furthermore, there was a tradition among the Jews that certain types of material were better transmitted orally than by writing; in this way the sayings of many of the rabbis circulated by word of mouth for several generations before they were written. Jesus was a teacher like some of the rabbis, and it is likely that his disciples memorized some of his teachings and treasured them in their memory rather than in written form.

The first Christians were very enthusiastic about converting others to the belief that Jesus was the Messiah—first the Jews in Jerusalem, and then Gentiles and Jews all over the Roman world. New converts had to be instructed in the faith and practices of the new religion. Christian communities or congregations met for worship, and in various ways they had to compose or adapt hymns, prayers, and confessions of faith for their services of worship. In this manner the materials of the Gospels were slowly accumulated. Some written collections may have been made of the teachings of Jesus (such as Q that we have mentioned), and collections were also made of the principal passages in the Old Testament which the Christians saw fulfilled in the life of their Messiah. The Old Testament was the Bible of the earliest Christians, and there was a Christian interpretation of it that was not entirely the same as the Jewish.

The earliest Gospel, Mark, was probably not written until the latter part of the sixties of the first century, after the persecution of Christians under the Emperor Nero, or even later. Threats to the Christian faith constituted one of the reasons for the writing of the earliest Gospel. Another was the fact that some of the apostles and followers of Jesus, eyewitnesses of what he had done and hearers of what he had said, had already died or were getting old. The time was ripe for the story of the good news to be set down in written form.

The four Gospel writers depended upon sources of various kinds, and thus handed down to some degree traditions they received. They wrote for the early Christian community. Yet, each was an individual who had his own style, his special interests and emphases, and his interpretation of the life and significance of Jesus. We should be aware of the individuality and special interests of the separate Gospel writers.

Mark wrote the first Gospel. The earliest tradition about him is preserved by Bishop Papias, early in the second century, who said: "Mark became the interpreter of Peter and he wrote down accurately, but not in order, as much as he remembered [or Peter related] of the sayings and doings of Christ." John Mark was not one of the twelve apostles. His mother's home was a center for the early Christian community in Jerusalem, and Mark was associated for a time in missionary work with Paul and Barnabas. He was estranged from Paul for a while, but later reconciled. Some scholars have suggested that Mark was the young man who fled from the scene of the arrest of Jesus, as recorded in Mark 14:51; this can only be conjecture. He probably wrote his Gospel in Rome.

Mark is the least artistic of the Gospels. Its author was probably the least educated of the evangelists. He writes a straightforward account of the life of Jesus, emphasizing action more than teaching. He stresses the humanity of Jesus more than the others, and yet to him Jesus was the Son of God and no mere man.

The Gospel of Matthew is attributed to the apostle of that name who was originally a tax-collector. Because the author depended so much upon Mark, a nonapostle, many scholars question that he was really the author of the Gospel itself, and conjecture that Matthew compiled the document we referred to above as Q. This might agree with what Bishop Papias reported: "Matthew recorded the oracles (or, teachings) in the Hebrew tongue, and each interpreted them to the best of his ability."

The author of this Gospel was a Jew before he was converted to Christianity. One of his main purposes was to show the relationship of Jesus to the Old Testament Law and prophecy, which he came not to abolish, but to fulfill (5:17). Matthew gives more of the teachings of Jesus than Mark, relating five long discourses of Jesus. It is he who gives the full account of the Sermon on the Mount, which he may have considered to be the new Christian Law, corresponding to the

Mosaic Law given on Mount Sinai. He has a special interest in the church, and is the only Gospel writer who mentions it (16:18; 18:17). One scholar has suggested that the Gospel was written largely to be a handbook for teaching and administration within the early Christian church, comparable to the Manual of Discipline among the Dead Sea Scrolls. It was probably written about A.D. 80 or 85.

The third Gospel was by Luke, the "beloved physician" of Paul (Colossians 4:14). Luke wrote both this Gospel and the Acts of the Apostles, the most ambitious literary undertaking in the New Testament. In these two works he sought to describe the beginnings of Christianity, from the birth of Jesus to the preaching of the gospel in Rome. At the outset he explains to "most excellent Theophilus," to whom he addressed his Gospel, that he wrote "having followed all things closely for some time past . . . that you may know the truth concerning the things of which you have been informed" (1: 3-4). Luke is the most self-conscious writer and historian among the evangelists, and writes excellent Greek in a most attractive style. The French scholar Renan called the Gospel "the most beautiful book ever written."

Luke was probably a Gentile before his conversion, and addressed his Gospel to Gentiles more than to Jews. He is convinced of the universal appeal of Christ, whose genealogy he traces back to "Adam, the son of God" (3:38).

Luke puts great emphasis on the love and compassion of God, and pictures Jesus as the friend of publicans and sinners, the champion of the outcasts. He shows much interest in problems connected with wealth, recording several parables and sayings dealing with it. In his version of the Beatitudes, Jesus says simply:

"Blessed are you poor, for yours is the kingdom of God.

But woe to you that are rich, for you have received your consolation" (6:20, 24).

Both the Gospel of Luke and the Book of Acts stress the role of the Holy Spirit in the life of Jesus and the early church. John the Baptist is a Spirit-filled prophet, and Jesus is often guided by the Spirit. In Acts, the Holy Spirit moves the apostles and the church on many occasions. Another emphasis in the Gospel of Luke is the place of prayer in the life of Jesus; he reports seven critical occasions when Jesus resorted to prayer.

The Gospel of Luke is characterized by a spirit of thanksgiving, and of joy and cheerfulness, which are not so prominent in the other Gospels. It is not surprising that his Gospel is one of the most popular and helpful of all the New Testament books. We do not know where he wrote, but it was probably around A.D. 85, later than Mark, not far from the time of Matthew.

The Gospel of John stands apart from the other three in that it cannot be fit into the synoptic pattern. Anyone who reads this Gospel will immediately see important differences from the other three.

There are differences regarding events in the life of Jesus. Here Jesus has a brief ministry in Judea parallel with that of John the Baptist, and seems to spend more time in Jerusalem than the Synoptics suggest. The cleansing of the temple comes at the beginning rather than near the end of his public career. The crucifixion takes place a day earlier than in the Synoptic Gospels. This Gospel omits some of the familiar features of the other Gospels, such as the baptism of Jesus by John, the temptation, and the agony in the garden—all of which might be taken as indicating too clearly the human side of Jesus' nature.

Another important difference is that in this Gospel there are long discourses by Jesus, who speaks of himself much more often than in the other Gospels. John does not give an account of the birth of Jesus, but begins by describing him as the *Logos* who was present with God at creation.

In this Gospel the miracles or wonders performed by Jesus are continually called "signs"; they are symbols of deeper truths about Jesus. Some of the miracles of this Gospel strike the modern reader as being extreme, such as the raising of Lazarus, and the turning of water into wine at the marriage at Cana.

These are only some of the differences between the Gospel of John and the others. On the whole it is much more an interpretation of the meaning of Jesus Christ, than a historical narrative. Where there are historical differences from the Synoptics, however, we must not in every case conclude that John is incorrect and the Synoptics correct.

Most scholars believe that this Gospel was written near the end of the first century, about A.D. 100, by someone named John. But what John? Bishop Irenaeus wrote about A.D. 180: "John, the disciple of the Lord, who also leaned on his breast, himself produced his gospel, while he was living at Ephesus in Asia." He apparently meant John the son of Zebedee. There is some good evidence that this John had died before A.D. 70, and many students believe that the Gospel as we have it is not the kind of book one would expect from an apostle. Many believe that the author was John the Elder of Ephesus, who may have been a disciple of the Apostle John.

The Life of Jesus

More books have been devoted to the life of Jesus than to any other figure in history. These have varied greatly in their interpretations, and have sometimes been contradictory. It is not possible for anyone to write a wholly satisfactory life of Jesus. This is true for at least two reasons.

One reason is the very nature of the materials from which the life of Jesus must be written. The Four Gospels constitute almost our only source, and we have seen how they were written and have recognized that they are not biographies. The other reason is that Jesus has been, since the time of his first appearance in public, an object of faith, and likewise an object of controversy. Men have believed deeply and felt strongly about him, either in his favor or in opposition to him. Some men crucified him, and others have been crucified for his sake. Such a person cannot be the object of a calm, scientific, historical appraisal.

The Gospels were written by men of faith in order to inspire faith in Jesus Christ. Yet, the figure they described was one who had lived in history, and no mythical figure. He had lived in Palestine, taught and done mighty works, and died on a cross in Jerusalem. At the same time he was the Risen One, the author of their salvation who had been sent by God.

In this present section we propose simply to sketch in broad outline the course of Jesus' life. The reader who wishes to fill in the details must read the Gospels for himself, and he can find assistance in the reading of modern books on Jesus.

Jesus was born before the end of the reign of Herod the Great (4 B.C.), probably around 7 B.C. He lived for nearly forty years, with a public ministry of perhaps three years (though some scholars believe it lasted only a few months, as the Synoptic Gospels appear to indicate). A recently suggested precise date for the crucifixion is April 7, A.D. 30.[2]

According to Matthew and Luke, Jesus was born to the virgin Mary in Bethlehem under unusual circumstances. The accounts in these two Gospels supplement rather than parallel each other. Jesus grew up in Nazareth of Galilee. Galilee had more Gentile inhabitants than Judea, and was more subject to foreign influences. The religious atmosphere there was freer and more open to change.

---

[2]G. B. Caird, *Interpreter's Dictionary of the Bible*, Vol. I, p. 603. However, astronomical calculations vary from A.D. 27 to 33.

Jesus grew up in a family in which there were four other sons and an unnamed number of daughters. Luke 2:41-52 is the only Gospel passage that manifests a direct interest in Jesus' childhood. He was taken to the Temple at the age of twelve probably in order to take upon himself the obligation to keep the whole Law, and become a "son of the Law." He probably learned the trade of carpentry, and if Joseph died at a fairly early age, Jesus must have had to work to help support the family before he could leave home. He attended the local synagogue services, and at least the elementary synagogue school. He probably learned to read the Old Testament in Hebrew, though his mother tongue was Aramaic; he probably could speak some Greek.

When John the Baptist began to preach and baptize in Judea, Jesus was attracted to him and his message. He was baptized by John. The Gospel of John says Jesus had a brief public ministry paralleling that of the Baptist, but the others indicate he began to preach in Galilee only after John was imprisoned.

Most of Jesus' public ministry was in Galilee, much of it along the shore of the Sea of Galilee. His message was basically this: " 'The time is fulfilled, and the kingdom of God is at hand; repent, and believe in the gospel' " (Mark 1:15). In the next chapter we shall consider in detail the content of Jesus' teaching. Let us note here that he was sometimes given the title of respect, "Rabbi," meaning "my master" or "teacher." In some ways he did teach like the contemporary rabbis. He answered questions; he commented on Scripture; he gave counsel on various subjects; and he told stories to illustrate his teachings. Yet he did not appeal to the past as the Jewish teachers did, and his followers included women and children, and tax-collectors, harlots, and sinners. These last were not necessarily flagrantly wicked people, but those who could not keep the Law as the Pharisees interpreted it. Jesus taught in various places—in synagogues, along the seaside, in homes, in the marketplaces. The people recognized that he spoke with an authority which was different from that of the other teachers. Many of his teachings, especially his parables, had a freshness and vigor about them that made them unforgettable.

In addition to teaching, Jesus performed wonders and miracles. These were of two kinds. Many were miracles of healing —of leprosy, palsy, blindness, epilepsy, fevers, and the like. In many cases the people of the time believed illness was caused by demon-possession, and cure demanded the exorcising of the demons. Jesus is reported to have exorcised demons in several cases, although the New Testament recognizes that others could do so (such as the disciples, Matthew 10:1, and the followers of the Pharisees, Matthew 12:27). Jesus was sometimes embarrassed by the demands for the performing of wonders, and did not wish to be known primarily as a wonder-worker. He could heal only where faith was present.

The other type of miracle is that known as nature miracles, including the stilling of the storm, the feeding of the multitudes, walking on the sea, and the raising of three individuals from the dead.

Jesus attracted a great deal of popular attention and a large following. People were impressed by his preaching of the imminent coming of the kingdom of God, though some may have misunderstood his real meaning; and they were impressed by his ability to heal and cast out demons. Jesus experienced some difficulty in proclaiming his message because of the popularity of his healings.

From among his followers Jesus chose an inner circle of twelve apostles. The lists are given in Matthew 10:2-4; Mark 3:16-19; and Luke 6:14-16. While the names do not agree absolutely, the discrepancies are of little importance. Most of them were obscure men, and very little is related concerning all but four or five. Mark states clearly Jesus' purpose in selecting them: "to be with him, and to be sent out to preach and have authority to cast out demons" (3:14-15). Their mission was to be very similar to his, and they were to be closely associated with him in order to receive more intensive teaching than the multitudes.

However, Jesus soon aroused opposition from several quarters. Some Pharisees were at first drawn to him, but they came to see that he was too lax in observing the Law as they interpreted it, and they objected to his consorting with sinners and outcasts. They particularly objected to his failure to observe the Sabbath strictly, and to keep the laws concerning personal purity. The political authorities became aroused by his popularity, fearing that he might be planning to lead a revolt against Rome. Even some of his friends and relatives seem to have felt they must rescue him from his own madness (Mark 3:21, 31-35).

The Gospels show little concern for the chronological order of Jesus' life. It appears, however, that after working in Galilee for a period of a few months or nearly three years, he withdrew into the territory north of Galilee for a time. He was informed that Herod Antipas was determined to kill him (Luke 13:31-33). Jesus' reply indicated he was not afraid of "that fox," but he believed a prophet should not perish outside Jerusalem. He may have felt that his mission was being misunderstood by the multitudes, who put too much emphasis upon his healing activities, and he may have wanted to rethink the nature of his work. In the Phoenician region of Tyre and Sidon he came into contact with a Greek woman who asked him to cast out a demon from her daughter. Jesus' reply indicated that his mission was to the Jews, but when she showed great faith in him, he cast out the demon.

At Caesarea Philippi, Peter made his great confession saying, "Thou art the Christ, the son of the living God." According to all of the Synoptic Gospels Jesus commanded them to tell this to no one, but according to Matthew, Jesus declared that this was a revelation to Peter from God (16:17).

Sometime after this Jesus left Galilee and northern Palestine to go to Jerusalem, in order to present there, the capital of the Jewish world, his message of the kingdom of God. Whether or not he knew beforehand that his presentation would lead to his death, he was prepared to meet death if it were necessary. The Gospels present many teachings in the time before he arrived in Jerusalem, among them some of the most memorable of Jesus' parables in the Gospel of Luke. It is difficult to make out just what was his route; he is represented as being both in Samaria and in Transjordan.

The events of Jesus' final days in Jerusalem are told with a fullness of detail that is unusual for the Gospels, and there is considerable agreement among them concerning what happened. This part of the life of Jesus probably became crystallized in narrative form sooner than the earlier years, because of the great significance to the early Christian community of the crucifixion and the various events surrounding it.

Jesus entered Jerusalem in triumph—but in a kind of triumph that differed strangely from that of other conquerors. He entered riding upon an ass, while many of his followers spread their garments and palm branches on his way, crying out: " 'Hosanna! Blessed be he who comes in the name of the Lord! Blessed be the kingdom of our father David that is coming! Hosanna in the highest!' " (Mark 11:9-10) The next day he entered the temple to cleanse it. He cast out those who bought and sold in the temple court, overthrew the tables of the moneychangers, and said: " 'Is it not written, "My house shall be called a house of prayer for all the nations?" But you have made it a den of robbers' " (Mark 11:17).

For about a week Jesus continued to teach in Jerusalem. He was challenged by many groups. The priests inquired by what authority he did such things as he had done in the temple. The Pharisees and Herodians tried to trap him by asking whether or not it was lawful to pay tribute to Caesar. The Sadducees asked him a question about the resurrection (in which they did not believe) that tried to make that doctrine appear ridiculous. Jesus answered his critics with great acumen so that they were unable to trap him.

Finally came the events that led up to the crucifixion of Jesus. The Last Supper, which clearly was an event carefully planned by Jesus, probably was not a Passover meal. This interpretation fits the chronology of the Gospel of John, and there are hints of it in the Synoptics, though the latter usually treat it as the Passover. Several important elements in a Passover meal are not mentioned. It was apparently a specially arranged "fellowship meal" in which Jesus wished to prepare his disciples for what was to follow. It was a preparation for the kingdom, for Jesus said, "I shall not drink again of the fruit of the vine until that day when I drink it new in the kingdom of God" (Mark 14:25). By eating of the bread and drinking the wine together, the disciples were bound with one another and with Jesus in a new covenant, succeeding to the old covenant made at Sinai.

Events moved swiftly thereafter. Jesus suffered the agony of Gethsemane—an agony of complete aloneness with God, when his closest disciples were sleeping, and he dedicated his will completely to the will of God. Judas betrayed his master: did he betray only his whereabouts, or did he betray the fact that Jesus claimed to be the Messiah?

There was a secret trial before the Sanhedrin, and a public trial before Pilate. Historians have argued endlessly over the legality of these trials, and over the question whether the Sanhedrin had at this time the right to sentence anyone to capital punishment. The truth is very probably that the "trial" before the Sanhedrin was only an informal and secret hearing, held hurriedly because of the Passover festival, in which the members decided what charge they would bring against Jesus. Whether or not the Sanhedrin could decree capital punishment, one fact is well established: crucifixion was a Roman method of execution, not Jewish. The Jewish method was stoning. Crucifixion was a ghastly form of execution, in which the victims often lingered for days. It was used especially for slaves. Cicero described it as "the most cruel and hideous of punishments." Mercifully, Jesus died within a few hours.

The priestly authorities in Jerusalem were no doubt greatly antagonized by Jesus' action in cleansing the temple, and by his saying he would destroy the temple (Mark 13:2; 14:58 and parallels). Jerusalem was the stronghold of the Sadducees, the priestly aristocracy, who were generally subservient to the Roman government; they had a strong vested interest in the Temple and its rites. For his part, Pilate was doubtless quite willing to do away with one who appeared to be a troublemaker among the Jewish people, and potentially a leader of a political revolt. Rome wanted him to keep peace and order in his domain, and Pilate needed the favor of the Jewish authorities.

The story of Jesus did not end with his crucifixion and his burial in the tomb of Joseph of Arimathea. At the time of the arrest and crucifixion, Jesus' disciples fled and deserted him. Judas had betrayed him, and Peter denied that he even knew him. The crucifixion must have seemed to the disciples only a stark tragedy, whatever Jesus may have done and said to prepare them for it in advance. But their discouragement and disillusionment turned into hope and great joy when they came to believe that Jesus had been resurrected from the grave.

The resurrection of Jesus cannot be the object of ordinary historical investigation. The historian cannot now discover exactly what happened. All of the Gospels contain accounts of resurrection appearances, but there is little agreement between them, and there are discrepancies that cannot be reconciled. In some of the accounts, Jesus seems to appear in spirit form; he was able to appear through closed doors and vanish suddenly, and some of the disciples thought he was a spirit (Luke 24:31, 37; John 20:19, 26). Other accounts emphasize the fact that Jesus was flesh and blood by saying that he ate with the disciples (Luke 24:43; John 21:13).

We are on soundest historical ground if we note that the earliest record of the appearances of Jesus is that given by Paul in 1 Corinthians 15:3-8:

For I delivered to you as of first importance what I also received, that Christ . . . was raised on the third day in accordance with the scriptures, and that he appeared to Cephas, then to the twelve. Then he appeared to more than five hundred brethren at one time, most of whom are still alive, though some have fallen asleep. Then he appeared to James, then to all the apostles. Last of all, as to one untimely born, he appeared also to me.

Here Paul makes no distinction between the appearance to himself and the appearances to the other persons. Paul did not see Jesus in the flesh, but had a vision of the risen Lord (Acts 9:3-9; Galatians 1:16). There are indications that an early tradition made no distinction between Jesus' resurrection from the grave and his exaltation to the right hand of the Father (Acts 2:33; 5:31; Philippians 2:9; Hebrews 1:3; 8:1; possibly John 3:14; 12:32, 34).

Many of the disciples and followers of Jesus—perhaps not all, but many—became convinced of the resurrection by vision appearances, or by the testimony of others who told of seeing him. Then they felt that they were forgiven for their desertion of him at the time of his arrest and crucifixion, and they came to a new understanding of the meaning of his life and his death. They could say as Paul did: "We know that Christ being raised from the dead will never die again; death no longer has dominion over him. The death he died he died to sin, once for all, but the life he lives he lives to God" (Romans 6:9-10).

The Life of Paul

After Jesus, the second most creative and influential person in the whole history of Christianity was the Apostle Paul. He wrote much of the New Testament, and figures prominently in the early history told in its pages. As a historical character Paul can be better known than anyone else in New Testament times, including Jesus, and his contribution to the Christian movement was crucial and many-sided.

We have two sources of information concerning Paul. The primary source is the letters which he wrote. We should think of them as real letters rather than as "epistles." The latter term suggests writings that are more formal and systematic than most of Paul's were. Like most letters, those of Paul are very revealing of his emotions and his thoughts, and of his personality. Some passages are more directly autobiographical than others, such as Galatians 1—2, 2 Corinthians 11—12, and Romans 7.

The other source of information is the Acts of the Apostles. We have already seen that this is the second half of a two-volume work written by Luke, who was for a time a companion and co-worker with Paul.[8] Acts includes a series of sections written in the first person plural (the "we sections"), 16:10-17; 20:5-16; 21:1-18; 27:1—28:16, that may have been taken from a diary kept by Luke. Acts was written to tell how the Christian gospel spread from Jerusalem to "all Judea and Samaria and to the end of the earth" (1:8). It was a defense of the Christian religion which sought to show that it was a logical and true development from Judaism, which was in no way antagonistic to the Roman government, though it was opposed by

---

[8]See p. 174.

the Jews themselves. Acts supplies much information about Paul, especially from chapter 9 onward, but it does not cover the whole of his life. It is largely silent on the first twelve or fifteen years of his life as a Christian, but goes into great detail about his final arrest in Jerusalem, his defense of himself before the authorities, and his trip to Rome—all constituting the "passion of Paul." At some points it is difficult to harmonize facts given in Acts with information derived from letters of Paul; in such cases, it is natural to give priority to the letters. For example, Acts tells of five visits of Paul to Jerusalem, while the letters mention only three; the problem of equating the visits in Acts with those in the letters has given rise to much debate among scholars.

Paul was born in Tarsus, Cilicia, in Asia Minor. His place of birth is significant, for he was at the same time a Jew, a Greek, and a Roman. His Jewish name was Saul, and his Roman name Paul (meaning "the little one"). Tarsus was a large city in his time, noted both as a center of Hellenistic culture and as a commercial center. Paul probably did not receive a Hellenistic education, but he spoke Greek and must have acquired at least a superficial knowledge of Greek philosophy and religion. Though a Jew, he was also a Roman citizen.

As a boy, probably in early adolescence, Paul went to Jerusalem to study. Speaking in his own defense at the time of his arrest in Jerusalem, he said that he was "brought up in this city at the feet of Gamaliel, educated according to the strict manner of the law of our fathers" (Acts 22:3). This was Rabban Gamaliel I, a noted teacher of Jerusalem who belonged to the more liberal school of rabbis, mentioned also in Acts 5:34 as adopting a moderate attitude toward Christianity.

We do not know whether Paul ever saw Jesus or heard him teach, or whether he witnessed the crucifixion. After the crucifixion he became an ardent persecutor of the Christian way; he must have known enough about Jesus and his teachings to know what he was opposing. He was present at the stoning of the first Christian martyr, Stephen, consenting to his death and guarding the garments of those who stoned him (Acts 7:58; 8:1).

Within two or three years after the crucifixion, Paul was converted to the very faith whose adherents he was persecuting. Acts describes his conversion in three places (9:1-9; 22:5-11; 26:12-18), and Paul refers to it in some of his letters. On the way to Damascus to continue his persecution of Christians, Paul saw a great light and fell to the ground, and heard Christ speaking to him. Smitten blind, Paul was led to Damascus, where he conferred with Ananias and received baptism at his hands.

Paul's conversion to the Christian faith was doubtless prepared for by several things. One was his own inability to find genuine communion with God and justification in the sight of God through the keeping of the Law, however hard he tried. Another was his observation of the way the Christians lived and the manner in which they met even death when persecuted by himself and others. For Paul, however, his conversion was an act of God in which God revealed his Son to him in order that he might preach Christ among the Gentiles (Galatians 1:16). The appearance of Christ to Paul was the final appearance of the risen Lord, similar to the appearance to other apostles and many disciples (1 Corinthians 15:8).

After remaining in Damascus a few days, Paul went away into Arabia and then returned to Damascus (Galatians 1:17). Arabia here probably does not mean the great Arabian peninsula, nor does it necessarily mean a desert region. It may refer to the kingdom of the Nabatean Arabs, extending from the region of Damascus down through Transjordan into southern Palestine and the Sinai Peninsula. It is possible that Paul merely went into the region south of Damascus, because he felt the need of a retreat for meditation and for thinking out some of the problems now arising in his mind. It is equally possible that he began immediately to preach the Christian gospel and to serve as the missionary to the Gentiles that he felt called to be. In Damascus he met so much opposition from the Jews that he had to escape from the city.

Three years after his conversion Paul went to Jerusalem (Galatians 1:18-19; cf. Acts 9:26-30). Paul says that he spent fifteen days in Jerusalem, seeing only James the brother of Jesus and Peter. The purpose of this visit was to discuss with the leaders of the mother church in Jerusalem his understanding and interpretation of the Christian message. Then Paul went into the region of Syria and Cilicia (Galatians 1:21). Acts gives no details of this period, but it may be that some of the things referred to by Paul himself in 2 Corinthians 11:23-27 took place in this time—beatings, shipwrecks, frequent journeys, and so forth. During these "silent" years Paul was really not at all silent, but preaching the gospel in his native city of Tarsus and in nearby regions. Barnabas, hearing of his work, brought him from Tarsus and introduced him to the church at Antioch, the place where the disciples of Christ were for the first time called Christians, and there they worked together for a year.

Beginning in the thirteenth chapter, Acts relates three missionary journeys undertaken by Paul, each beginning in Antioch and ending in Jerusalem. On the first journey he went to Cyprus and various places in Asia Minor (within the borders of the modern Turkey). On the second he revisited some of these and crossed over into Europe, going to places such as Philippi, Thessalonica, Athens, and Corinth. In the third journey he visited many of the same places, remaining at Ephesus almost three years. These journeys are to be dated between A.D. 47 and 57.

It is artificial to think of Paul as conducting only three "missionary journeys," each well organized and carefully planned in advance. He had many missionary journeys, for he preached the gospel of Christ wherever he went, and he followed the leading of the Spirit. Sometimes he remained for only a short time in a given place; sometimes he remained a long time—nearly three years at Ephesus (Acts 19:8-10), and eighteen months at Corinth (Acts 18:11), a city which he visited at least three times. Paul's purpose was to visit the influential cities, centers of commerce and culture, and establish in them communities of Christian believers.

Paul's general pattern of activity was to go first to a Jewish synagogue and there preach that Jesus was the expected Messiah. Paul considered Christianity to be the true Judaism, and the church the Israel of God (Galatians 6:16). He did not make many converts among the Jews, and he was often expelled from the synagogues, sometimes arousing much disorder. He would then turn to the Gentiles, to whom he felt he had a special mission. The "Gentiles" were not only non-Jewish pagans, but also non-Jews who had been attracted by some of the features of Judaism. They adopted the monotheism and high ethical standards of Judaism, but did not undergo circumcision nor take the obligation to keep the whole Law. Paul may have made many of his converts from among these half-proselytes to Judaism, called in ancient times "God-fearers." While Paul felt that he had a special mission to the Gentiles, he did not turn against his fellow countrymen, but earnestly sought their salvation also. He once wrote, "I could wish that I myself were accursed and cut off from Christ for the sake of my brethren, my kinsmen by race" (Romans 9:3).

At some point in his career, probably A.D. 49, Paul had a conference with the leaders of the mother church in Jerusalem regarding the relationship of Gentiles to the Christian church.

This conference, often called the Apostolic Council in Jerusalem, is told about in Acts 15; Paul's own report of the same conference may be in Galatians 2:1-10, though the two reports do not correspond entirely. Some scholars believe that the conference of Acts 15 took place at the time of the visit of Paul and Barnabas to Jerusalem recorded in Acts 11:29-30. The issue was very clear and was exceedingly important for the future of the Christian church. Some of the leaders of the Jewish Christians believed that Gentiles who wished to become Christians should keep the Mosaic Law. They insisted that two requirements of the Mosaic Law were especially important: circumcision, and the observance of the Jewish food laws. The food laws were complicated, but one of the most important regulations was that in the eating of meat no blood should be eaten, for "the blood is the life, and you shall not eat the life with the flesh" (Deuteronomy 12:23). Paul, on the other hand, taught that salvation is through faith in Christ, not through the keeping of the Law. He did not believe that anyone was saved by the keeping of the Law; thus he could not insist that Gentiles had to be circumcised, observe the dietary regulations, and otherwise live as if they were Jews. To do so would have greatly hampered his work, and was not in accord with his understanding of the gospel.

As Acts 15 tells the story, a compromise was reached: Gentile Christians did not have to undergo circumcision, but they were enjoined to refrain from eating meat that had been offered to idols, from eating blood (and thus to refrain from eating animals that had died by strangulation), and from unchastity —from the kind of sexual immorality to which the heathen were often prone (15:20, 29). Paul in Galatians 2:1-10 does not know of any compromise on the issue; he says simply that he was entrusted with the gospel to the uncircumcised, as Peter had been entrusted with the gospel to the circumcised, "only they would have us remember the poor, which very thing I was eager to do." In his letters Paul shows no evidence of compromise on the food laws, though of course he objected strongly to sexual impurity. In any event, Paul's point of view eventually won the day, but his letters show that the extreme party of the Jewish Christians often gave him much trouble.

On his final journey to Jerusalem, Paul was arrested when he entered the temple with some Jewish Christians who were fulfilling a vow; he was accused of defiling the temple by bringing Greeks into the holy area. Roman soldiers had to rescue him from an angry mob of Jews. The remaining chapters of Acts record in considerable detail Paul's speeches defending himself before the Jewish mob, the Sanhedrin, the Roman governor Felix, and King Agrippa II. He spent two years in prison at Caesarea, and finally appealed his case to Rome, since he was a Roman citizen. On the way to Rome his ship was wrecked off the island of Malta; the Book of Acts gives a vivid description of the shipwreck and of Paul's fortitude and leadership throughout the storm. But Paul finally reached Rome, where he remained in house custody for two years. Acts ends with the statement that Paul "lived there two whole years at his own expense, and welcomed all who came to him, preaching the kingdom of God and teaching about the Lord Jesus Christ quite openly and unhindered" (28:30-31).

What was Paul's final fate? We have no accurate information, but the tradition arose early that he met a martyr's death at Rome by beheading. Perhaps at the end of the two years just mentioned he was tried and condemned (A.D. 61). Some scholars think, however, that Paul was acquitted or that his case was dropped for lack of accusers, and that he lived three or four years longer, finally being put to death in Rome in A.D. 64 or 65. If so, he may have visited Spain, as he said in Romans 15:24 he hoped to do; and he may have revisited various places in the Aegean region, such as Crete, Ephesus and Macedonia, and Troas (1 Timothy 1:3; 2 Timothy 4:13; Titus 1:5).

It is not easy for a modern Christian to appreciate fully the accomplishments of the Apostle Paul. Some interpreters have accused him of corrupting the simple religion of Jesus and making of it an elaborate Christ cult and intricate theology. What he did in fact was to help make it possible for Christianity to break out of its narrow geographical and national bounds and become a universal religion, acceptable to Gentiles as well as Jews, and to do this while remaining true to the spirit of Jesus and to the earliest Christian message.

Paul lived in a day when travel was difficult and dangerous, yet he traveled far and wide in spreading the gospel. He probably went usually on foot, when he was not on the sea, and took only the barest of necessities. Furthermore, he worked at his trade of tentmaker or leather-worker, accepting only a meager support from some of his churches, and collecting funds for the relief of the church in Jerusalem. He had to face all kinds of conflicts and opposition: from the Jews who rejected the gospel, from the civil authorities who arrested him for disturbing the peace, from converts who misunderstood his gospel in one way or another, and—perhaps worst of all—from those Jewish Christians who continually disagreed with his presentation of the Christian message. When he had still ten or more years to live, he summarized his experiences in this way:

Five times I have received at the hands of the Jews the forty lashes less one. Three times I have been beaten with rods; once I was stoned. Three times I have been shipwrecked; a night and a day I have been adrift at sea; on frequent journeys, in danger from . . . my own people, danger from Gentiles . . . danger from false brethren; in toil and hardship, through many a sleepless night, in hunger and thirst, often without food, in cold and exposure. And, apart from other things, there is the daily pressure upon me of my anxiety for all the churches. (2 Corinthians 11:24-28)

The Letters of Paul

Thirteen of the twenty-seven books of the New Testament are letters ascribed to Paul (not counting Hebrews), making up a fourth of the New Testament. These letters were written mostly to churches and individuals to deal with problems that come to Paul's attention in one way or another.

Some are more like modern letters than others. The Letter to Philemon has only one chapter, and could have been written on a single sheet of papyrus. It is addressed to Philemon to commend to him a runaway slave named Onesimus, entreating Philemon to receive him not as a slave but as a beloved brother. Yet, this short letter is addressed also to "the church in your house." The Letter to the Romans is the longest of Paul's letters, and is more like a formal treatise than an ordinary letter; we are more justified in calling it an "epistle" than most of the others.

Paul very likely wrote many more letters than have been preserved,[4] and some of those which are ascribed to him may not actually be from his pen (or dictation). Hebrews did not bear Paul's name originally, and was not ascribed to him until the end of the second century. It is certainly not by Paul; on this most scholars are today agreed.

Of the other letters, 1 and 2 Timothy and Titus are very likely not by Paul in their present form, although they may contain some fragments of Pauline letters. Some scholars have questioned the genuineness of Colossians and 2 Thessalonians, but on grounds that are not convincing. Many scholars today question that Paul wrote Ephesians. While it contains many ideas that are like those of Paul, it seems to go beyond Paul at some points, and it may have been written—as many prominent

---

[4]On the making of the canon of the New Testament and the collection of Paul's letters, see pp. 268-70.

New Testament critics maintain—by a close disciple and follower of Paul.[5]

We shall discuss very briefly the nine letters of Paul that are certainly original, and also Ephesians, in the order in which they probably were written.

First and Second Thessalonians were probably his earliest letters. They can be easily dated, and their purpose is clear. Soon after landing on European soil, Paul went to the seaport city of Thessalonica. There he converted many people, particularly among the Gentiles. But some of the Jews raised a riot against him, and Paul had to leave before finishing his work. Later, while he was in Corinth, Silas and Timothy brought a report of the church in Thessalonica, and Paul wrote to them his first letter, probably in A.D. 50. He commended the Thessalonians for their fidelity to the gospel and for withstanding persecution, and admonished them to live purely. He then answered two questions they had raised concerning the second coming of Christ: Will those who die before the second coming share in its blessings? When will the second coming occur? He answered the first affirmatively; at the second coming both the living and those who had died in Christ will meet the Lord in the air (4:13-18). As for the second, he replied that no one knows when the second coming will take place; all must live and work, and be prepared for it when it does occur.

Second Thessalonians was written not long afterward, to attempt to clear up further misunderstanding concerning the second coming. Paul said that the coming of Christ was not imminent, and could not occur until after widespread apostasy and the defeat of the Antichrist. He admonished the people not to be idle in expectation of the second coming, but to be diligent, as he had been when he was with them, supporting himself by his own labors.

---

[5]On Goodspeed's theory of the composition of Ephesians, and its connection with the collection of Paul's letters, see p. 268.

First and Second Corinthians contain parts of an extended correspondence of Paul with the church at Corinth, which he had founded and from which the letters just discussed had been written. Four letters were involved, and Paul made at least three visits to Corinth. This city in Greece was noted in the ancient world for its very mixed population and its low moral standards.

On his "third" missionary journey, Paul spent three years in Ephesus (about A.D. 53-55). Hearing there about conditions in the Corinthian church, he wrote a letter to it concerning association with immoral people within the church (1 Corinthians 5:9). It may be that 2 Corinthians 6:14—7:1 is a fragment of that letter, for it deals with such a matter.

A little later Paul received a letter from Corinth, asking his advice on various questions relating to Christian faith and practice; he also received news from "Chloe's people" (1 Corinthians 1:11) about conditions in the Corinthian church. In reply Paul wrote the letter which we call 1 Corinthians. He gave his judgment regarding various matters reported to him, particularly the strife among various cliques within the church at Corinth, and immorality (including gross sexual immorality). Then, beginning with chapter 7, he turned to the questions about which the Corinthians had written to him, and discussed marriage, the eating of food that had been sacrificed to idols, the veiling of women in public worship, the proper observance of the Lord's Supper, spiritual gifts (including speaking with tongues), and the resurrection. This letter contains some of the most valuable chapters ever written by Paul: the earliest account of the first Lord's Supper (11:23-26), the great poem on Christian love (chapter 13), and the chapter on resurrection (15).

Unfortunately even this splendid letter did not clear up all the problems in Corinth, and Paul found it necessary to visit Corinth. We know little of what happened, but Paul called it a "painful visit" (2 Corinthians 2:1). When he returned to Ephesus, he wrote a severe letter to the Corinthians (2 Corinthians 2:3-4; 7:8), a part of which may be preserved in 2 Corinthians 10—13, for it fits this description and is quite different from the earlier part of 2 Corinthians. Later, Paul left Ephesus and went into Macedonia, and there received better news of conditions in Corinth; then he wrote his fourth letter—2 Corinthians 1—9, minus 6:14—7:1. This is one of the most personal of Paul's letters. He shows how much he glories in his apostolic office, and defends his work and character against various charges. Before long he went to Corinth, and spent the winter of 55-56 there, writing in that city the Letter to the Romans.

These various letters of Paul to the Corinthian church reveal in a vivid manner the conditions in a first-century Christian congregation that was made up largely of converts from paganism in a city noted for its low morality; many of the converts were from the lower strata of society, including slaves. It was far from being a peaceful and harmonious assembly of Christian saints. We see Paul in these letters as the theologian and practical administrator, wrestling with thorny questions and seeking to do so within the bounds of his Christian faith.

Romans is the longest, most influential, and most theological of Paul's letters. We may call it "the gospel according to Paul," because in it he deliberately sets forth his understanding of the Christian message of salvation. It is well organized and systematic, apparently written with great care. Paul wrote the letter in Corinth before he set out for Jerusalem to deliver the collection he had been making for the church there; he hoped thereafter to visit the Roman church on his way to Spain (15:23-29). He wrote to pave the way for his visit, and probably enlist the help of the Roman church for his mission to Spain. We do not know when and by whom the Roman church had been founded. The 16th chapter of Romans probably was not originally a part of the letter to the Romans, which ended with the benediction in 15:33.

Romans expounds Paul's understanding of the gospel as "the power of God for salvation to every one who has faith, to the Jew first and also to the Greek. For in it the righteousness of God is revealed through faith for faith" (1:16-17).

The Letter to the Galatians is one whose purpose and message is very clear, but it is hard to know at what point in Paul's life it was written. Paul had established churches in Galatia, but after he left them certain Judaizers—Jewish Christians who insisted on the need to observe the Jewish Law —went to those churches and stirred up trouble. They denounced Paul's credentials as an apostle, and preached that Christians ought to be circumcised and observe the Law. Paul wrote with considerable passion to counteract their teaching. In a long autobiographical section (chapters 1-2), he sought to defend his position as an apostle, and to prove that his gospel came to him by revelation, not from men. Then Paul proceeded to set forth his view that salvation comes not from keeping the law, but from "faith working through love" (5:6). He admonished the Galatians to hold fast to their Christian freedom, neither taking on a yoke of slavery nor interpreting freedom as license.

The difficulty in fitting this letter into Paul's life, and thus of dating it, comes from differences of opinion as to what Paul meant by "the churches in Galatia" (1:2). Galatia was a Roman province that covered a large strip of territory running through the center of Asia Minor. Were Paul's churches in southern or northern Galatia? We know from Acts 13:13—14:23 tha: Paul evangelized several cities in southern Galatia —Pisidian Antioch, Iconium, Derbe, and Lystra. Acts 16:6 and 18:23 speak of Galatia in a general sense, and some scholars think these refer to the northern part of the province, what was known as "Galatia" in its older geographical sense. Since we are certain that Paul established churches in southern Galatia, it is more probable that this letter was addressed to them. As for the date, scholars differ very widely, partly depending upon their view of the destination of the letter. The similarity of its contents to Romans and parts of the Corinthian correspondence suggests a date in the middle fifties, but some scholars date Galatians even before the Jerusalem Council (A.D. 49), and thus make it the earliest of Paul's letters. A date near that of Romans is likely, but we cannot say anything very definite as to the place of its composition; Paul may have written it during his long stay in Ephesus, or a little later in Corinth.

The remaining certain letters of Paul—Philippians, Colossians, and Philemon—are known as the captivity epistles because they were written while Paul was in prison. It has generally been assumed that they were written from Rome, for we know that Paul was imprisoned there. He also was in prison at Caesarea for at least two years, awaiting trial (Acts 24:27). Many scholars now believe that Paul was imprisoned also in Ephesus, and wrote one or more of these letters there. Acts does not record an imprisonment of Paul in Ephesus; it has been inferred from passages such as 1 Corinthians 15:32, where Paul says, "I fought with beasts at Ephesus," and 2 Corinthians 1:8-10, where he speaks of a deep affliction he experienced in Asia that led him to despair of life itself and to feel he had received the sentence of death. Further, some scholars think that the runaway slave Onesimus, about which the Letter to Philemon was written, is more likely to have fled from Colossae to nearby Ephesus than to faraway Rome; and that Paul's travel plans outlined in Philippians 2:19-24 sound very similar to 1 Corinthians 4:17-19 and Acts 19:22. It is at least a plausible theory that one or more of the so-called captivity epistles (especially Philippians) was written from Ephesus (around A.D. 54 or 55) rather than from Rome (around A.D. 61).

Philippians was written to a church with which Paul always had good relationships and of which he was very proud. He had established it as his first church in Europe. There Paul and Silas were imprisoned, and had an experience which led to the conversion of their jailer (Acts 16:12-40). He visited the church later (Acts 20:6).

Paul wrote the letter to the Philippians to thank them for a gift they had sent him in prison at the hands of Epaphroditus. He fell ill while visiting Paul, but when he recovered, Paul sent him back to Philippi with the letter. It is filled with thanksgiving to the Philippians for their generosity and faithfulness, and with expressions of joy. The words "joy" and "rejoice" occur no less than sixteen times; even in prison Paul writes, "Rejoice in the Lord always; again I will say, Rejoice" (4:4). He takes occasion to warn the Philippians against Judaizers, and to admonish them to heal any divisions in their fellowship. Philippians 2:5-11 expresses a very lofty view of Christ in words Paul may have taken from an early Christian hymn. Philippians is one of the most personal and most serene letters Paul ever wrote, and one of the easiest and most comforting to read today.

Colossians was written to a church Paul had not founded. Its founder was a fellow servant, Epaphras, who came to Paul to report on conditions there. Colossae was in Asia Minor, about a hundred miles east of Ephesus. Epaphras apparently reported that the Colossian church was threatened by a heretical teaching combining Judaic and Gnostic elements. Paul wrote to warn the Colossians against being led astray by such false teaching. Paul calls it "philosophy and empty deceit" (2:8). Its proponents held that Christ was only one among the supernatural powers, and so the angels and "elemental spirits" were to be worshiped; it required also rigid observance of food laws and of religious seasons, and certain ascetic practices. Paul stresses in opposition to these beliefs the supremacy and all-sufficiency of Christ for the individual, for the church, and for the cosmos. Paul says that Christ is the image of the invisible God, in whom all things in heaven and on earth were created. In him dwells the fullness of God, and through him God has reconciled all things to himself. The Christian should not submit to rigid ritualistic and ascetic practices, for he has put off the old nature and its practices, and has put on a new nature. This letter emphasizes, as none of the other letters we have surveyed, the cosmic work of Christ in overcoming the forces of darkness and evil in the universe, and contains the most exalted conception of Christ to be found in all of Paul's writings.

Ephesians is denied to Paul by many modern scholars, as we have seen. In some of its leading ideas it goes beyond the ideas of Paul, as in its conception of the church and its attitude toward marriage, and the style and vocabulary are different from the nine letters of Paul generally conceded to be genuine. Its sentences are longer and generally more involved than in the other letters. As for its vocabulary, Ephesians contains 82 words that are not found elsewhere in Paul's letters, and sometimes it uses phrases and words in a manner different from Paul. It gives the impression that it comes from a second generation of Christians, who believed that the church is built upon the foundation of the apostles and prophets (2:20; 3:5), and could make Paul say: "When you read this you can perceive my insight into the mystery of Christ" (3:4). The evidence indicates to many scholars that Ephesians was written by an admirer and disciple of Paul, who carried some of his ideas to their logical conclusion. However, since we do not know all of the details of Paul's life nor how long he lived, we must not affirm dogmatically that he *could not* have written this letter.

Since the words "in Ephesus" are not found in the earliest Greek manuscripts in 1:1, and since the letter does not sound as if it were written to a specific local church, Ephesians may have been originally a circular letter—whether by Paul or not—sent by the hand of Tychicus (6:21) to several of the churches in Asia Minor.

Whoever wrote it, Ephesians is a sublime work, and has had great influence in the history of Christianity. Its theme is that the Christian church is the body which fulfills in history the eternal purpose of God revealed in Jesus Christ. The church is the body of Christ (1:23; 4:16), the temple of God (2:19-22), and the bride of Christ (5:23-32). The letter is addressed especially to Gentiles, to show how they may become members of the body of Christ according to the eternal plan of God.

Ephesians has great value for us because of its high doctrine of the church and the type of life it demands, and because it emphasizes the unity of all believers in Christ. "There is one body and one Spirit . . . one Lord, one faith, one baptism, one God and Father of us all, who is above all and through all and in all" (4:4-6).

The Postapostolic Age

The decade from A.D. 60 to 70 marked a turning point in the history of New Testament times. Both Peter and Paul suffered martyrdom in this decade. James the brother of Jesus, leader of the Jerusalem church, was stoned to death A.D. 62. Other leaders had died, or would die soon. It is likely that by A.D. 70 few of those who had been disciples and eyewitnesses of Jesus in Palestine remained alive.

The Jewish revolt against Rome, A.D. 66-70, resulted in the capture and destruction of Jerusalem, and the imposition of harsh measures by the Romans on the Jews. About the time of the outbreak, the members of the Christian church in Jerusalem fled to the town of Pella in Transjordan. Thus came to an end the mother-church of Christianity during Paul's career. For the ensuing years no center of Christianity dominated, but the churches at Antioch, Ephesus, and Rome were especially important.

We cannot write a satisfactory history of the postapostolic age, from 70 to the end of the New Testament period, around A.D. 150. The Acts of the Apostles ends with the imprisonment of Paul in Rome, and no other narrative book in the New Testament carries the story on. We can trace out some of the history by reading the New Testament books written in this era, as well as some Christian writings that were produced at this time but were not included in the New Testament.[6]

In this period the lines between Judaism and Christianity hardened, and the Christian church became more and more Gentile in its membership, though it did not lose its Jewish roots. The Christian faith had to struggle for its identity, and the church became more efficiently organized.

Early Christianity suffered some persecution from the Roman government. In its earliest stages the Roman officials could hardly distinguish between Judaism and Christianity. When they did learn to distinguish Christianity, they considered it a "novel and mischievous superstition," as Suetonius said in describing the Neronian persecution. But there were few periods of open hostility and outright persecution; most notable were those under Nero, and later under the Emperor Domitian, about A.D. 95.

The more serious threat to the Christian faith came from within, from teachers of false doctrines. We can see the nature of these from writings that were produced to combat them. Many of these doctrines were of a Gnostic variety. On the general nature of Gnosticism, which was a strange combination

---

[6]On some of these writings see pp. 154, 266. Especially important are the writings of the "apostolic fathers," such as Ignatius, Polycarp, Papias, and Clement.

of various teachings, see below, p. 275. One of the most dangerous teachings of Gnosticism was that Jesus did not actually live in the flesh, but only "appeared" or "seemed" to live, a teaching called Docetism. Many writings of the New Testament did battle against this heresy. The Christian faith was in danger of becoming on the one hand a kind of theosophy or "higher thought," and on the other hand of becoming too ascetic, but it resisted these dangers and others. The Christian faith maintained its identity, but kept its roots in history and in the teachings of Jesus and the apostles.

We must recall that the Gospels were written in this period (with the possible exception of Mark, which may have been composed before A.D. 70). Luke wrote both his Gospel and the Acts of the Apostles, about A.D. 85. The Letter to the Ephesians, if not from Paul himself, was composed in the early part of this period.

The remaining books of the New Testament are the Pastoral Epistles, Hebrews, the Catholic Epistles, and Revelation. As we discuss these in the order in which they appear in the Bible, we shall see that many of them are pseudonymous—that is, written in the name of great men of the earlier era, usually apostles. We should not consider this as in any way fraudulent or dishonest; it was simply in accord with literary practice of the time, and many examples of the same practice can be seen in both the Old Testament and the intertestamental literature. The name of a great person of the past, particularly an apostle, gave to a writing the possibility of a hearing, and then of authority, which it would not otherwise have secured.

First and Second Timothy and Titus are called the Pastoral Epistles, because they purport to be written by Paul as a chief pastor, to his younger helpers and companions, Timothy and Titus, who also are pastors. They were written to give advice and encouragement in the work of the ministry, especially in church administration and worship and the promoting of sound Christian doctrine.

In their present form these epistles are not by Paul, though they may contain Pauline fragments. The vocabulary and style, as well as the ideas and the general background, are not those of Paul and his time. A careful study of the Greek vocabulary of these three short epistles has shown that 306 of the words used, a little more than one third of the total, are not found in the ten letters of Paul. Furthermore, certain key words are used in a manner different from Paul's usage. "Faith," for example, means a body of Christian doctrine, or Christian religion in general, rather than a relationship of trust in Jesus Christ. There is more emphasis on good works than Paul made, and much less on the Spirit. If there are genuine Pauline fragments in these letters, they may be found in 2 Timothy 1: 15-18; 4:9-22; and Titus 3:12-15. Some scholars believe these fragments come from the time between Paul's two imprisonments in Rome.

The Pastoral Epistles are thus an early manual for the clergy, written probably in the early years of the second century A.D. to strengthen the church and give it guidance in important matters.

These books have much value because they reflect church organization of the time and the false teachings in the church which the Christians had to combat. The organization of the church has progressed considerably beyond that reflected in Paul's letters (as in 1 Corinthians 12-14).

In the Pastoral Epistles we encounter the following ministers or workers in the church: bishops, elders, deacons, and enrolled widows. It seems likely that bishops and elders are synonymous terms, with the term bishop (meaning "overseer, supervisor") designating the function, and elder the office. However, some scholars think that at this time there was a single bishop for each Christian congregation or each city, and associated with him were elders and deacons. A bishop would be an elder, but not all elders were bishops. The "enrolled widows" (1 Timothy 5:9-16) were widowed women not less than sixty years old who devoted themselves to fulltime church work in return for their support.

The Pastorals reflect false teachings against which the church had to struggle. Readers are warned against "myths and endless genealogies which promote speculations" (1 Timothy 1:4), "the godless chatter and contradictions of what is falsely called knowledge" (6:20), and various ascetic practices (4:3). These heresies probably were mostly of Gentile Gnostic origin, though we do hear of "Jewish myths" (Titus 1:14) and "the circumcision party" (1:10). The Pastoral Epistles insist upon a religion which sees God as both Redeemer and Creator of man and his world, and grounds its faith upon what God has done in Christ in history. While it does not give up hope in the return of Christ and the coming day of judgment, it seeks to find ways in which the Christian and the church can live on in the world as it is, without compromising with worldly standards.

The Epistle to the Hebrews is an epistle only in part. It is really a treatise or tract that ends like a letter. This book is certainly not by Paul. Ancient writers sometimes attributed it to Barnabas or Clement; some said Luke translated it into Greek from Paul's original Hebrew or Aramaic. It lacks many of that apostle's major emphases, and goes its own way in its teaching. The author wrote to show the superiority of Christianity over Judaism, to people who were tempted to give up their faith and return to Jewish beliefs and practices in a time of persecution and false teachings. The book is a careful and well-organized discussion, which makes three points: (1) Jesus Christ is superior to the prophets (1:1-3), the angels (1:5—2:18), and Moses (3:1-6); (2) his priesthood is superior to the Levitical priesthood, since he belongs to the eternal order of Melchizedek (4:14—7:28); and (3) Christ's sacrifice offered in the heavenly sanctuary is superior to the numerous animal sacrifices offered by the priests on earth, so that he is the mediator of a new covenant (8:1—10:39). Interspersed with these arguments are sections of admonition or warning, often beginning with "Therefore," which exhort the readers to give attention to these teachings, accept them, and live as Christians should, particularly in a time of affliction.

The author supports his views by numerous quotations from the Old Testament, and by using an idea which goes back to Plato: things which are seen on earth are only shadows of the eternal realities in heaven. For example, he says that the Hebrew temple was "a copy and shadow of the heavenly sanctuary" (8:5) and "the law has but a shadow of the good things to come instead of the true form of these realities" (10:1). An unusual teaching in Hebrews is that apostates from the true Christian faith have no chance of a second repentance (6:4-6; 10:26-31).

Little is known of the time and place when Hebrews was written. It may have been written in Rome, for it was first quoted by Clement of Rome about A.D. 95, and 13:24 may be translated, "They of Italy salute you." As for the date, it may have been written any time between the sixties (before the destruction of the Jerusalem temple in 70) and about A.D. 90.

The next seven books in the New Testament are grouped together as the Catholic Epistles. This is an ancient designation used because they were addressed mostly to Christians in general, to the universal Church, rather than to local churches, as Paul's letters had been. Most of them are not really letters, but tracts dealing with various problems faced by the church at the time of writing. All of these books, except 1 John and 1 Peter, were slow in being recognized as canonical and authoritative.

The Book of James is a sermon in the form of a letter, consisting largely of ethical instruction without clear order. The author was from early times thought to be James the brother of Jesus. While this is possible, the fact that it is written in excellent Greek, the absence of references to Jesus, and other considerations speak against this identification. The principal topics are temptation, the right conduct and proper relationships of rich and poor, bridling of the tongue, and the relationship between faith and works. The most famous verse is: "So faith by itself, if it has no works, is dead" (2:17). Luther called this a "right strawy epistle," because he thought it contrary to Paul's doctrine of faith. Actually the letter is not in basic disagreement with Paul. Paul could speak of the "fruits of the Spirit" (Galatians 5:22-23), and of "faith working through love" (Galatians 5:6), whereas James speaks of faith proving or demonstrating itself through works (2:18-20). It may have been directed against a misunderstanding or perversion of Paul's teaching about faith and Christian freedom which led to lax morality. The date is impossible to fix accurately, but many scholars put it near the end of the first century.

First Peter was written to give hope and encouragement to Christians in Asia Minor in a time of persecution. They are urged to "rejoice in so far as you share Christ's sufferings" (4:13), and to show that they are "a chosen race, a royal priesthood, a holy nation, God's own people" (2:9). This is one of the finest of the short books in the New Testament, filled with hope and wise teaching. Some scholars believe it was not written by the Apostle Peter, because it is in excellent Greek (which a former Galilean fisherman could hardly write), and seems to show acquaintance with some of Paul's letters. However, it is quite possible that the letter was written by Silvanus, who had been a missionary companion of Paul (in Acts he is called Silas), at the direction of Peter. It was written from Rome ("Babylon" of 5:13), probably after the beginning of the Neronian persecution A.D. 64.

Second Peter is the latest book in the New Testament, composed about A.D. 150. It was certainly not written by the Apostle Peter. Several early church fathers had doubts about his authorship, and it won its way into the canon of the New Testament very slowly. Its second chapter borrows wholesale from the little epistle of Jude. The author of 2 Peter knew a collection of Paul's letters which was recognized to be scripture (3:16). These facts, as well as others, point to a very late date, and authorship by someone other than Peter.

The letter was written to Christians in general primarily to counteract the teachings of heretics. They were libertines who are described as licentious, greedy, and despisers of authority. They follow "cleverly devised myths" (1:16), and above all they scoff at the second coming of Christ, saying, "Where is the promise of his coming?" (3:4). "Peter" reminds his readers that "with the Lord one day is as a thousand years, and a thousand years as one day" (3:8); so they must not lose hope that the day of the Lord will come like a thief, and must live in such a manner as to be ready for its coming.

First, Second and Third John are from the same author, probably John the Elder who, we said above, was very likely the author of the Fourth Gospel. There are many similarities between these three letters and the Gospel. First John does not have the form of a letter, but rather a treatise or written sermon, and does not name its author. Second and Third John name as the writer simply "the elder," but they are in letter form. All were written near the end of the first century, probably at Ephesus.

First John is a long meditation on the theme of the nature of God and the Christian life. God is light and love, and the true Christian walks in the light and loves his neighbor. It is also directed against the false teaching of antichrists; the spirit of antichrist is that he denies that "Jesus Christ has come in the flesh" (4:2). The false teachers were also living unlovely lives.

Second John is written to some local church and repeats in brief form the principal teaching of 1 John, and warns against showing hospitality to false teachers. Third John, addressed to a man named Gaius, commends him for receiving messengers from the elder, and condemns one Diotrephes. The latter is one "who likes to put himself first" and refuses to acknowledge the elder's authority; he refuses to welcome messengers from the elder and puts out of the church those who do. The tone of these three letters suggest that John the Elder was a man in a position of some authority over several churches, in and around Ephesus. He sent missionaries around in the area; some Christians welcomed them and recognized John's authority, but others did not.

The letter of Jude was written with a specific purpose: to appeal to its recipients "to contend for the faith which was once for all delivered to the saints." This faith was a body of doctrine that was being endangered by false teachers, similar to those described in 2 Peter. According to tradition Jude, brother of James, was the brother of Jesus (Mark 6:3). So little is known about him that we can hardly affirm or deny that he wrote this little letter; and nothing definite can be said about its time and place of origin.

The last book of the New Testament is the Revelation to John. Most readers of this book today find it very strange and puzzling, even weird and fantastic. It is misused by some Christians as a book of predictions of our own time, but it is ignored by most. In the early days of Christianity it was not readily accepted into the canon, and the Greek Orthodox Church does not now consider it as fully authoritative and scriptural.

This book—note that its proper name is Revelation to John, not Revelations as it is often called—is an apocalypse, the only one in the New Testament. It belongs to a specific type of literature and thought, called apocalyptic, and must be understood in the light of earlier books such as Daniel and Ezekiel in the Old Testament, and some of the intertestamental books.[7] The New Testament contains apocalyptic chapters, such as Mark 13 and its parallels, and apocalyptic ideas appear in other books.

Revelation was written in a time of crisis and persecution for the Christian church probably around A.D. 95 when the Roman emperor Domitian vigorously promoted the cult of emperor worship and persecuted Christians who refused to participate in it. The author was someone named John; he was certainly not the same John who wrote the Gospel and 1, 2, 3 John, for those books and Revelation are poles apart in style and contents. Thus he was probably not John the son of Zebedee, nor John the Elder. He was a leader in the churches of Asia Minor who had been exiled for his faith to the island of Patmos. He was probably Jewish in origin; he writes in very poor Greek, with a strong Semitic cast.

Anyone who reads this book today should do so with a good commentary at hand so that he may understand its symbolism; and he should try to understand it in terms of its own time and its original purpose. John wrote to fortify the Christians of Asia Minor under persecution with the assurance that God and Christ would ultimately conquer the forces of evil. As examples of correct interpretation, let us point out that the great harlot Babylon of chapter 17 is Rome; and that the number 666 of 13:18, the number of the beast that is overthrown, probably stands for the Emperor Nero. This is derived by writing *Neron Caesar* in Hebrew letters and then taking

---

[7]For brief description of what is meant by apocalyptic literature and thought, see pp. 32, 34-5, 85, 217.

the total of the values of the letters, which is 666. There was a widespread legend in the first century that Nero would be revived and become the Antichrist. Properly interpreted, Revelation can be seen as a book of deep faith and great hope.

The New Testament characteristically ends with a vision of the new heaven and new earth, and with promise of the ultimate triumph of God over all the forces of evil.

VI

the message of the
new testament

THE TITLE PAGE OF THE SECOND PART OF THE
Christian Bible often reads: "The New Covenant, Commonly
Called the New Testament of our Lord and Savior Jesus
Christ." New Covenant is indeed a better title than New Testa-
ment, for it is the story of the appearance on earth of Jesus
Christ to be the mediator of a new covenant, and of his followers who made up the people of a new covenant. When
Jesus gave his disciples the cup at the Last Supper, he said:
"This cup is the new covenant in my blood" (1 Corinthians
11:25; cf. Mark 14:24). Paul considered himself to be the
minister of a new covenant (2 Corinthians 3:6), and Hebrews
sees the fulfilment of Jeremiah's prophecy of a new covenant
(Jeremiah 31:31-34) in the covenant of which Jesus was the
mediator (8:8-13; 10:16-18). In our discussion of the faith
of the Old Testament (pp. 88-9) we said that the concept
of a covenant is central to the understanding of the Old Testament. It is also central to the New, in spite of the fact that
the word itself occurs infrequently. The new covenant is a
fulfilment of the old, bringing to realization its promises, and

not a sharp break from it. The concept of covenant binds together, rather than separates, the Old and New Testaments.

The message of the New Testament is not the setting forth of new ideas about God. It tells of a new and climactic act of God in sending Jesus Christ, and in forming the Christian community as his own people, the true Israel. Some parts of the New Testament are proclamation of the good news concerning what God has done in Christ for the saving of mankind, and is intended to convert believers. Other parts are teaching or instruction, intended to build up the faith and life of believers so that they may be mature Christians. Proclamation and teaching cannot always be clearly separated, but it is well to remember that it does contain both.

We shall discuss the message of the New Testament in a different manner from that of the Old Testament. Instead of discussing topics, we shall discuss the message of Jesus first, then the earliest Christian proclamation, next Paul's message, and the viewpoint of John. Finally we shall summarize the unifying elements in the New Testament message.

Jesus and the Kingdom of God

" 'The time is fulfilled, and the kingdom of God is at hand; repent, and believe in the gospel.' " These were the words with which Jesus began his career of preaching the gospel of God (Mark 1:15). The message of John the Baptist was very similar: " 'Repent, for the kingdom of heaven is at hand' " (Matthew 3:2). John had called upon men to repent and prepare themselves for the coming judgment, had baptized his followers, and had summoned specific groups of people to " 'bear fruit that befits repentance' " (Matthew 3:8). All of the Gospels, except John, make Jesus' announcement of the coming of the kingdom of God and his teachings about it central to his ministry. What did he mean by the kingdom of God? What did he think men should do in order to be prepared to enter it? What was his own relationship to the coming of the kingdom? All of these are crucial questions in the message of Jesus.

When Jesus used the phrase "kingdom of God," he was not talking about a territory, a nation, or any piece of land. It would be much more accurate for us to speak of the kingship, or reign, or sovereignty of God. Furthermore, the phrase "kingdom of heaven," used only in Matthew, is an exact equivalent. It does not mean the kingdom *in* heaven; the word "heaven" is simply used as a synonym for God. At this time the Jews were sometimes reluctant to use the word "God" and substituted for it certain synonyms or circumlocutions, of which "heaven" was a common one.

Jesus never clearly defines what he means by the kingdom of God, but the phrase would have been familiar to his hearers. The idea, though not the exact phrase, goes back to the Old Testament, and the phrase itself was used by the Jews in their prayers, and on other occasions in the first century.

As far back as the days of Gideon the judge, the Israelites tried to get him to serve as king over them and establish a ruling dynasty, but Gideon replied: " 'I will not rule over you, and my son will not rule over you; the LORD will rule over you' " (Judges 8:23). When the monarchy of Saul was established, there were some who interpreted this as a rejection of Yahweh as king over Israel (1 Samuel 8:7). Throughout the history of Israel, the prevailing belief was that Yahweh was the true King of Israel; the king on the royal throne was anointed to be God's representative and agent on earth.

In ancient Israel, however, there were two aspects to the kingship of God: (1) on the one hand, they believed God was the eternal King of Israel, the Creator of the world and its Ruler; and yet (2) on the other hand, they realized that God was not in fact King because his sovereignty was not recognized and his will was not obeyed—neither throughout all of Israel, nor among the nations of the world. Second Isaiah could prophesy of the time when every knee would bow to Yahweh as God and King (Isaiah 45:23). Thus it could be said: God *is* King, and he is *not yet King,* for his sovereignty is not everywhere recognized. The full realization of the sovereignty of God was a hope for the future.

In late Old Testament times and in the intertestamental literature, an idea developed in apocalyptic thought which was to be very important for the conception of the kingdom of God. A dualism arose which made an important distinction between the present age and the age-to-come. Many Jews came to believe that the present age is under the rule of Satan, Beelzebub, or other evil powers (see Luke 4:6; 11:20; John 12:31; 14:30; 16:11; the idea is found in the Pseudepigrapha and the Dead Sea Scrolls). Thus, the dominion of Satan must be broken before the ushering in of the age-to-come and the appearance of the kingdom of God.

Some of the teachings of Jesus speak of the kingdom of God as future. One of the clearest is Mark 9:1: " 'Truly, I say to you, there are some standing here who will not taste death before they see the kingdom of God come with power.' " He taught his disciples to pray, " 'Thy kingdom come' " (Matthew 6:10). He spoke of a future judgment in which a separation would be made between the sheep and the goats, the righteous and the wicked, and to the former the King would say, " 'Come, O blessed of my Father, inherit the kingdom prepared for you from the foundation of the world' " (Matthew 25:34). At the Last Supper, Jesus said regarding the cup, " 'I shall not drink again of the fruit of the vine until that day when I drink it new in the kingdom of God' " (Mark 14:25). In these, as well as other passages, Jesus appears to envisage a future coming of God's kingdom.

On the other hand, some of his teachings clearly sound as if he believed the kingdom had already come and was already present. When explaining the meaning of his exorcism of demons, he says, " 'If it is by the Spirit of God that I cast out demons, then the kingdom of God has come upon you' " (Matthew 12:28; in Luke 11:20 the expression "finger of God" is used instead of "Spirit of God"). Jesus interprets the casting out of demons as evidence of the breaking of the power of Satan, so that the kingdom of God may come, and speaks of it as already in some manner present. Another significant passage is Luke 17:20-21. The Pharisees ask when the kingdom of God is coming, and Jesus answers that the kingdom does not come with signs that can be observed, and so people will not say "Lo, here it is!" or "There it is." " 'For behold,' " says Jesus, " 'the kingdom of God is *in the midst of you.*' " The italicized phrase can be rendered "within you," and some scholars have interpreted this as meaning that the kingdom is something entirely spiritual, within the hearts of the believers. It is more likely, however, in view of the passage as a whole, that Jesus is really saying that the kingdom of God is already in your midst. In Matthew 11:11-14 and Luke 16:16 Jesus makes a distinction between the era of the law and the prophets which lasted to the time of John the Baptist, and the kingdom of God which—as he says—people are now entering. Other teachings of Jesus, especially some of his parables, can be cited as evidence for his belief that the kingdom of God was already present in his own time.

How can we reconcile these two ideas that appear to be quite different? Did Jesus believe that the kingdom of God had already come in his own time and through his ministry, or did he look for it in the future? Interpreters have resorted to various devices to eliminate one set of teachings or the other, or to say that one set belongs to one period of Jesus' life and the other set to another period. It is wise to retain both sets of teachings, and try to see how they are related in Jesus' teaching as a whole. Jesus believed that in his ministry, notably in his casting out of demons, he was destroying the power of evil and enabling God's rule to manifest itself, and yet he foresaw that the complete realization and manifestation of God's reign lay in the future. In the person and the whole ministry and life of Jesus the kingdom of God is already present in principle, and men may enter it by giving to God their absolute obedience; but the full realization of the kingship of God, the consummation of his kingdom, lies in the future. His teachings indicate he thought it would be in the near future, so that he could say, "The kingdom of God is at hand."

In his teachings about the kingdom of God, Jesus did not show interest in setting precise dates and giving all of the details of its coming (see Mark 13:32). His aim was to announce its coming, and to summon men to be prepared to enter it or receive it. Yet in his own career a new era had opened up, and the powers of the age-to-come had already begun to be realized. God had already begun to rule in the world in a more complete sense than he had ever done before.

Thus, the kingdom of God in Jesus' teaching is not something that men are called upon to build on earth; nor is it something that gradually grows on earth. Above all it is *God's* kingdom, in which *his* will is done and which comes in *his* own way. Yet, men may prepare themselves to enter it and receive it by repentance, and by doing what John the Baptist called "bear fruit that befits repentance."

Many of Jesus' teachings speak of the way of life of those who are disciples of the kingdom of God. Much of his teaching in this regard is summed up in the Sermon on the Mount (Matthew 5—7). This Sermon does not set forth the conditions one must meet in order to enter the kingdom of heaven—for who could fulfill such conditions entirely? Yet, it does describe the ideal way of life for those who are members of the kingdom of God. The first beatitude sets the tone and announces the purpose: " 'Blessed are the poor in spirit, for theirs is the kingdom of heaven." Those who are in the kingdom are humble, meek, merciful, pure in heart, ready to endure persecution and affliction. They aim at a righteousness that exceeds that of the scribes and Pharisees, not abolishing the law but fulfilling its deeper meaning. Murder consists not simply in the act of killing, but in the anger and hatred which inspire it. Adultery is not just an act of infidelity, but the lustful desire. The disciple of the kingdom learns to love his enemy as well as his neighbor. In giving alms, in praying, and in fasting, he avoids public display and the desire to please men, but seeks to please God. He is single-hearted in his devotion to God, knowing that he cannot serve God and Mammon at the same time. Jesus holds up before his disciples as the goal of their way of life the imitation of God, the summons to "be perfect, as your heavenly Father is perfect" (5: 48). This does not mean sinlessness, but rather impartiality and integrity such as God shows in making the sun rise on the evil and on the good, and sending rain on the just and the unjust.

Repentance and preparation for the kingdom of God meant, in Jesus' teaching, radical and concrete obedience to the will of God in all kinds of situations. Jewish teachers sometimes spoke of the need to take upon oneself the yoke of the kingdom of God, or the yoke of God's commands. So, Jesus did not teach that men could earn the right to enter God's kingdom, for it was the gift of God, but that those who were ready for the kingdom of God must see that it meant discipline and obedience, as well as joy and fulfilment. Jesus' emphasis was upon what men should *be* rather than what they should *do,* but what they were would inevitably express itself in positive action, for a good tree must bring forth good fruit.

We may turn now to the question: what was Jesus' own relationship to the coming of the kingdom of God? Did he consider himself to be only a prophet, heralding the coming of the kingdom and teaching men how to prepare themselves for it? Or, was he the Messiah with a very special relationship to the kingdom? If he considered himself to be the Messiah, in what sense did he interpret messiahship?

The answers to these questions are most varied. Some scholars of outstanding reputation maintain that we cannot really know anything about Jesus' self-conciousness, about how he thought of himself. They say we can know only what the writers of the Gospels and the other New Testament books thought and believed about him. All were written after the resurrection of Jesus, and everyone in the Christian community believed that Jesus was the Messiah, though they may have had different ways of expressing and explaining it. We must admit it is extremely difficult for anyone to know just what was Jesus' own conception of his mission, and the fact that all of the New Testament was written after the resurrection should rule out all dogmatism in discussing this question.

The earliest Christians believed, after the resurrection of Jesus, that he was the Christ, the Son of God, one who had a unique relationship to God and to the coming of his kingdom. Peter said at the conclusion of his sermon on Pentecost: "Let all the house of Israel therefore know assuredly that God has made him both Lord and Christ, this Jesus whom you crucified" (Acts 2:36). The Christian church used many titles to express its belief in the special role of Jesus—Christ, Son of God, Son of Man, Son of David, Lord, Servant, Savior, *Logos* (Word), and many others.

Our word "Christ" is the Greek *Christos,* which translated the Hebrew word *Mashiah,* "the anointed one." Sometimes Christ (or the Christ) is used in the Gospels in the sense of the Messiah, as in Mark 12:35; 13:21; John 1:20, 25; 3:28, etc. However, it soon became, after the resurrection, a proper name for Jesus, so that he could be called Christ, Jesus Christ, Christ Jesus, Our Lord Jesus Christ, and the like. These occur especially in Acts and the epistles. It is doubtful that Jesus ever referred to himself directly, in the earliest sources, as Messiah or Christ.

There is one fact of which we can be certain: Jesus did not fulfill any of the normal Jewish expectations concerning the Messiah. There was no orthodox, generally accepted doctrine of the Messiah, but Jesus did not fit any of the types of Messiah that the Jews hoped for. He was not a king seated upon a royal throne, dispensing justice and righteousness; he recognized the need to " 'render to Caesar the things that are Caesar's' " (Mark 12:17). He was not a warrior at the head of a great company of soldiers, ready to lead a revolt against Rome. He deliberately rejected the temptation to overthrow the Roman government by force. He was not a supernatural, angelic being who had come from heaven on clouds of glory. He was a human being living very much as other men did; some of the religious leaders thought he was too human when he associated with sinners and the outcasts of society. No, Jesus was not the Messiah in any of the generally accepted senses, and we should not be surprised that the majority of the Jews did not hail him as such.

In the Synoptic Gospels Jesus does not say much about his own role, and speaks relatively little about himself. In this respect the Gospel of John is different, for there he speaks often of himself. In the earlier Gospels, he wants to be known for what he does and for his teachings, not for the claims he makes for himself. The story in Matthew 11:2-6 is typical. When John heard in prison about the deeds of Jesus, he sent some of his disciples to inquire, " 'Are you he who is to come, or shall we look for another?' " Jesus did not directly answer their query, but replied: " 'Go and tell John what you hear and see: the blind receive their sight and the lame walk, lepers are cleansed and the deaf hear, and the dead are raised up, and the poor have good news preached to them. And blessed is he who takes no offense at me.' " Jesus' answer might be paraphrased: "Look at what I am doing, and from that draw your own conclusion as to whether I am the expected Messiah."

The Gospel of Mark has a theory concerning the "messianic secret" of Jesus. Mark says that many demons and unclean spirits that Jesus cast out recognized him, but Jesus ordered them not to reveal who he was (1:24, 34; 3:11-12). Mark also says that Jesus told the parables in order to mystify the people, but taught their meaning to his own disciples in secret (4:11-12). Immediately after Peter's confession at Caesarea-Philippi, Mark says that Jesus "charged them to tell no one about him" (8:30). Most interpreters believe that to some extent this theory of a messianic secret is Mark's way of explaining why the multitudes did not recognize Jesus as the Messiah and accept him; certainly his explanation concerning the parables is at variance with Jesus' real purpose in teaching through parables. Nevertheless, there may be behind Mark's theory the fact that Jesus was very reluctant to be looked upon as the Messiah, for there were connotations in that term that he did not like. He rejected the nationalistic, political, and materialistic aspects of the messianic expectations that were abroad among the people.

In view of all this, some scholars believe that Jesus did not claim to be the Messiah, nor wish to be considered as such. They believe he wished to be known simply as a teacher or rabbi, and a prophet. He announced the coming of a kingdom and of a Messiah, and he called upon his hearers to repent, as the Old Testament prophets did, but had no special relationship to that kingdom. Some of the words of Jesus give evidence that he did think of himself as a prophet. At Nazareth he said, " 'A prophet is not without honor, except in his own country, and among his own kin, and in his own house' " (Mark 6:4). He said that it was not appropriate for a prophet to perish away from Jerusalem (Luke 13:33). Immediately after the triumphal entry into Jerusalem, when the people asked, "Who is this?" the crowds replied: " 'This is the prophet Jesus from Nazareth of Galilee.' " (Matthew 21:11) Other passages could be cited that show Jesus was considered as a prophet in his own time. To be a prophet, a spokesman for God like the prophets of the Old Testament, was a high calling and a difficult mission.

Nevertheless, there are many things in the earliest traditions concerning Jesus and his life that make it hard to believe that he wished to be considered only as a prophet, and that he made no claim to be the Messiah in any sense.

When Jesus was baptized by John, he heard a voice from heaven saying, " 'Thou art my beloved Son; with thee I am well pleased' " (Mark 1:11). These words combine two Old Testament verses, Psalm 2:7 and Isaiah 42:1. Peter confessed the belief of the disciples when he said: " 'You are the Christ' " (Mark 8:29). Jesus did not reject this designation, nor rebuke Peter for his answer, though he did accept it with some reservation. The story of the triumphal entry of Jesus into Jerusalem at the beginning of his last week has every appearance of being a planned entry of a messianic figure, and he was hailed as such. At the Last Supper, he offered the cup as representing the blood of the covenant, and spoke of looking forward to drinking the cup in the kingdom of God. At the trial before the high priest, we read that Jesus was asked, " 'Are you the Christ, the Son of the Blessed?' " and Jesus replied, " 'I am' " (Mark 14:61-62).

In addition to these specific incidents, we should notice that Jesus summoned men to follow him, to become his disciples. He called upon them to repent and prepare for the kingdom, but he also called upon them to renounce many material things and come after him. The number of the disciples who followed him in this way was much greater than the twelve apostles.

Jesus thus spoke with an authority, and with an urgency for personal decision to follow him, that was greater than one would expect from a rabbi (teacher) or prophet.

It is most likely, then, that Jesus did consider himself as the Messiah, but not in the popular sense. He reinterpreted the idea of messiahship in a new and creative way, giving to the word "Messiah" a new meaning. The clue to this reinterpretation is in his use of the unusual term, Son of man.

The term Son of man occurs more often in the Gospels than any other messianic term, and it always occurs in sayings of Jesus. It is used very rarely outside the Gospels.

This term has three different meanings. Sometimes it is only another way of saying "mankind" or "a human being," as in Psalm 8:4. This is its meaning in Mark 2:27: " 'The sabbath was made for man, not man for the sabbath; so the Son of man is lord even of the sabbath.' "

Another use of the title, Son of man, was to describe the supernatural, angelic figure that many Jews expected the Messiah to be; they looked forward to his coming on clouds of glory to bring deliverance and judgment. This use is based on Daniel 7, where we read that "one like a son of man" came before the Ancient of Days and was given eternal dominion, glory, and kingdom. The Son of man in the Book of Enoch[1] is specifically a messianic figure. He is described as coming to sit on the throne of glory and judge the nations; he is pre-existent; and he is "the anointed one" and "the light of the gentiles."

In many passages of the Gospels the Son of man is described as coming in the future with the angels, to sit on his glorious throne, judging the nations and saving the righteous. Some

---

[1] For brief discussion of this intertestamental book, see above, pp. 147-8. The Son of man occurs especially in the section known as the Similitudes of Enoch, chapters 48, 69, and 71.

of these passages are Mark 8:38; 13:26; 14:62; Matthew 19:28; 25:31; Luke 18:8.

There is a third meaning to the term, Son of man, that is entirely new, and is unique with Jesus. He speaks of the suffering of the Son of man, and combines in his sayings about the Son of man some of the characteristics of the Suffering Servant of the Lord depicted in Isaiah 53 and related passages of Second Isaiah. Immediately after Peter's confession, Mark says that Jesus "began to teach them that the Son of man must suffer many things, and be rejected by the elders and the chief priests and the scribes, and be killed, and after three days rise again" (8:31). Peter rebuked Jesus, for he could not understand this kind of messiahship. But twice Jesus repeated these predictions of his coming suffering (Mark 9:31; 10:33). Concerning himself Jesus further said, " 'For the Son of man also came not to be served but to serve, and to give his life as a ransom for many' " (Mark 10:45).

We conclude, then, that Jesus considered himself as the Messiah, but accepted the designation with some reluctance and reinterpreted the idea it involved in a new, creative manner. For his reinterpretation he chose the figure of the Son of man, probably because it was not associated with political and nationalistic ambitions, and it could be connected with his suffering as a human being. It was a somewhat mysterious title, perhaps impossible for Gentiles to understand. Jewish disciples of Jesus had great difficulty understanding that the Messiah must suffer; that is why they deserted him at the time of the crucifixion.

The early Christian community combined the last two meanings of the term "Son of man": they thought of Jesus as the Son of man who had suffered, died, and risen again, and they looked forward to the time when he would return on clouds of glory with the heavenly angels as a triumphant Son of man. Did Jesus himself hold both of these meanings, expecting to return in bodily form as a triumphant Messiah? This is a question we cannot answer, and it is better to say that we do not know whether he had such an expectation. After 1900 years he has not returned in this manner, but it is a fact that he has returned in spirit to many individuals and in his Church, the "body of Christ."

The important question we must ask concerning Jesus is this: did God truly send him, and—whatever designation he used or accepted—did God through him usher in the kingdom of God? To this question the Christian answers in faith: Yes.

The Earliest Christian Preaching

Soon after the resurrection of Jesus, his disciples had the experience of Pentecost; as Acts 2 relates it, they were filled with the Holy Spirit, and men from various nations heard them speaking each in his own language. The apostles accomplished many signs and wonders. The members of the Christian community enjoyed a very close fellowship, expressed for a time in the common ownership of possessions. They continued to worship in the temple, and "breaking bread in their homes, they partook of food with glad and generous hearts, praising God and having favor with all the people" (Acts 2:46-47). The apostles and others proclaimed Jesus as the Messiah, and additions were made to the church. On more than one occasion some of the apostles were arrested by Jewish authorities, but subsequently released. The first Christian martyr, Stephen, was put to death by stoning. After that, the Christians were persecuted in earnest, and many of them were scattered throughout Judea and Samaria to preach the gospel of Jesus Christ.

Various expressions are used to indicate the nature of the early preaching; in the Synoptic Gospels and Acts we read of Jesus or the apostles "preaching the kingdom of God," whereas in the Pauline epistles the usual phrase is "preaching Christ."

In a study of fundamental importance, C. H. Dodd has sought to define the contents of this earliest Christian preaching, or apostolic preaching.[2] He finds its contents primarily in the five speeches of Peter recorded in Acts 2:14-40; 3:12-26; 4:8-12; 5:29-32; and 10:34-43, and the speech of Paul at Pisidian Antioch given in Acts 13:16-41. In addition, he believes that traces of it can be seen in some of Paul's letters, such as 1 Corinthians 15:1-7, 23-28; Romans 1:1-4; 8:31-34; 10:8-9; Galatians 1:3-4; and in 1 Peter 1:10-12; 3:18-22.

This early Christian preaching was a proclamation of the good news of what God had done and would do in Christ for man's salvation. It is often referred to in modern works on the New Testament by its Greek name, Kerygma.[3] In Greek this word could mean either the act of preaching or the content of what was preached. It is in the latter sense that the word is most often used today, virtually as a technical term. In many respects the word gospel, "the good news," is synonymous; in fact, New Testament writers themselves more often use the word gospel *(evangélion)* for the content of the earliest preaching than the word *kérygma.*

The content of the kerygma, or the gospel as it was preached in its earliest form, was as follows:

(1) The age of fulfilment of God's promises to Israel has now dawned. The prophecies of the Old Testament are now coming to pass. The individual items of the kerygma are usually supported by quotations from the Old Testament, such as passages of Joel 2, Psalms 2 and 110, Deuteronomy 18, Isaiah 53, and others.

(2) This fulfilment has taken place through the ministry, the death, and the resurrection of Jesus.

---

[2] *The Apostolic Preaching and its Developments,* new edition (London: Hodder & Stoughton Ltd., 1944).

[3] The correct pronunciation of this word is *kay'-rig-ma,* with accent on the first syllable (not on the second, as it is frequently pronounced). Some writers even form an adjective from this word and speak of kerygmatic preaching, kerygmatic theology, and the like.

(a) He was born of the seed of David.

(b) In his ministry " 'God anointed Jesus of Nazareth with the Holy Spirit and with power . . . he went about doing good and healing all that were oppressed by the devil, for God was with him' " (Acts 10:38). In such a manner Jesus of Nazareth was "a man attested to you by God with mighty works and wonders and signs which God did through him" (2:22).

(c) But Jesus was put to death on the cross. This was done through the plan and foreknowledge of God, but at the hands of wicked men who denied the Holy and Righteous One.

(d) God raised up Jesus from the dead, loosing the pangs of death, and made him Lord and Christ. Of his resurrection many of the early disciples were witnesses.

(3) The risen Jesus has been exalted to the right hand of God in heaven, as Prince and Savior, the messianic head of the new Israel.

(4) The presence of the Holy Spirit in the church is the sign of Christ's power and glory. Thus the Holy Spirit was poured out on the Church on the day of Pentecost. Luke often emphasizes the presence and the leading of the Spirit, and so also does Paul in his letters.

(5) Christ will soon return from heaven to consummate the messianic age, and be judge of the living and the dead. The expectation of the return of Christ was vivid in the early years of the church; though it became less vivid as time went on, and the expectation of the second advent was replaced by other ideas in some writings (as we shall see), it is found even in the latest books of the New Testament.

(6) The kerygma closes with an appeal for repentance and belief in Christ, sometimes for baptism in the name of Jesus;

and with the offer of forgiveness of sins and the coming of the Holy Spirit. One of the most complete statements of this is in the words of Peter in Acts 2:38: " 'Repent, and be baptized every one of you in the name of Jesus Christ for the forgiveness of your sins; and you shall receive the gift of the Holy Spirit.' " Those who accepted the appeal would experience the salvation promised to the members of the elect community, the true Israel.

The kerygma was addressed to those who were not believers in Christ to convert them to the Christian faith. Its purpose was to evangelize. In the course of time teaching was developed for the Christians, so that they might become mature. We need not suppose that all of the above elements were included in every Christian sermon addressed to possible converts, nor that there was no variation from these elements. The above summarizes in a convenient way the total message as it was preached to convert Jews or Gentiles to faith in Christ.

This preaching is closely related to the message of Jesus, expanding it in the light of his whole career. We have seen that the heart of his message is in Mark 1:15, which has three elements: (1) The time is fulfilled; (2) the kingdom of God is at hand; therefore, (3) repent and believe in the gospel. The kerygma follows the same outline, but gives the significance of the whole career of Jesus—from birth to the second advent—for the Christian believer.

The kerygma apparently did not put great emphasis on the ministry of Jesus. As time went on, when the apostles and eyewitnesses of his ministry died, and the return of Jesus was delayed, the Gospels were written. They follow in general the pattern of the kerygma, but fill in many of the details of the life and teaching of Jesus. They were intended both for the conversion of believers and for the instruction of Christians in the content of their faith.

The New Creature "in Christ" (Paul)

"I am not ashamed of the gospel: it is the power of God for salvation to every one who has faith, to the Jew first and also to the Greek. For in it the righteousness of God is revealed through faith for faith; as it is written, 'He who through faith is righteous shall live' " (Romans 1:16-17). "If any one is in Christ, he is a new creature; the old has passed away, behold, the new has come" (2 Corinthians 5:17). These two passages summarize many of the characteristic features of Paul's message.

His message was built upon the early kerygma we have outlined. Though Paul apparently did not know Jesus in his earthly career, he must have known the earliest Christian message during the time he was persecuting the Christians. He surely must have listened to the earliest preachers of the gospel; to him their claim that the crucified Christ was the Messiah, and that he had risen from the dead, must have seemed to be blasphemy. When he was converted on the road to Damascus, Paul saw the risen Christ and, before long, he began to preach Christ. Three years after his conversion he went to Jerusalem and spent a fortnight talking with Peter and James the brother of Jesus (Galatians 1:18-20); and then fourteen years later he was in Jerusalem, apparently at the time of the Jerusalem Council, and conferred with the apostles again. This time he said that the leaders of the church, "those who were of repute," added nothing to his gospel (2:6). In writing to the Corinthians, he spoke of "what I also received" (1 Corinthians 15:3). Paul believed that he received his gospel by revelation; it was not man's gospel (Galatians 1:11). Nevertheless, it was based on the earliest Christian preaching, going beyond it and interpreting it in the light of Paul's own experiences and contemplation. Paul's theology constitutes his attempt to explain the meaning of his conversion, against the background of his earlier training and experience in Judaism, and in the light of his subsequent life as a Christian missionary.

Paul's letters were addressed to individuals and churches that were already Christian; hence they contain more that should be called teaching than appeals for conversion. Because Paul's message is contained for us in these letters, we cannot expect to find in them a system of doctrine. Paul was a complex character, in whom the man of action and the thinker were remarkably combined. It was his nature to see many things in terms of absolute contrasts, of black-or-white, that others did not see so clearly contrasted. His message thus contains elements that are paradoxical, if not inconsistent; it is not strange that 2 Peter 3:15-16 says that "our beloved brother Paul" wrote in his letters "some things hard to understand."

Paul believed that all men are sinners, and stand in need of rescue from the power of sin, and reconciliation to God. "All have sinned and fall short of the glory of God" (Romans 3:23). For Paul, sin was not just an act or a series of acts; it was a state or condition in which men live, a fundamental wrongness in all men. It is the very opposite of faith: "whatever does not proceed from faith is sin" (Romans 14:23). He does not say much about the origin of sin. Sometimes he says that sin originated with Adam, the ancestor of the human race, or the representative, typical man (Romans 5:12-14). At other times he seems to believe that sin originates with "elemental spirits," the demonic powers of the universe that are at war with man and God. Man living in sin lives according to "the flesh." This does not mean for Paul that the material side of man's nature is in itself sinful, as contrasted with the spiritual side, or the soul. "Flesh" sometimes does signify man's lower nature, but usually it is man's whole nature apart from and in opposition to God. Living according to the flesh is the opposite of life in the Spirit, the life of faith.

Man thus stands in need of rescue from sin, and God in his love has provided the means of rescue. "God shows his love for us in that while we were yet sinners Christ died for us . . . sending his own Son in the likeness of sinful flesh and for sin, he condemned sin in the flesh" (Romans 5:8; 8:3). Christ, sent by a loving Father to the world, is his answer to man's need of rescue from slavery to sin.

Man, on his part, is saved from the power of sin by faith. This, of course, is a central word for Paul. Paul himself had tried to find salvation from sin and communion with God through the keeping of the Law, but he failed. Romans 7:7-25 is a description of how Paul in his pre-Christian days sought to find peace with God by the keeping of the Law, but could not do so; it is also a description of typical man seeking salvation in this manner. He says, "I delight in the law of God, in my inmost self, but I see in my members another law at war with the law of my mind and making me captive to the law of sin which dwells in my members. Wretched man that I am! Who will deliver me from this body of death?" Paul's own answer is: "Thanks be to God through Jesus Christ our Lord!" (Romans 7:22-25.)

By faith Paul did not mean simply an opinion about Christ, nor an assent to a set of doctrines about him. He meant trust in the living Christ, confidence in the faithfulness of God. In the fullest sense, faith is man's wholehearted acceptance of the good news that the saving grace of God has been freely offered to him in Christ. It is the precondition for receiving God's salvation, but it involves the continuous need for submission to God and obedience to him (Romans 1:5). Faith is the response of man to the revelation of God in Christ. "For by grace you have been saved through faith; and this is not your own doing, it is the gift of God—not because of works, lest any man should boast." (Ephesians 2:8-9.)[4] Faith means the abandonment of all dependence upon one's self and one's own merit, and complete reliance upon the grace of God, as revealed most of all in Jesus Christ.

The Christ of whom Paul most often speaks is the crucified and risen Christ, the living Lord. He says little about the life and teachings of Jesus before the crucifixion, although he believed in the full humanity of Christ and he must have assumed that his readers knew of the earthly career and teaching of Jesus. For Paul the cross and the resurrection were of central importance.

The titles and names which Paul uses for Jesus are revealing. He uses the name Jesus alone for the earthly man. Christ, the equivalent of Messiah, has become for him virtually a part of the name, rather than a title, so that he can speak of Jesus Christ or Christ Jesus, or simply Christ. He does not use the title Son of man, which would have been meaningless to Hellenistic readers of his letters. He speaks of Jesus as born of the seed of David, but does not call him Son of David, possibly because it would have seemed too nationalistic. His favorite title is Lord *(kyrios)*. This title probably did not originate with Paul, for it is found in the Aramaic phrase which was probably used in the Palestinian churches, *Marana tha,* meaning "Our Lord, come!" (1 Corinthians 16:22). Lord is a title which would have been readily understood in the Hellenistic world as the head of a religious cult. Because it is used in the Old Testament of God (the same word *kyrios* in the Septuagint), it is sometimes difficult to determine whether Paul is speaking of God or of Christ.

Paul often calls Christ "Son of God." He says that he was "designated Son of God in power according to the Spirit of holiness by his resurrection from the dead" (Romans 1:4).

---

[4]Though Ephesians may not be from Paul himself (see above, pp. 193-4, 200), we quote it sometimes in this section because it is usually Pauline in its attitude.

There are a few passages in which Paul may call Christ "God," particularly Romans 9:5 and 2 Thessalonians 1:12. In these passages the translation is not certain, and they may refer to God apart from Christ. In Colossians 1:19; 2:9 he says that the "fulness of God" dwelt in Christ. Yet, Paul in a number of places makes a clear separation between God and Christ, and maintains his strict Jewish monotheism. For example, in 1 Corinthians 8:6 he says, "for us there is one God, the Father, from whom are all things and for whom we exist, and one Lord, Jesus Christ, through whom are all things and through whom we exist." It is perhaps surprising to most readers to learn that Paul uses the term Savior of Christ only once, Philippians 3:20 (cf. Ephesians 5:23). This term appears frequently in the pastoral Epistles and 2 Peter, later than Paul.

Paul uses many different terms to express what God through Christ, particularly in his death and resurrection, does for the man of faith: redemption, justification, reconciliation, adoption, victory over demonic powers, sacrifice, forgiveness, and new creation. Most of these terms are to be considered as synonymous; they are varying attempts on Paul's part to explain what God in Christ has done for him, and can do for any believer. It was difficult to put this into precise words. Paul knew that in his conversion he had experienced a tremendous revolution in his life. He was overwhelmed by the fact that, even while he was a sinner, Christ died for him and brought him into fellowship with God. In Christ, Paul found release from his inner turmoil, freedom from the Law, and a life of joy and peace. It was not easy to put into words what Christ could do for the man of faith, and Paul tried several different ways. His figures are drawn from various areas of life—the law court, the marketplace, the cult, the battlefield, and so on.

Like a slave ransomed from his master, the believer is redeemed from slavery to sin. As an accused man standing before a bar of justice may be acquitted and declared innocent, the believer is "justified" by God; he is acquitted, and set in a right relationship with his accuser. Salvation means reconciliation between God and man, who had been estranged before: "God was in Christ reconciling the world to himself" (2 Corinthians 5:19). The believer is no longer a slave, but is adopted as a son by God, and as an heir of God, he is a fellow heir with Christ (Romans 8:17; Galatians 4:5-7).

The work of Christ meant not only that he conquered sin for the individual, but also that he won a victory over the "elemental spirits," the demonic powers of the universe that lead man into sin. In Colossians 2:15 a vivid metaphor is used: God "disarmed the principalities and powers and made a public example of them, triumphing over them" in the cross of Christ. The salvation secured by Christ is a cosmic salvation, rescuing the whole universe from the power of sin and death.

Sometimes the death of Christ is described as a sacrifice. This is not as prominent in Paul's letters as in some other parts of the New Testament (as, for example, in Hebrews), but it is present in passages such as Romans 3:25; 5:9 and others. As a sacrifice, the death of Christ served to set man in a favorable relationship with God.

Paul strangely makes little use of the concept of forgiveness of sins, and the related appeal for repentance. Forgiveness of sin is mentioned only in Colossians 1:14 and Ephesians 1:7. No doubt forgiveness of sins is implied in some of Paul's other metaphors. Possibly the reason he speaks so little of forgiveness is that he was concerned not so much with the forgiveness of sins already committed as with the rescue of man from the power of sin. He says little of repentance also, but it is implied in faith.

In all of these metaphors for the work of Christ, Paul is attempting to say that man is delivered from his slavery to sin and his estrangement from God, and is set in the right relationship with God, a relationship of fellowship and love, best expressed by the figure of the son who can call out to God, "Abba! Father!" (Romans 8:15; Galatians 4:6)

The man who in faith accepts what God has done for him in Christ becomes a new creature, a new man. He puts on a new nature, and has put off his old nature. "If any one is in Christ, he is a new creature" (2 Corinthians 5:17). Paul explains what happens in this manner. When the pre-existing Christ came to earth and became a man, he took upon himself a full humanity, identifying himself completely with all of mankind. He lived a fully human life, being tempted to sin but not sinning. His life was indeed more completely human than any that has been lived, for he lived as God desires man to live; he was fully obedient to God, even to death on the cross. In the cross the love of God and the wickedness of man were both fully revealed, and God's love conquered man's sin.

The man who has faith identifies himself with Christ; he accepts what God has done, and he becomes a new man "in Christ." As Christ had identified himself with sinful humanity, so the believer identifies himself with the perfect Christ. Thus he becomes a new creature, a new man "in Christ." Paul put great emphasis on the solidarity of mankind. Just as he could say that in Adam all sin, so he can say that in Christ all have the possibility through faith of a new life (Romans 5:12-21).

For Paul, the symbol for the death of the old nature and creation of the new nature was the rite of baptism. "Do you not know that all of us who have been baptized into Christ Jesus were baptized into his death? We were buried therefore with him by baptism into death, so that as Christ was raised from the dead by the glory of the Father, we too might walk in newness of life." (Romans 6:3-4; see also Colossians 2:12.) In Galatians 3:27, he says: "As many of you as were baptized into Christ have put on Christ." Baptism was thus the sign and seal of man's death to an old nature and resurrection to a new; it was also the act of initiation into the church which, as we shall see, Paul called "the body of Christ."

The life of the Christian was for Paul a life "in Christ." This is one of the most characteristic and typical phrases of Paul. He uses the phrase "in Christ" or "in the Lord" 164 times; a few times he uses the similar phrase "in the Spirit," obviously with the same or very similar meaning. Paul sometimes speaks of Christ as being "in you," or in the believer, but not nearly as often as he speaks of the believer being in Christ.

The believer who is "in Christ" has all of the benefits of salvation—peace, joy, freedom, ability to live a life of love of God and of his fellow men, and many others. He has what Rudolf Bultmann aptly calls "openness for the future—openness, that is, for every fresh claim of God both to action and to the acceptance of his fate."[5]

Paul's view of the Christian life has been called by some interpreters Christ-mysticism. This is appropriate, provided we see clearly what Paul did not mean, and what kind of mysticism it was. It was not the type of mysticism in which man could become completely absorbed in the divine, in God or Christ. Paul was always conscious of the fact that God remains God and man remains man; they cannot become one. Man seeks fellowship with God, not absorption in the divine. Furthermore, Paul did not have in mind an ecstatic mysticism, though he himself was capable of ecstatic experiences (see his conversion, and 2 Corinthians 12:1-5). It was ethical mysticism, in which the believer seeks to live a life worthy of the Christ with whom he has union.

Paul's view of the Christian life as a new life "in Christ" leads us to a discussion of his attitude toward the Law and

---

[5]*Primitive Christianity in its Contemporary Setting* (Living Age Books; New York: Meridian Books, 1956), p. 204.

toward moral standards in general. His point of view is by no means easy to grasp, and involves paradoxes.

Paul had sought as a Pharisaic Jew to keep the Law and thus to be justified in the sight of God, but he felt continually frustrated in his effort. He could not wholly keep the Law, and he found no true peace. Peace came to him only through faith in Christ. Therefore, Paul often stated unmistakably that no man can be justified, saved, or reconciled to God by keeping the Law, or by doing good works. By the Law, Paul usually meant the legal part of the Old Testament, or the Old Testament as a whole; yet he recognized that even Gentiles have a concept of natural law, and of conscience (Romans 2:13-16). Abraham, the ancestor of the Hebrews, was saved by his faith, not by the Law, which came after his time (Romans 4).

For Paul "Christ is the end of the law, that every one who has faith may be justified" (Romans 10:4). The Christian is dead to the Law. Nevertheless, Paul could say: "The law is holy, and the commandment is holy and just and good" (Romans 7:12). The Jewish law had value in that it told man what sin is, awakened his conscience, and led him to Christ. The Christian, then, is not wholly exempt from law as a principle of life: Paul can speak of fulfilling the "law of Christ" (Galatians 6:2), and can say, "he who loves his neighbor has fulfilled the law. The commandments . . . are summed up in this sentence, 'You shall love your neighbor as yourself' " (Romans 13:8-9). Paul never does actually distinguish in his letters between the moral law and the ceremonial law, but he implies that the Christian should fulfill the moral law of the Old Testament, and he himself (as one who had been born a Jew) did on some occasions keep regulations of the ceremonial law.

The logical way of stating Paul's position is to say that the man of faith, who is a new creature in Christ, will do what he *ought* to do because he now *wants* to do it. He does from inward desire what the man under the Law did from outer compulsion. His life naturally produces the fruit of the Spirit, and his faith works through love (Galatians 5:6). Paul himself could say:

> I through the law died to the law, that I might live to God. I have been crucified with Christ; it is no longer I who live, but Christ who lives in me; and the life I now live in the flesh I live by faith in the Son of God, who loved me and gave himself for me. (Galatians 2:19-20)

This is the true Christ-mysticism of Paul.

With this view of the Christian's freedom from law and his new life "in Christ," Paul should logically not have needed to give ethical advice to his readers. But in reality he does just that to a great extent. His letters often contain a large section dealing with practical matters that give specific moral injunctions or admonitions, sometimes with advice on special problems on which he was consulted. One reason for this is that Paul's message was widely misunderstood, especially among Gentiles who did not have the high moral standards of the Jews. Some thought he meant the Christian is free from all law and can do whatever he likes to do; they mistook freedom for license. Another reason is that there is in Paul's message (and often in the Christian message in any form) an ultimate paradox: the Christian must be admonished to strive, with the help of God, to *become* that which he already *is* by the grace of God. Paul often exhorts his readers to live worthily of their calling, to live according to the new nature that they have put on, and the like. The paradox is most clearly stated in Philippians 2:12-13: "Work out your own salvation with fear and trembling; for God is at work in you, both to will and to work for his good pleasure."

As for ethical motivation, Paul sometimes appealed to the words or the example of Jesus, especially his humility and meekness. Sometimes he even admonished others to follow his own example. But his appeal above all was for Christians to live worthily of their union with Christ; this union was to be both their motive and their dynamic for living.

Paul's ethics are based largely upon the Old Testament and arise out of his Jewish background, though at some points he may have been influenced by Hellenistic ethical ideals of the times, particularly of the Stoics. Morton S. Enslin has summarized the four basic moral precepts of Paul as follows:[6] (1) "Separate yourselves from all that would defile." Paul warns especially against sexual laxity of the sort which was widespread in the Roman world among non-Jews. (2) "Be steadfast in all the conduct of life." "Stand firm" is a favorite injunction; the Christian is to persevere, be courageous, be willing to suffer affliction. Paul says the slave should obey his master, and the master be fair and just toward his slave; the church member should obey those set above him; the Christian should respect the Roman authorities. (3) "Through love serve one another." Here Paul reveals very close kinship to the teaching of Jesus. (4) "Rejoice in the Lord always; again I will say, rejoice." These words of Paul, written in prison (Philippians 4:4), may sound strange as an ethical precept, but they are characteristic of him. He realized how evil this world is, but he believed that Christ had overcome the world and the Christian should rejoice because of his hope for the future.

Paul did not think of his converts as being saved merely as individuals, and did not expect the Christian to live a solitary life. He established churches in many parts of the world, and had constant anxiety and care for them. He saw the Chris-

---

*The Ethics of Paul (Apex Books; Nashville: Abingdon Press, 1957), pp. 133-307.

tian as a member of the church, of the community of the
new covenant, the true Israel. Paul's most characteristic term
for the church is "the body of Christ." In 1 Corinthians 12:
12-30 and Romans 12:4-8 he uses the figure to emphasize the
variety of gifts within the church, the mutual dependence of
the members, and the full importance of all the members. In
Colossians 1:18 and Ephesians 1:23; 4:16; 5:23, the figure
is used to stress the unity of the church and the headship of
Christ. Paul may have used the term "body of Christ" in a
very realistic sense: the church is the material and earthly body
of the spiritual Christ who is exalted to heaven. In other passages, the church is the temple in which God dwells (1 Corinthians 3:16; 2 Corinthians 6:16; Ephesians 2:19-22), the bride
of Christ (Ephesians 5:23-32), or the "Israel of God" (Galatians 6:16).

Individual members of the churches were to Paul "saints"
or "brethren." The former term was not used because all Christians were considered to be perfect and upright in their lives.
"Saint" does not imply godliness, but rather a certain relationship to God. Paul addressed the church of Corinth as follows:
"To the church of God which is at Corinth, to those sanctified
in Christ Jesus, called to be saints. . . ." It is perfectly clear
from 1 Corinthians that there were members of the church
in Corinth who were far from saintly in the moral sense; the
letter reveals both serious party division and sexual immorality
of an unspeakable kind (5:1). Those who were in the church
were "saints" because they had surrendered themselves to God
through faith in Christ, and had been set apart by God and
called to a new life.

Paul believed in the second coming of Christ. This belief
appears throughout his letters, but the hope of the second
coming is more vivid in the early letters than in later ones.
His earliest letters, 1 and 2 Thessalonians, were written to deal
specifically with problems of the second coming. In the first

of these Paul seems to look for the advent of Christ in the near future. In later letters, the hope is not abandoned, but the emphasis comes to be placed more upon the life of the believer "in Christ" from day to day. Paul never indulged in apocalyptic speculations of a detailed sort, and his letters are far different from the Book of Revelation. One specific teaching of Paul's was influenced by his belief in the return of Christ. In reply to a question from Corinth regarding marriage of those who were single, Paul advised them to refrain from marriage "in view of the impending distress" and because "the appointed time has grown very short" (1 Corinthians 7:25-35). Paul never gave up belief in the second coming of Christ, and the coming of a day of judgment, as a time when God would punish evil and those who had received Christ would see the consummation of their salvation. He constantly appealed to his readers to live so as to be ready for the return of the Lord, for he might come at an unexpected time "like a thief in the night."

Eternal Life (John)

The Gospel of John stands apart from the Synoptic Gospels, as we saw in the last chapter. It is the latest of the four, and follows a somewhat different historical framework; it has a tone that is different from the others. It seems likely that the Gospel and the three Epistles of John (but not Revelation) were written by the same man—John the Elder, who lived and wrote in Ephesus toward the end of the first century A.D.[7] The greatest difference between his Gospel and the others is that his is much more a theological interpretation of the life

---

[7]While most scholars think that the Gospel and Epistles have a common authorship, there are outstanding scholars who do not. There are indeed some subtle but significant differences between the Gospel and the Epistles (particularly 1 John; 2 and 3 John are so brief that their content is very meager). Even if 1 John was not written by the same man as the Gospel, it shares with it many ideas; if not by the same author, 1 John was composed by a close companion or disciple of the Gospel writer. In our discussion, quotations from the Gospel are indicated simply by chapter and verse, while quotations from the Epistle are prefixed by "1 John."

of Jesus than they are. None of the Gospels is a wholly objective, straightforward history of Jesus' life; each has its own interpretation. But the Gospel of John presents the life of Jesus in a different light, and seeks to show above all the meaning of his life for the world and the believer.

John the Elder, probably born a Jew, was one who had a deep Christian experience, and meditated long upon the significance of Christ's life. Perhaps he was a Christian preacher —a "prophet" he would have been called in the first century— and had often spoken on the themes he finally treated in his writings. He wrote in order to counteract errors into which some Christians of his day had fallen, and to set forth a very positive evaluation of Jesus Christ in terms that would be understood by Hellenistic readers. His writings have a style and vocabulary of their own, and present a few great ideas over and over.

John thought of life and the world in terms of great contrasts: light and darkness, good and evil, truth and error, life and death, God and the world. He did not think so much of the contrasts between "this age" and "the age to come," as many other New Testament writers did, as between the temporal order and the eternal order. Many of these contrasts remind us of the ideas presented by the Essenes in the Dead Sea Scrolls. They do not constitute a thorough and genuine "dualism," for John believed that God created this world and is in control of it; his final victory over darkness and evil is assured. The present age is under the temporary control of Satan, "the ruler of this world" (12:31; 14:30; 16:11), but Christ has defeated him and made possible his defeat in the life of the believer (12:31; 1 John 3:8).

John presents Jesus above all as the revealer of God. In his writings we find three of the great affirmations about God: "God is spirit" (4:24); "God is light" (1 John 1:5); and

"God is love" (1 John 4:8, 16). God is frequently called Father by Jesus, and he may become Father to the believer.

In the Gospel of John, Jesus is an eternal divine being who existed with God from the very beginning, who came to earth and lived among men as a thoroughly human being in the flesh, was crucified, and returned to heaven, but would return (apparently in spiritual form) to be with his own and receive them to himself. In this Gospel, Jesus lives his life on earth serenely and with great confidence. He knows the end from the beginning. Not only does he know God completely, but he knows all men (2:25).

Jesus reveals God in his whole life and in his person. "No one has ever seen God; the only Son, who is in the bosom of the Father, he has made him known" (1:18). " 'I and the Father are one' " (10:30). " 'He who has seen me has seen the Father,' " he says to Philip (14:9). For John the whole of the ministry of Jesus is important; he does not place the same great emphasis on the crucifixion and resurrection that Paul does. In his Gospel, the crucifixion is the glorification of Jesus; in most of the rest of the New Testament, the glorification comes after the crucifixion.

The message of the Gospel of John is set forth clearly in the opening words:

In the beginning was the Word, and the Word was with God, and the Word was God. He was in the beginning with God; all things were made through him, and without him was not anything made that was made. In him was life, and the life was the light of men. . . . And the Word became flesh and dwelt among us, full of grace and truth; we have beheld his glory, glory as of the only Son from the Father. (1:1-4, 14)

Here the English "Word" translates the Greek word *lógos*, which it can render only imperfectly. As the *lógos*, Jesus is the "utterance" of God, but he is also the agent of God in creation, and the mediator between man and God. After the opening sentences, the Gospel does not employ this word in this sense, but the presentation of the life of Jesus accords with the opening sentences, and they serve to set the life of the human Jesus against the background of eternity.

John uses for Jesus virtually all the titles that are found in other parts of the New Testament. He is teacher, rabbi, prophet, the Messiah (left untranslated in 1:41; 4:25), the Christ, Lord, the Lamb of God, Savior of the world, Son of man (used primarily of the heavenly being, not to emphasize his humanity), the King, and Son of God. The last of these titles is the most frequent. As Son of God, Jesus knows the Father perfectly, is at one with him, and reveals him to man. The climax of the Gospel is reached in the confession of Thomas when he sees the risen Lord and cries out: " 'my Lord and my God!' " (20:28) This is one of very few verses in the New Testament in which Jesus is called God.

One of the characteristic features of the Gospel of John is that in it Jesus frequently speaks of himself. John presents Jesus as saying seven great "I ams": " 'I am the bread of life; he who comes to me shall not hunger, and he who believes in me shall never thirst' " (6:35). " 'I am the light of the world; he who follows me will not walk in darkness, but will have the light of life' " (8:12). " 'I am the door of the sheep' " (10:7). " 'I am the good shepherd. The good shepherd lays down his life for the sheep' " (10:11). " 'I am the resurrection and the life; he who believes in me, though he die, yet shall he live, and whoever lives and believes in me shall never die' " (11:25-26). " 'I am the way, and the truth, and the life; no one comes to the Father, but by me' " (14:6). " 'I am the true vine, and my Father is the vinedresser' " (15:1). In these statements we can see a great deal of what John thought concerning the person of Jesus, and what believing in him would accomplish for the disciples.

In the writings of John the word "faith" occurs only once: "This is the victory that overcomes the world, our faith" (1 John 5:4). Yet he very frequently uses the verb "believe," and calls upon men to believe. The purpose of the Gospel is stated in this way: "These [words] are written that you may believe that Jesus is the Christ, the Son of God, and that believing you may have life in his name" (20:31). First John 5:1 says, "Every one who believes that Jesus is the Christ is a child of God, and every one who loves the parent loves the child." Belief is, therefore, in the first instance, a belief *about* Jesus, that he is the Christ and God's Son. But it is also belief *in* Christ, and self-surrender to him, as Paul had emphasized. Belief in Christ leads to union with Christ, which John usually calls "abiding in" Christ.

The one who believes in Christ experiences, according to John, a new birth, or birth "from above." The same Greek phrase can mean either "born anew" or "born from above." To Nicodemus Jesus says, " 'Truly, truly, I say to you, unless one is born anew, he cannot see the kingdom of God.' " (3:3) Aside from chapter 3 of the Gospel, the idea of being born again, or born of God, appears frequently in 1 John. The new birth is a supernatural transformation of man's nature, very similar to Paul's idea of the Christian's being a new creature in Christ.

While John is concerned for the salvation of the individual, he is also interested in the formation of the church as the body of the believers. The word "church" does not appear in the Gospel, but it surely has in view the church when it speaks of the believers in Christ as the flock, of which he is the shepherd (10:16); and of the branches, of which Christ is the vine (15:1). And the church was also in John's mind when he spoke of Jesus' gathering "into one the children of God who are scattered abroad" (11:52). One of the remarkable passages in the Gospel is the section in Jesus' intercessory prayer in which he prays for the unity of his disciples in his lifetime and of those who believe in him through their word. His prayer is " 'that they may all be one; even as thou, Father, art in me, and I in thee, that they also may be in us, so that the world may believe that thou hast sent me' " (17:21). John lived at a time when the unity of the church was threatened by dissensions and false teachers, as the Epistles show.

To those who believe in him, Christ gave the promise of the Paraclete. This is one of the unique words of John's writings, occurring in 14:16, 26; 15:26; 16:7, and 1 John 2:1. The Greek word of which Paraclete is a transliteration is rendered in the Gospel by the Revised Standard Version as Counselor, and by the King James Version as Comforter (in the sense of "strengthener"); in 1 John 2:1 both render it as advocate. The *paráklētos* was literally "one who was called alongside another" to serve as legal counsel, witness, or the like. He was the counselor in this sense, or one's advocate before a judge. Twice the Paraclete is called the Spirit of truth, and once the Holy Spirit. Jesus promises that the Paraclete will come to the disciples after he leaves them, to guide them into all truth, and glorify Jesus by convincing men that unbelief in him is sin (16:7-14). In 1 John 2:1 the "advocate" with the Father is "Jesus Christ the righteous." To some extent these passages are difficult to harmonize. But we should note that in the first mention of the Paraclete, the promise is of "another Paraclete." This suggests that Jesus himself on earth is an advocate and counselor of men. There are indications in the Gospel that Jesus expected to return to earth as spirit, so that he is the Paraclete. First John, written long after the lifetime of Jesus, can thus write of Jesus himself as the Paraclete.

The gift of God to those who believe in Jesus is eternal life. This is one of the most characteristic phrases of John, and he uses it in a special way. Sometimes the single word "life" means the same thing.

The unique feature of John's view of "eternal life" is that he considers it to be a present possession of the believer. " 'Truly, truly, I say to you, he who hears my word and believes him who sent me, *has* eternal life; he does not come into judgment, but has passed from death to life' " (5:24). " 'Truly, truly, I say to you, he who believes *has* eternal life' " (6:47). There are many such passages in John's writings.

Judgment, likewise, is something which is already present in the lifetime of Jesus.

He who believes in him is not condemned; he who does not believe is condemned already, because he has not believed in the name of the only Son of God. And this is the judgment, that the light has come into the world, and men loved darkness rather than light, because their deeds were evil (3:18-19).

Yet, there are passages which speak of future judgment and of the future coming of Christ. " 'Do not marvel at this; for the hour is coming when all who are in the tombs will hear his voice and come forth, those who have done good, to the resurrection of life, and those who have done evil, to the resurrection of judgment' " (5:28-29). Jesus sometimes talks of his returning to earth: " 'When I go and prepare a place for you, I will come again and will take you to myself, that where I am you may be also' " (14:3). In some cases it is clear, however, that the coming of Christ is a coming of the spiritual Christ to the believer, as in 14:23: " 'If a man loves me, he will keep my word, and my Father will love him, and we will come to him and make our home with him'."

Interpreters of John have had difficulty in reconciling the two sets of ideas. Is eternal life a present or a future possession? Is judgment present or future? Some scholars think that passages such as 5:28-29 which speak of future judgment are additions to John's own writing. Others believe that the author has not made a complete integration of his own view of eternal life with the traditional Christian hopes for the future. Perhaps there is some truth in the latter, but the differences between the two are not really great.

For John "eternal life" is not so much immortality or life that is endless, as it is a new quality of life. One who is born from above has infused into his life a new being. Eternal life is like life "in Christ" in Paul's writings, a mystical-ethical union with Christ. Yet it is a life whose consummation and full realization lie in the future, rather than in the present life of this world. The ideas appear together, with an implied moral exhortation, in 1 John 3:2-3: "Beloved, we are God's children now; it does not yet appear what we shall be, but we know that when he appears we shall be like him, for we shall see him as he is. And every one who thus hopes in him purifies himself as he is pure."

John gives this definition of eternal life in 17:3: "This is eternal life, that they know thee the only true God, and Jesus Christ whom thou hast sent." To know God is to know that he is one and to know his true nature as revealed in Jesus Christ; to know Jesus Christ is to believe in him and accept his revelation. Eternal life is similar to the kingdom of God, a phrase used in 3:3, 5. Nicodemus is told that he cannot see the kingdom of God unless he is born anew, and that he cannot enter the kingdom unless he is born of water and the Spirit. Eternal life implies, then, recognition of God's sovereignty so that one is reconciled to him; it means that one has passed from death to life, and escaped the power of death to destroy him; it brings him the ability to obey God and bear much fruit. When one has eternal life, he is in Christ and Christ is in him.

First John clearly states that one who is born of God has escaped from sin's power, and is capable of living a sinless and perfect life: "No one born of God commits sin; for God's nature [or seed] abides in him, and he cannot sin because he is born of God" (1 John 3:9; see also 3:6; 5:18 and cf. John 8:31-47). Yet, there is a realistic note in 1 John 5:16-17, in which the reader is bidden to pray for a brother who has committed a sin that is not mortal.

Love is one of the key words in John's writings, found over and over in the Gospel and 1 John. It was out of love for the world that God gave his only Son, to bring to every believer eternal life (3:16). The life of Jesus was a life based upon love of God and love of man; "having loved his own who were in the world, he loved them to the end" (13:1). The life of the Christian is a life of love toward God and Christ and toward his fellow men. Again and again the Christian is told that to obey God means to love his brethren. Some of the strongest and most memorable words are in 1 John:

> Beloved, let us love one another; for love is of God, and he who loves is born of God and knows God. He who does not love does not know God; for God is love. . . . We love, because he first loved us. If any one says, "I love God," and hates his brother, he is a liar; for he who does not love his brother whom he has seen, cannot love God whom he has not seen. . . . For this is the love of God, that we keep his commandments. (4:7-8, 19-20; 5:3)

Unity in Diversity

The three great creative figures of the New Testament are Jesus, Paul, and John. Now that we have discussed their message, and the earliest Christian preaching, we have covered the essentials of the New Testament message. For the remaining books, the reader should consult our discussion in the last chapter (pp. 201-11). They present few if any new ideas, and some were concerned with counteracting false teachings.

The New Testament as a whole shows a rich diversity in its message. In part this is to be attributed to paradox, or even inconsistency. Much of the richness is the result of development in the course of the spread of the Christian faith from its small beginnings in Palestine.

Is there a unity within this diversity? There is, and it is to be found in the person and life of Jesus Christ, and his meaning for those who believed in him. At the risk of oversimplification, we may summarize the unifying themes of the New Testament message as follows:

(1) Jesus' birth and earthly career were purposed by God for the saving of mankind. This is expressed in two ways: Jesus fulfilled the Old Testament prophecies; and he was a pre-existing divine being, present with God even at the creation. Thus Jesus was not a man who became divine; nor was he a good man who was deified by his followers. He was the incarnation of God, and a true revelation of the divine nature.

(2) In his earthly career Jesus lived as a real man. He lived in the flesh, being completely human, tempted as other men were but without sin. The New Testament rejected as false all teaching that Jesus only "seemed" to exist as a human being.

(3) While the whole of Jesus' earthly life was important, the crucifixion and resurrection were of central significance. The story of these events crystallized early; they occupied almost an exclusive place in the theology of Paul. Their significance was explained in a variety of ways, but at the least the crucifixion demonstrated man's utter wickedness, for it meant the cruel murder of an innocent man; it revealed God's grace and mercy; and it showed Christ's complete obedience to God and his love for his fellow men. The resurrection of Jesus meant that he had conquered death, and that the Christ in whom men believed was a living, risen Lord.

(4) Throughout the New Testament is found the hope of Christ's return in glory and judgment. This was at first vivid, and controlled many aspects of the life of the church. As

the return was delayed, the hope became less vigorous, but was not abandoned. John's Gospel offered an alternative to expectation of the visible, material return of Christ with its emphasis on eternal life as a present possession and the coming of Christ in spirit into the lives of believers. Throughout the New Testament, the hope of Christ's return is one of the bases of the appeal for purity of life, and preparedness to receive him whenever he may come.

(5) The New Testament message has a variety of ways of expressing the manner in which the believer appropriates for himself the benefits of Christ's life, death, and resurrection. Jesus summoned men to repent, follow him, and be prepared for the kingdom of God. Paul stresses faith as the doorway to man's becoming a new creature "in Christ." John called for belief that Jesus is the Christ, in order that one might be born again and receive eternal life. There is a basic unity in these three different ways of putting the Christian message, in spite of the different terms they employ.

(6) The New Testament message called men to life in the Christian church. Whether or not Jesus specifically intended to found a church, he summoned men to follow him as his disciples, and from them he chose a select group of apostles. After the resurrection, the Christian community was a party within Judaism, distinguished by the fact that it believed the Messiah had already come. In the course of time the church separated itself completely from Judaism, and became organized. It was considered to be the true Israel, the body of Christ, God's own people, the community of the new covenant.

(7) The New Testament message always insisted on a high standard of morality. It could not abandon its roots in Judaism, and did not wish to do so. Among Gentiles the Christian message of freedom in Christ was sometimes misunderstood as allowing license and even lawlessness. Against such misunderstanding Paul and others strove vigorously. The ethical

standards of the New Testament are largely the same as those of the Old. There is a remarkable agreement that love is the fulfilment of God's command, so that man's ethical duty may be summarized in the Old Testament injunction (Leviticus 19:18) " 'You shall love your neighbor as yourself' " (Matthew 22:39; Romans 13:9; James 2:8; 1 John 3:11). With respect to the dynamic of the moral life, Jesus was convinced that "every sound tree bears good fruit" (Matthew 7:17). Paul taught that the man who is a new creature "in Christ" will show in his life the fruit of the Spirit (Galatians 5:22). John said that he who is born anew (or from above) abides in Christ, and Christ abides in him, so that he obeys because he loves.

VII

why sixty-six books?

THE ENGLISH WORD BIBLE GOES BACK TO A
Greek word *biblia* that meant literally "books." Our Bible is
in fact a collection of books—sixty-six books as Protestants
usually count them, thirty-nine in the Old Testament, twenty-
seven in the New. A Roman Catholic Bible contains seven
additional books in the Old Testament, and supplementary
material in Daniel and Esther not ordinarily found in Protestant Bibles.

Yet we know that these are not the only books of a religious
nature that were produced in ancient times by the Israelites
and by the early Christians. Why was this group of sixty-six
books selected to constitute the Bible? By what process and
with what standards were they chosen? Why is there a difference between Catholic and Protestant Bibles? Can we have
confidence today that exactly these sixty-six books—no more
and no fewer—should constitute our sacred Scripture?

The Idea of a Canon of Scripture

The word "canon" is used to designate the list or collection
of books that are considered by the adherents of a religion to

be sacred and authoritative. This word has a great variety of meanings in English. It goes back to a Semitic word that meant "reed." Since reeds were used as measuring rods, *kanōn* in Greek came to mean measure, standard, rule, and the like. It was used in the New Testament with the meaning of "rule" or "limit" (Galatians 6:16; 2 Corinthians 10:13-16). It apparently came to be applied to the list of books considered to be Scripture for two different reasons: those books were thought to measure up to a certain standard, and they in turn came to constitute the standard by which right belief and conduct could be determined.

Most Christians grow up taking the Bible for granted, and Jews have their own Bible—the Old Testament. But the existence of a collection of authoritative books is not as obvious as the reader might think. In ancient times, for example, the people of Mesopotamia, Egypt, and Greece had religions that were highly developed in many respects. They had prayers, hymns, myths, and other writings of various types that they used in their life and worship, but they apparently did not have Bibles, for they did not have canons of Scripture. The religions of the Far East have many sacred books, but in some instances they are quite voluminous because they have not passed through a process of selection. The three great monotheistic faiths of the world today—Judaism, Christianity, and Islam—all have Scriptures in the strict sense. Christianity adopted the idea of a canon from Judaism, and Islam from Judaism and Christianity. We have to inquire, then, why the ancient Israelites had the idea that a specific collection of books ought to be considered sacred and authoritative. Why did they have a canon?

The Israelites believed that Yahweh had a concern for his chosen people, and a will for their total life. They believed that Yahweh communicated this concern and will to them in various ways. One way was through their history; he was constantly active in their history, sometimes performing saving acts, at other times sending punishment to discipline them. Another way was through the spoken words of special representatives, especially the prophets. Jeremiah thought of himself as the very "mouth" of Yahweh (Jeremiah 15:19). A third way was through the written word.

The various types of literature which the Hebrews produced were believed to be of divine origin, or to be sacred because of their association with sacred places and activities. The prophets had faith that Yahweh put his words into their mouths, and it was his word they spoke, not their own. They prefixed their messages with: "Thus saith the Lord." The Hebrews believed that all of their laws and legislation, of whatever nature, originated with God, not with Moses or with their kings. They could even say that Yahweh wrote upon the two tables of stone in the time of Moses (Exodus 34:1). In some cases books which contained law were deposited in a sanctuary; thus they could acquire sanctity in part by their association with a sacred place (Deuteronomy 31:9; Jos. 24:26; 1 Samuel 10:25; 2 Kings 22:8).

The historical narratives of Israel told about the actions of God in the events of the past, and Israel considered Yahweh to be the principal Actor in history. The Israelites used the psalms in their worship, in their hymns praising God, in prayers confessing their sins and seeking forgiveness, in some psalms proclaiming the kingship of Yahweh or celebrating his acts in history, in the laments pouring out their souls in grief and seeking his aid, and so on. Other books that came to be called Scripture were used in worship, in one way or another. The wisdom writers believed they were speaking the will of Yahweh, though they did not express the belief as prominently as the prophets. Finally, some of the books which were originally secular, or largely secular, came to be considered as sacred because of the religious interpretations given to them (such as the Song of Solomon).

The idea of a very specific canon of Scripture, which was closed and to which no additions could be made, arose only after Israel came to believe that the authentic voice of divine authority could no longer be heard, and so God's word must be consulted in written form. We shall see that they developed the belief that inspiration ceased in the time of Ezra. Scripture thereafter could be interpreted, in oral or written form, but interpretation never had the authenticity of the words of Scripture.

Formation of the Old Testament Canon

The various books of the Old Testament, we have seen, were written over a period of nearly a thousand years. The formation of the canon took place by a gradual process, in three main phases.

In order to understand these three phases, we must know that the Jews divide their Bible differently from Christians. They divide it into three parts, as follows:

(1) *The Law* (which Jews call *Torah*), consisting of the Pentateuch: Genesis, Exodus, Leviticus, Numbers, and Deuteronomy.

(2) *The Prophets,* consisting of (a) *the Former Prophets,* Joshua, Judges, 1-2 Samuel, and 1-2 Kings, and (b) *the Latter Prophets,* Isaiah, Jeremiah, Ezekiel, and the Book of the Twelve (which we call Minor Prophets)—Hosea, Joel, Amos, Obadiah, Jonah, Micah, Nahum, Habakkuk, Zephaniah, Haggai, Zechariah, and Malachi.

(3) *The Writings,* or *Hagiographa*: Psalms, Proverbs, Job, Song of Solomon (or Song of Songs), Ruth, Lamentations, Ecclesiastes, Esther, Daniel, Ezra, Nehemiah, 1-2 Chronicles.

The Law was the first part of the Old Testament to be canonized, and Jews have usually considered it to be more highly sacred and authoritative than the other books of the Old Testament. It is probable that it was canonized by approximately 400 B.C., near or in the time of Ezra.

The original edition of Deuteronomy, which formed the basis of Josiah's reforms in 621 B.C. (see above pp. 50, 75), was probably the first book to be considered authoritative, and thus it was the nucleus for the Law and for the whole canon of Scripture. The description of the discovery of the book and the reformation of Josiah in 2 Kings 22-23 speaks of a "book of the law" or "book of the covenant." It was found in the Jerusalem temple by Hilkiah the high priest in the course of repairs to the temple. The book was taken to Huldah, a prophetess, who in effect put her stamp of approval on it. Then the king gathered the elders of Judah and Jerusalem to the temple and had the book read to them. Next the king made a covenant before the LORD, and instituted far-reaching reforms. This book therefore not only had the full weight of the king's authority behind it, but was approved by both prophet and priest. Its contents (if it was Deuteronomy in its original form) show the influence of both prophetic and priestly ideals. Under these circumstances, it is hard to see how any book could have been made any more authoritative in the life of the nation.

Subsequently the narratives we have called J and E (which had already been combined) were prefixed to Deuteronomy, and the Priestly narrative was added to the whole work. All of this material together made up the first division of the canon. Though it is sometimes called the Law, it consists of much more than law or legislation in the usual sense. It presents a narrative of the history from creation to the death of Moses. The laws are contained within a framework of historical narrative.

The Jews call the first division of their Bible by the name *Torah*. While this word is sometimes rendered by Law, and it sometimes means that in the narrow sense, it often means a great deal more. More properly, as applied to the Pentateuch, it means "instruction" as to what the believer must *know* about his history, and what he must *do* both in ritual and in everyday life. The orthodox Jew today seeks to live very literally by the *Torah*, insofar as that is possible under modern conditions; the liberal or reformed Jew interprets the *Torah* freely, and often puts more emphasis on the prophetic books than the *Torah*.

As the probable date of the canonization of the Law we have given 400 B.C. That is only approximate, and may be too early. It was completed and made authoritative before the break between the Samaritans and the Jews. This break may have taken place in the time of Ezra, and some scholars look upon the event described in Nehemiah 8, telling how Ezra read a book before a great assembly of the people, as the formal institution of the Torah. We cannot be certain of this; there is some evidence (particularly in the Jewish historian Josephus) for placing the break between the Samaritans and the Jews in the fourth century or even later. The Samaritans have the *Torah* in virtually the same form as the Jews, and consider only it to be sacred, not accepting the other two divisions of the canon of Scripture.

The division of the Old Testament called The Prophets contains both books of prophecy in the usual sense and narrative books. The books beginning with Joshua and continuing through 1-2 Kings record the history of Israel from the entrance to Canaan to the Babylonian exile. We do not know certainly why these are called Prophets: perhaps because they were written in the spirit of the prophets and emphasize the principle of divine retribution and reward (they were edited by the Deuteronomists); or because they were thought to have been written by prophets; or because they told about certain prophets. The Book of Daniel, which in English Bibles is usually classified with the prophets, is not in this group, but in the third division. It is not a book of prophecy in the Hebrew sense, but an apocalypse, and probably was written after the Prophets were canonized.

It can readily be seen that this division contains books, and materials within books, that are very old; many of the prophets lived before the Torah was canonized, and the events recorded in the historical books took place before that time. Amos, the earliest literary prophet, lived in the eighth century B.C. It is likely that the books in this division gradually acquired authoritative status, in part because of their reading in the worship of the temple or the synagogue, or both. The synagogue, as a place for common worship of the people and for religious instruction, came into existence during the Babylonian exile or in the postexilic age; we have no definite information as to the time of its origin. In the services of the synagogue (at least in later times) both the Law and the Prophets were read.

In ancient Israel very few people could read and write. While we have no statistics, a conjecture of one per cent literacy may be too high. The ability to read and write was confined largely or exclusively to the priesthood and to professional scribes (who wrote out legal documents, letters, and the like for a fee). Therefore, the great majority of the people acquired their knowledge of the contents of the sacred books from public reading in services of worship. In the Jewish Talmud a name for Scripture means literally "reading" (*miqrá*).

The time when the Prophets were canonized was approximately 200 B.C. This date is indicated by the fact that the writer of the Prologue to the apocryphal book of Sirach says that his grandfather, the author of Sirach, had devoted himself to the reading of "the law and the prophets and the other books," and he uses a similar phrase two other times. "The law and the prophets" here seem to be the first two divisions of the Old Testament which had been accepted as authoritative by this time. Sirach was written shortly after 200 B.C.

The New Testament contains evidence that the Law and the Prophets had already been canonized, but the third division of the canon was still unsettled. When Jesus uttered the Golden Rule, he closed by saying, "This is the law and the prophets" (Matthew 7:12), meaning that he was giving a very concise summary of the Scriptures which were considered as canonical in his day. A similar phrase is used in Luke 16:16, and in verses 29 and 31 of that chapter there is mention of "Moses and the prophets." In Luke 24:44 Jesus refers to "the law of Moses and the prophets and the psalms," indicating that at least Psalms in the third division may have been considered as Scripture.

The third division, The Writings (also called Hagiographa, "sacred writings"), was not definitely canonized until the end of the first century A.D., between A.D. 90 and 100. The Jewish rebellion against Roman rule, A.D. 66-70, failed; the Romans captured Jerusalem and burned the temple, and Rome adopted an iron policy against the Jews. The religious capital of Judaism passed to the little town of Jamnia in western Palestine, to which many of the leading rabbis moved. There the Academy of Jamnia debated the contents of the third division of the canon and settled its contents, fixing on the books named above. In addition to the crisis brought on by the fall of Jerusalem to the Romans, there was serious tension at this time between Judaism and Christianity. The Christians accepted the Jewish Bible as they knew it (usually in its Greek translation) as their sacred Scripture. They quoted from it, and read it in their worship. But the Jews objected to the way the Christians interpreted their Scripture, and there was confusion regarding the exact number of books which should be considered as authoritative. Of course the Jews objected especially to the Christians' use of apocalyptic thought, and their belief that the Messiah had already come.

We should not think of the Academy of Jamnia as being the same as an ecclesiastical council, with formal authority. The rabbis of Jamnia discussed various books over a long period of time, and settled matters by reaching a consensus or a majority opinion. Their opinions were accepted, not because they had formal delegated authority, but because they had great prestige as rabbinical leaders.

The rabbis discussed a large number of books, but certain books were especially debated: Ecclesiastes, Song of Solomon, Esther, and Ezekiel, and Sirach among the books that came to be called Apocrypha. Ecclesiastes was questioned because it contains many unorthodox opinions, but was probably accepted because of its supposed authorship by Solomon. The Song of Solomon appears to be a group of very secular love songs, with little religious value; it was accepted because of its ascription to Solomon, and because it was interpreted as singing of the love between Yahweh and Israel (as the Christian Church came to interpret it as speaking of the love between Christ and the Church, his bride). Esther never mentions the name of God, and is very nationalistic; it was accepted because of its great popularity and its use at the festival of Purim. Ezekiel conflicts in some of its legal sections with the *Torah;* one rabbi is said to have burned many jars of midnight oil in making the two harmonize. Sirach was highly valued by many because of its lofty teaching; it is in fact a very fine book, its contents being up to the standard of several of the books which were accepted into the canon. It was rejected because of clear indications it was written a little after 200 B.C., long after the date of Ezra.

The New Testament gives evidence of the fluidity of this third division. A number of the apocryphal books are alluded to in the New Testament, or influenced the thought of New Testament writers; this is particularly true of the books of Sirach and the Wisdom of Solomon. The New Testament even quotes, virtually as Scripture, books that are outside both the Hebrew canon and the Apocrypha. For example, Jude 14-15 quotes the Book of Enoch 1:9.

The final decision regarding the canonicity of books rested in part upon popular acceptance of books, and in part upon a formal standard: the rabbis believed that divine inspiration began with Moses and ended with Ezra. The opinion that inspiration did not begin until Moses ruled out many of the apocalyptic works written in the name of very early worthies such as Enoch. The belief that it ceased with Ezra ruled out books such as I-II Maccabees that dealt with events after his time, and books that obviously were written after Ezra (Sirach, Wisdom of Solomon, and others). Daniel was accepted because, though it probably was written in the second century, it made Daniel appear to have lived in the time of the exile. The Psalter, of course, had been used in worship and was very popular. Not all of the Writings, however, were read in worship, as the Law and the Prophets were, though the so-called Five Scrolls (Song of Solomon, Ruth, Lamentations, Ecclesiastes, and Esther) eventually came to be read at five important Jewish festivals.

The Jewish Talmud and other works have a strange phrase to indicate that books are canonical: those that are canonical "defile the hands." Noncanonical books, such as the Apocrypha and the Christian Scriptures, were said not to defile the hands. This is the opposite of what one would expect. The phrase obviously means that sacred books must be approached and handled with great care and reverence; if not, they produce ritual impurity that is defiling.

So far as Israel and Judaism are concerned, the Academy of Jamnia made the only official decision regarding the canon of Scripture on which we have information. We have seen that we really do not know the date and circumstances of the canonization of the Law and the Prophets. Perhaps we should not speak of canonization at all except that which took place around A.D. 100. There was apparently a difference between books' being "sacred" and their being "sacrosanct." For a long time the books of Scripture were sacred in that they were considered as of divine origin and authoritative, but additions could be made to them, and they could be changed to some degree. After the Academy of Jamnia the accepted books were sacrosanct, in that their text could not be changed.

In the chapter on the Apocrypha we have seen that the policy of the various branches of the Christian church has varied with regard to the contents of the canon. The Apocrypha are those books which are in the Latin Vulgate but not in the Jewish canon (all of them being also in the Greek Septuagint, except II Esdras). Some scholars speak of a Palestinian canon and a longer Alexandrian canon, that of the Septuagint, since it was translated in Egypt. However, we do not know of any official pronouncement concerning an Alexandrian canon. The Roman church wavered in its attitude and did not reach an official decision until the Council of Trent (1546), when all of the Apocrypha were accepted as thoroughly authoritative except I-II Esdras and the Prayer of Manasseh. The Eastern churches have usually accepted some or all of the Apocrypha. Protestant churches, following Martin Luther and others, have usually clung to the Hebrew canon, rejecting the books of the Apocrypha as not a part of the Old Testament, though many Protestant Bibles print the Apocrypha and they are considered to be of value. We must defer to the end of this chapter a discussion of the attitude which Christians should take toward the problem of the canon, and thus toward the books of the Old Testament Apocrypha.

Formation of the New Testament Canon

The New Testament is less than one third as long as the Old, and the books comprising it were written within a period of about a hundred years. The formation of the canon of the New Testament was a long and gradual process, as with the Old Testament. We cannot divide it into clearly defined phases, and regarding some of the steps involved we are not well informed from ancient sources.

Our New Testament consists of four types of books: Gospels, the Acts of the Apostles, Letters of Paul and others, and the Revelation of John. In addition to these which have been accepted in our New Testament, others of each type were produced in the early years of Christianity. Among others there were Gospels of Peter, of the Hebrews, and of the Egyptians; the Acts of Paul; the Letter of Barnabas, the Letter of Clement of Rome to the Corinthians, the Letter to the Laodiceans, and Letters known as II Clement and III Corinthians; and the Revelation of Peter, and an apocalyptic work known as the Shepherd of Hermas. In addition there were the Teaching of the Apostles (the *Didaché*), and the Preaching of Peter. Most of these competed for inclusion in the canon, and were considered as Scripture in certain places and certain times; some almost became canonical. We shall see that of the books that did find acceptance into the New Testament, some were accepted very widely at an early date, while others were slow in winning canonical status.

The first Bible of the early Christians was the Old Testament, in the form we have discussed above, usually in a Greek translation. This was their only Bible for many years. Christian preachers and missionaries quoted from it (sometimes rather freely from memory), especially to prove that Jesus was the long-promised and predicted Messiah; and it was read and expounded in services of Christian worship. When New Testament writers speak of "sacred writings" or "Scripture," they usually mean the Old Testament. In 2 Timothy 3:15-17 the recipient of the letter is reminded that

> from childhood you have been acquainted with the sacred writings which are able to instruct you for salvation through Jesus Christ. All scripture is inspired by God and profitable for teaching, for reproof, for correction, and for training in righteousness, that the man of God may be complete, equipped for every good work.

The writer is certainly referring to the Old Testament here, though it is not impossible that he has in mind also some Christian writings that had already been recognized as scriptural, since this is one of the latest books of the New Testament to be written. First Timothy 5:18 quotes as Scripture both Deuteronomy 25:4 and a saying of Jesus which is found in Luke 10:7.

From very early days Christians treasured the words and deeds of Jesus. Their teachers and preachers quoted what he had said, and told about what he had done. Probably little collections of his words and deeds were made. Eventually the Gospels were written, between about A.D. 60 and 100 or a little later. Some sayings of Jesus survived outside the Gospels (see Acts 20:35 and 1 Corinthians 9:14).

The earliest Christian writings about which we now know were the Letters of Paul. This great missionary to the Gentiles wrote them, not as formal theological treatises, but as real letters, mostly to churches he had established or had a special interest in, to deal with acute problems that had arisen in those churches. In some cases he learned about their problems from letters they wrote to him. He wrote some letters to individuals. Paul expected the churches to which he wrote to read the letters in their church meetings. To the Colossians he said, "When this letter has been read among you, have it read also in the church of the Laodiceans; and see that you read also the letter from Laodicea" (4:16). Some letters, such as Romans, may have been addressed to several churches. It was, of course, quite natural for the letters of Paul to be read in church meetings, in order to inform the members; we must remember that few of them were able to read for themselves. Paul's letters were not at first read as if they were equal in value to the Old Testament. But the churches must have kept and treasured his letters, and some may have made small collections of them. It is altogether probable that Paul wrote more letters than have been preserved to the present.

An attractive theory regarding the collection of Paul's letters has been elaborated by E. J. Goodspeed, the noted American scholar and New Testament translator. He thinks that the publication of Acts about A.D. 90 led to a new understanding of Paul's importance and a desire to know more about him. Some Christian—probably someone living in Asia Minor who had long known Colossians and Philemon—started on a search for the letters of Paul in the various churches mentioned in Acts. Finding seven letters, he combined them with the two he knew, and then wrote a covering letter in which he summarized the most important and permanently valid teachings of the apostle; this was what we now call the letter to the Ephesians. He then issued the first collection of Paul's letters.[1] This theory suggests a possible method by which Paul's letters were assembled, but it has some weaknesses, such as the implication that there had been little interest in Paul before Acts was published. In any event, we may suppose that by the end of the first century A.D. all of the large and influential Christian churches had one or more letters of Paul, and some may have had small collections; they read them in their services, without necessarily considering them as sacred in the same way

---

[1]*The Meaning of Ephesians* (Chicago: University of Chicago Press, 1933).

that they did the Old Testament. The letters were treasured, and were on the way to being counted as canonical.

In the early second century some Christians still valued the oral traditions they had received from the apostles more highly than the written word. Papias, bishop of Hierapolis, claimed that he made a special point of talking with those who were followers of the apostles, to learn what the apostles said. "For," said Papias, "I did not consider that I got so much profit from the contents of books as from the utterances of a living and abiding voice."[2]

By the middle of the second century the Gospels were being read in Christian services of worship along with Old Testament books. Justin Martyr, writing in Rome about 150 A.D., says that on Sunday the Christians living in towns or in the country would gather together in one place, and "the memoirs of the Apostles or the writings of the prophets are read, as long as time permits."[3] After the reading, the president would deliver a sermon exhorting the people to "imitate these excellent examples"; they would pray together, and then observe the Lord's Supper. From other references in Justin's writings, we know that by "the memoirs of the Apostles" he meant Gospels. Here it looks very much as if the Gospels are put on the same level as the books of the Old Testament prophets.

About the same time there lived a man who did a great deal to stimulate the formation of an official canon. This man was Marcion, one of the first heretics of the church and one of the first men to attempt to reform the church. He was a wealthy shipowner, born in Asia Minor, who came to Rome and joined the Christian congregation there. His heretical ideas led him to be excommunicated in A.D. 144, but he gathered his followers into a separate church.

---

[2]Eusebius, *Ecclesiastical History* III, 39 (Henry Bettenson ed., *Documents of the Christian Church* [Oxford, 1943], p. 38).

[3]*Apology* I, 67 (Bettenson, *op. cit.*, p. 94).

Marcion was a strong antagonist of Judaism and the Old Testament, and a great admirer of Paul, partly because Paul had carried on successful contests with the Jews and with Judaizers in the church. Marcion believed that the Jewish Scriptures and the Christian writings present to us two different Gods: one is the God of the Old Testament who is just, demanding "an eye for an eye and a tooth for a tooth," and the Creator of the material universe; the other is the God of the Christians who is good and merciful, the Redeemer of mankind, and the Father of Jesus Christ. Marcion completely rejected the first God and the Old Testament which told about him. For his followers Marcion made a canon of sacred books, which consisted of two parts: the Gospel of Luke, which he edited in such a way as to remove passages suggesting that Christ considered the God of the Old Testament to be his father (recall that Luke had been associated with Paul); and ten letters of Paul, also edited to some extent.

By his heresy Marcion stimulated the Christians in the main stream of the church to formulate their beliefs more clearly and to think of establishing a list of books which would express their beliefs authoritatively. The church would not give up the Old Testament, and insisted that there were Four Gospels, not just one, and that there were other books in addition to the ten letters of Paul. Probably Marcion's views aroused interest in Acts because it showed Paul in association with other apostles and leaders. The church really owes a great debt to this early heretic, as it does to many another.

In the latter part of the second century, Irenaeus could insist that there are Four Gospels just as there are four zones of the world in which we live, and four principal winds, while the church is spread over all the earth; he wrote that God "gave us the gospel, fourfold in form but held together by one Spirit."[4] Tatian, a disciple of Justin, compiled a harmony of the Four Gospels into a single book called the Diatessaron.

From near the end of the second century comes an important document known as the Muratorian Canon, a fragmentary list in Latin, translated from a Greek original. It indicates the canon of Rome around A.D. 200: Four Gospels, Acts, 13 Letters of Paul (not Hebrews), 2 Letters of John, Jude (here mentioned for the first time), Revelation of John, and also the Revelation of Peter, "which some of us refuse to have read in the Church." The Shepherd of Hermas is to be read privately, but not publicly in the church. This list also accepts "Wisdom, written by the friends of Solomon in his honor"; this may be the Wisdom of Solomon of the Old Testament Apocrypha. It names various books that are rejected, because "it is not fitting for gall to be mixed with honey."[5]

In the second century a development took place in the technical preparation of books that may have facilitated the formation of the canon, and certainly made easier the reading of Christian writings. That was the adoption of the *codex* form for the making of books. Before this time books were produced in the form of scrolls, like those which are used in Jewish synagogues at the present. A scroll is a long, continuous piece of writing material that can be rolled up, the writing being placed on it in columns. The scroll of a long work is bulky and awkward to handle. The codex form is the same as we use today in printing books: a series of separate leaf pages are bound together between covers. This form was in use in the second century, and some scholars think it was a Christian invention. A codex is much more convenient to handle than a scroll, and it is far easier to look up a passage in a codex. It would have been easy to place in one codex all Four Gospels,

---

[4]*Against Heresies* III 11:8 (Cyril C. Richardson, ed., *Early Christian Fathers* [The Library of Christian Classics, Vol. I; Philadelphia: Westminster Press, 1953], p. 382).
[5]Bettenson, *op. cit.*, pp. 40-41.

or all the letters of Paul; in time, the whole New Testament, and even the whole Bible, was written in a single codex. Two outstanding inventions that greatly facilitated the distribution and use of Scriptures were the codex form of the book, and the printing press (about A.D. 1450).

It would be tiresome to give here all of the evidence for the development of the canon and record all of the lists known to us. In the third century Origen, one of the greatest scholars of the early church, who taught in Alexandria and later Caesarea, tried to analyze the situation in his time by classifying the various books as "accepted" or "disputed." He listed among the former twenty-two: Four Gospels, fourteen letters of Paul (including Hebrews, though he doubted its authorship by Paul), Acts, 1 Peter, 1 John, and Revelation of John. Among the "disputed" books were James, Jude, 2 Peter, 2-3 John, the Letter of Barnabas, and the Shepherd of Hermas. Origen seems, however, to have considered all of these books to be scriptural. Concerning Hebrews he once wrote: "God only knows who really wrote it."

The situation gradually developed to the point that in the year A.D. 367 Athanasius, Bishop of Alexandria, in his annual Easter letter to the churches of his diocese gave a list of the books that rightfully belong in the Old and New Testaments. The New Testament list contains exactly the same twenty-seven books we have in our Bibles today. But he added concerning the Teaching of the Apostles and the Shepherd of Hermas, that they were "to be read by those just coming forward to receive instruction in religion." The council of Hippo (393) and the Synod of Carthage (397) repeated the same New Testament list. We should not think that Bishop Athanasius really settled the matter by his authority, but rather that he reported the situation that generally prevailed in his time. The canon of the New Testament has not varied from this list of twenty-seven in the Roman Catholic and Protestant churches.

The Pauline authorship of Hebrews was often questioned in the West, but that did not keep it from being accepted. The Eastern churches wavered over the Revelation of John, and many did not fully accept it into their canon. The Greek Orthodox Church even today does not read from this book in its church services.

Now that we have traced the development of the canon to the form it now has we can discuss the criterion, or criteria, by which writings were deemed appropriate for inclusion in the authoritative list. The only formal criterion of which we know was that of apostolic origin—that is, a writing had to be from the pen of an apostle or of someone closely associated with an apostle. Thus, Mark's Gospel could be accepted because it was believed he recorded the preaching of Peter, and Luke and Acts because Luke had been associated with Paul. The epistles of James and Jude were thought to have been written by the two brothers of Jesus bearing those names. But this criterion of apostolic origin was to a degree artificial. Even in ancient times serious doubts were raised as to Paul's authorship of Hebrews. Some satisfied their consciences by saying that Paul wrote it in Hebrew and a friend translated it, or that Paul "wrote" it but a friend did the actual composition. It is not at all likely that Paul had anything to do with the writing of it. Furthermore, modern biblical criticism has shown that several of the books of the New Testament were not actually written by those to whom they were ascribed, as we have seen in our survey of the New Testament literature.

In practice, the criteria that primarily determined admission into the canon were usage in the life of the church, especially in its worship, and general conformity in outlook and teaching to the main stream of Christian thought. Jerome knew that some people thought Hebrews was written by Barnabas or Clement, but he said, "it makes no difference whose it is, since it is from a churchman, and is celebrated in the daily readings of the churches."[6] This is a very honest statement, and indicates an important reason for the inclusion of various books. Also, accepted writings had to conform generally with what was believed in most of the churches; no really heretical writings were admitted. No book in the New Testament departs as far from generally accepted beliefs as Ecclesiastes does in the Old Testament; the Jews did not emphasize right belief as much as Christians did.

There were several reasons why Christianity came to the point of fixing a canon of New Testament Scripture to stand alongside the Old Testament in its Bible. We have hinted at some of these in our discussion.

One was to preserve in permanent form the words and deeds of Christ and his immediate apostles. In time the apostles died, and the companions of the apostles died, and Christians found themselves further and further from the sources of their faith. They could not rely indefinitely on oral tradition and, since they knew of books that told of the words and deeds of Christ and his apostles, and that set forth the Christian gospel, it was natural for them to decide which of these were reliable for their purposes.

A New Testament canon was necessary also in order to provide believers with the proper and correct interpretation of the Old Testament. We have seen that the Old Testament was the first Bible of the Christians. But their interpretation of it differed at important points from Jewish interpretation. A need was felt for setting forth the correct interpretation and fulfilment of the Jewish Scriptures.

A third purpose in forming the New Testament was to combat heresy. If we think of the first two or three hundred years of Christianity as being a time that was ideal, with the church unified in its faith and practice, we are badly mistaken.

---

[6]Letter to Claudianus Postumus Dardanus, quoted by M. S. Enslin, *The Literature of the Christian Movement* (Harper Torchbook, 1956), p. 472.

There were many heresies, and some of them came perilously close to succeeding.

One heresy that we have already noticed was that of Marcion and his followers. They wanted to reject the Old Testament, and had a very restricted interpretation of the Christian faith. In a negative way Marcion stimulated the formation of a definite canon of Scripture.

Another heresy was that of Gnosticism. This is a name given to a conglomeration of beliefs that originated in pre-Christian times and became strong in certain circles of the early church. The Gnostics believed that salvation comes through knowledge *(gnosis)*, but they did not mean the kind of knowledge ordinarily gained in schools, or the knowledge of God about which Old Testament prophets talked; they meant knowledge of certain secrets and mysteries that had been supernaturally revealed, and into which one must be initiated. These were mysteries about the origin of the world, about the nature of the highly supernatural God they worshiped, and about man's own nature. Gnostics believed that this world is evil; it was not created by the high and holy God, but by intermediaries, or by an inferior deity known as the Demiurge. Salvation required illumination with knowledge, and often certain ascetic practices to overcome the evil of the flesh. Some Christian Gnostics believed that Christ did not really live in the flesh; he only seemed to live, and appeared in ghostlike form.

Still another heresy was that of Montanism. This was an ancient "revivalism" whose adherents believed that the spirit of prophecy was still alive and could lead them into ecstasy. It derives its name from Montanus of Phrygia, in Asia Minor, who was reputed to have been a priest of the pagan goddess Cybele before his conversion to Christianity. His followers believed that the Paraclete promised in John 14:16 dwelled bodily in him, and that the heavenly Jerusalem would soon come to Asia Minor. This heresy taught a very strict asceticism, and won many converts. By teaching that the new age of the Spirit had arrived, Montanism put Christ and the apostolic message on a secondary level.

The Christian church developed its canon in order to define the true faith and combat these and other errors. By holding on to the Old Testament the church insisted that the Creator of the world was the same God found in the rest of the Bible, that God's creation is not essentially evil, and that its religion was firmly rooted in history. The Gospels portrayed a Christ who really lived as a man on this earth among men. The Book of Acts formed a good bridge between the Gospels and the Letters. Taken as a whole the books accepted into the New Testament gave a well-balanced, realistic view of the Christian faith, with strong roots in history. And it showed the Christians how the promises of the Old Testament had come to fulfilment.

The Christian's Attitude toward the Canon

At the outset of this chapter, one of the questions we raised was this: can we have confidence that exactly the sixty-six books in our Bible—no more and no fewer—should constitute our sacred Scripture? We are now in a position to suggest some answers to that question.

First, let us summarize four factors in the formation of the canon that apply to both the Old and the New Testaments.

(1) The Jewish and Christian communities formed definitive collections of Scripture only when they had come to believe that the authentic voice of God could no longer be heard in spoken words, but could be read in written words. In ancient Israel the prophets valued highly the spoken word, which they believed they had received from Yahweh, and the people must have believed the prophets were spokesmen for him. In

one instance Jeremiah spoke scathingly of some writing, probably Deuteronomy:

> "How can you say, 'We are wise,
>   and the law of the LORD is with us'?
> But, behold, the false pen of the scribes
>   has made it into a lie." (Jeremiah 8:8)

But eventually the time came when the Jews believed that the spirit of prophecy extended only through the time of Ezra. Just when they arrived at this view is not certain, but the final fixation of the canon by the Academy of Jamnia took place some five hundred years after Ezra.

For the New Testament we have seen that Bishop Papias in the early part of the second century said he valued the spoken word of those who had known the apostles above the written word. This view was widespread as long as the apostles and other eyewitnesses of the life of Jesus, and those who had known the apostles, were alive, and probably for some time after they had all died. The final fixing of the New Testament canon occurred about two hundred years after that time.

(2) In determining what books should be in the two Testaments, the primary consideration was the experience of the religious community: those books were accepted which had become popular, especially in public worship, perhaps to a limited extent in personal devotion and guidance. Most people must have acquired their knowledge of the contents of sacred writings from hearing them read in public rather than from personal reading, because of the low rate of literacy and the expensiveness of books. The formal decisions of councils, academies, and individual rabbis or bishops did little more than record the general opinion of the religious communities; their decisions were probably of real significance only for certain marginal books.

(3) In both Judaism and Christianity a principal motive in the drawing up of official lists of authoritative books was to combat heresy. The final decision about the Old Testament, and the only official one about which we know, was made only after Christianity had become a threat to Judaism and there was conflict between the two faiths. The Christian canon was formed, as we have seen, to combat various heresies— Gnosticism, Marcionism, Montanism, and others. In combating heresy Judaism and Christianity were both compelled to define their faith more clearly. Fortunately the Christian church refused to define its faith in a narrow way, but allowed room for several emphases.

(4) The process of forming the canons of the two Testaments was certainly in part a human process. We should believe that to some degree there was divine guidance in the formation of the canons, but at various stages human decisions had to be made. These decisions were largely group decisions, with certain outstanding leaders exerting influence from time to time, but they were human decisions. In the process there was wavering over certain books, which showed uncertainty as to whether they should be considered authoritative or not. In the Old Testament there were debates especially concerning Esther, Ecclesiastes, Song of Solomon, and the books of the Apocrypha. It appears that Sirach almost made the canon. In the New Testament the books that were latest to be settled on, about which there were more serious debates, were Revelation, Hebrews, James, 2 Peter, 2-3 John, and Jude. The Shepherd of Hermas almost made the canon.

In the light of all these facts and factors, what should be the attitude of the Christian toward the canon today?

First, what should we think of the Old Testament Apocrypha? There have been various attitudes within the several branches of the Christian church. The Roman Catholic finally settled its attitude by adopting most of them as fully authoritative. Protestants have usually rejected them, either wholly or for public reading. Should we today feel ourselves bound only to the Hebrew canon as it was fixed by the Academy of Jamnia? Or can we find genuine value in these books of the Apocrypha? A decision should be based upon knowledge of what is in these books. An impartial reading will probably show that the two wisdom books, Sirach and the Wisdom of Solomon, are as helpful as the Book of Proverbs and more than Ecclesiastes. As history I Maccabees ranks higher than 1-2 Chronicles, and deals with a dynamic period in Jewish history. Other books vary in their value; the ordinary reader may find that he gets little religious aid from Judith, Tobit, and II Esdras. The least we may say is this: all of the Apocrypha, as well as other books written in the intertestamental period (such as those we call the Pseudepigrapha and the Qumran scrolls), are of fundamental importance to the historical understanding of various movements in Judaism just before the life of Jesus and during the early years of Christianity.

Second, what should we think of the sixty-six books in the ordinary Protestant Bible? Must we look upon all of them as sacred and authoritative? Are they equally so, or are some more authoritative than others? The history of the development of the canon may seem to justify a free attitude toward some of the books, at least toward those about which there was the most question in forming the canon.

Many of the early Protestant Reformers adopted a free attitude toward the canon of Scripture. Martin Luther went a little further than most, but we may take him as an example.

Luther had a clear principle by which he judged whether books of the Bible were truly canonical or not. He asked the question: do they lead us to Christ? Within the New Testament he valued certain books more highly than others. In the Preface to the first edition of his New Testament he said that the Gospel and first Epistle of John, Paul's letters (especially Romans, Galatians, and Ephesians), and 1 Peter "are the books which show Christ to you. They teach everything you need to know for your salvation, even if you were never to see or hear any other book or hear any other teaching."[7]

He showed elsewhere that he gave an inferior status particularly to Hebrews, James, Jude, and Revelation. He called James "a right strawy epistle," and said he would refuse to James "a place among the writers of the true canon of my Bible."[8] Luther thought James put entirely too much emphasis on works rather than on faith in Christ.

As for the Apocrypha, Luther judged the individual books differently according to their contents, considering most favorably Sirach and the Wisdom of Solomon; in general he thought the Apocrypha were not "equal to the sacred Scriptures, and yet are useful and good for reading." In the Old Testament he particularly rejected Esther. He said that he was so hostile to the Book and to Esther that he wished they did not exist, for "they Judaize too much and have much heathen perverseness."

Many Protestants have not, of course, manifested as much freedom as Luther did in dealing with the canon of Scripture. There are indeed dangers in such an attitude. But may we not exercise a truly Protestant and evangelical attitude of freedom toward the canon of the Bible? Should we not feel free to consider as less authoritative than others Esther, Song of Solomon, Ecclesiastes, Revelation, and even others? Can we not with great profit read some if not all of the Apocrypha?

Everyone who reads and uses the Bible frequently has of necessity his own "private canon." It can be determined by looking through his Bible to see which passages or books are well-worn from reading and study, and which pages are still

---

[7]Quoted from John Dillenberger ed., *Martin Luther: Selections from His Writings* (Anchor Books, 1961), p. 19.
[8]Preface to the Epistle of St. James, *ibid.*, p. 36.

clean. No one can fail to be moved by some of the great passages of Scripture, but all of us can readily be pardoned if we neglect the dreary wastelands of the "begots" and the ancient rules concerning sacrifice and similar matters.

Our final word concerning the canon should be one of immense gratitude to God, not only that we have a written Bible, but that we have one which has passed through a process of sifting and selection. A sacred book is not always a blessing. In Moslem lands the Koran has too often served as a barrier to progress. Sometimes the Christian Bible—we must honestly admit—has been a brake upon progress in science and culture, sometimes even in religion. It can represent the "dead hand of the past." But rightly used our Christian Bible can be an asset to be treasured and read and followed with gratitude, for it provides us with a firm anchorage in history, a necessary link with our past, and a source from which the church and the individual Christian can continually renew their faith and their knowledge of the right way to serve our Lord.

VIII

how we got
our english bible

THE BIBLE WAS NOT WRITTEN IN ENGLISH. THIS statement is so obvious that it should not need to be made, but many people are not aware of the implications of it. The Bible was written in foreign languages that were used long ago, and has come down to us only through a long and complicated process of copying, editing, and translation. Can we now really understand the languages in which it was written? Can we rely on the English translations available to us today?

The Bible is a *book of the people*. It was not written to be a treasure of mysteries and secret lore, or a private manual for use only by priests and ministers. It was compiled to be read and used by people in their everyday life and worship.

The story of the transmission and translation of the Bible through the centuries is a story that underlines the fact that it is, and always has been when properly used, a people's book. It is a story marked by long hours of patient and diligent work on the part of many people, sometimes by heroic courage that led to martyrdom, and always by dedication to the task of making the Bible available for those for whom it was intended.

283

The Hebrew Old Testament

The Old Testament was written in the Hebrew language, except the following passages which are in Aramaic: Ezra 4:8—6:18; 7:12-26; Daniel 2:4b—7:28; and Jeremiah 10:11. Hebrew and Aramaic are members of the family of languages known as Semitic, which is quite different from the Indo-European family to which belong English and most of the languages with which we are acquainted. Hebrew was the spoken and written tongue for most of the Old Testament period, but after the return from Babylonian exile Aramaic gradually replaced it in everyday use.

As we have seen, the Old Testament was written over a period of a thousand years or more. Not a single book of either the Old or New Testament has come down to the present in its autograph form—that is, in a manuscript written by the author. What we have are copies of copies of copies . . . going back ultimately to the originals. The oldest complete manuscript of the Hebrew Bible that can be definitely dated is in the Public Library of Leningrad, Russia, made in A.D. 1008. There are portions of the Old Testament in manuscripts that are some two or three hundred years earlier. The oldest manuscript of a single Old Testament book is the Qumran manuscript of the Book of Isaiah (one of the so-called Dead Sea Scrolls), which was copied about 100 B.C. A few biblical fragments found at Qumran are even older.

You might suppose that many errors were made during the long period of time in which the Hebrew was being copied by hand. Some errors did arise—from carelessness, from misreading of Hebrew letters that looked alike, from hearing incorrectly when a manuscript was being copied by a group of scribes from dictation, and other causes. Sometimes scribes tried to "improve" the text they were copying. But the Jews were extremely careful in copying their Bible, and relatively few errors were made, as can be proved by comparing the very ancient Qumran manuscript of Isaiah with the later copies. A fairly standard text was fixed around A.D. 100. In the period between the sixth and tenth centuries A.D. there lived a series of biblical scholars known as "Masoretes," who made a definitive Hebrew text, called the Masoretic Text. The surviving copies of this text show very little variation from one another. The Jews had the fortunate practice of destroying defective and worn-out manuscripts of their Bible.

In spite of the great care exercised in the copying of Hebrew manuscripts, some errors in the text can be discerned by modern scholars, when the Hebrew or Aramaic is not understandable or is obviously not correct. Sometimes they can recover the correct text by consulting one or more of the ancient versions of the Old Testament which may give the right reading because they were made before the standard Hebrew text was finished. At other times a scholar may recover the correct text by intelligent conjecture based upon his knowledge as to the kinds of mistakes ancient scribes were prone to make.

The Greek New Testament

The New Testament books were written in Greek, not classical Greek, the language of Plato and Aristotle, but the kind of Greek known as *koiné*. That word means "common," and is so used because it was the language that was in common use throughout the Roman Empire. As a result of the conquests of Alexander the Great and the policies of his successors, this had become the international tongue, much more widely used than Latin. The mother tongue of Jesus and of many of his followers must have been Aramaic; a few of his actual words have survived, as in *Talitha cumi,* "Little girl, arise" of Mark 5:41, and *Ephphatha,* "Be opened" in Mark 7:34. He could probably speak some Greek, for it was used more widely in

Galilee than in Jerusalem, but his teaching would have been in Aramaic.

The New Testament was written in a much shorter space of time than the Old Testament, about a hundred years; and a shorter period intervened between the writing of the separate books and our earliest manuscripts. As with the Old Testament, we have no autograph copies. The earliest fragment of a New Testament book known at present is a tiny scrap containing a few words of the 18th chapter of John, written about A.D. 150, now in the John Rylands Library, Manchester, England. The earliest complete manuscript of the New Testament, however, is from the fourth century—the Codex Sinaiticus, now in the British Museum, so named because it was found in a monastery at the traditional site of Mount Sinai. Another manuscript from the same century, the Codex Vaticanus (in the Vatican Library in Rome), is not complete. From the third century there are a large number of papyri found in Egypt and bought by A. Chester Beatty and the University of Michigan; they contain all or parts of 18 of the New Testament books. A more recent discovery is a manuscript (Bodmer papyrus) containing the gospel of John which was written about A.D. 200, which is not much more than a century after that gospel was written.

There are altogether nearly five thousand Greek manuscripts of all or parts of the New Testament. In addition, there are early translations into other languages and quotations from the New Testament in early Christian writings. No other text from ancient times is nearly so well known as the New Testament. Nevertheless, it is often no easy task to recover the reading of the original for particular passages, for no two manuscripts agree absolutely. Ancient scribes made mistakes, and sometimes they attempted to improve the text they were copying. A scribe sometimes made changes to harmonize a Gospel with others known to him, to adjust a quotation from the Old Testament to a copy known to him, to remove supposed heresy from a text, or to explain some obscurity.

The scholar who wishes to recover the original text is cursed with an abundance of riches. There is no simple method by which he works. He cannot necessarily depend on the earliest manuscripts, for a mistake may have been made even before they were copied; nor can he depend on the reading of a majority of the manuscripts, for a given error once made could have been copied many times over. The method used today is a complicated one. Manuscripts are divided into a small number of families or text types, and certain families seem to be more dependable than others. Then, each individual reading is examined and the preference is given to that one which best explains the origin of all variant readings. On very rare occasions, intelligent conjecture may be used, but it is not used nearly so often as with the Old Testament text.

Lest you should think that the differences in texts are not important, and that scholars make much ado over nothing, let us look at one which has an important bearing on religious belief. Romans 8:28 reads in the King James Version: "All things work together for good to them that love God," a translation of the late medieval text used by the King James translators. But a slightly different text appears in manuscripts brought to light since the time that version was made, one of them a Beatty papyrus of the third century. The correct rendering is given in the Revised Standard Version: "In everything God works for good with those who love him." There is really a big difference in those two statements, and it is important to know that the latter is what Paul wrote.

Ancient Versions

As a book of the people, the Bible was translated very early into foreign languages, so that it might be read and understood by the common man. The earliest translation of the

Old Testament was made before the lifetime of Jesus, and it is to that translation we first turn.

We saw above in discussing the history of Old Testament times (p. 84) that a large Jewish colony flourished in Alexandria, Egypt, in the third century. Many of the Jews there lost the ability to understand Hebrew, and adopted Greek as their vernacular. The Greek version known as the Septuagint was made so that they might hear and read their Scripture in a language they understood.

Legend has it that King Ptolemy Philadelphus of Egypt wrote a letter to the high priest in Jerusalem saying he wished to have the Jewish Law translated into Greek for his royal library in Alexandria. The high priest sent to Egypt seventy-two elders with a copy of the Law, which they translated for the king in seventy-two days. A late legend says they worked in separate cells and miraculously produced identical translations. The probability is that the Jews of Egypt took the initiative to provide themselves with a version they could use in their synagogue worship and study. They made it over a period of about two centuries, completing it by the beginning of the Christian Era. Some books were translated much more carefully and accurately than others. The version is called the Septuagint, from the Greek word for "seventy," because of the tradition as to the number of elders who made it.

You can readily see that this Greek version was made before the standard Hebrew text of the Old Testament was fixed, and even before the early Qumran manuscripts. Thus it is frequently valuable in helping us to recover the original reading of passages in the Old Testament. A striking example is in 1 Samuel 14:41, where the Septuagint shows that several lines were accidentally omitted by a scribe in copying the Hebrew. The Hebrew text reads: "And Saul said to the Lord, God of Israel, 'Give Thummim.' And Jonathan and Saul were taken, but the people escaped." The Septuagint version of this verse is much longer. It was made from a Hebrew text that read as follows, the additional words being italicized:

> And Saul said, "O Lord, God of Israel, *why hast thou not answered thy servant this day? If the iniquity is in me or in my son Jonathan, O Lord, God of Israel, give Urim; but if thou sayest, 'The iniquity is in thy people Israel,'* give Thummim." And Jonathan and Saul were taken, but the people escaped.

In this instance the eye of the scribe accidentally skipped from the first occurrence of the word "Israel" to the third, aided by the fact that the two words "Israel, give" came together in the second occurrence. Mistakes like this are made by modern stenographers using typewriters. Here the Septuagint preserves the older, original reading, and helps greatly in showing what happened on this occasion in the life of Saul.

The Septuagint was essentially the Bible of the early Christians, before the New Testament was written and considered as authoritative. It was the Scripture on which their religion was nurtured. In many cases quotations in the New Testament from the Old Testament are from the Septuagint rather than the Hebrew.

As Christianity spread in the Roman Empire, it made converts among people who could not understand the New Testament in Greek, nor the Old Testament in either Hebrew or Greek. So the Bible had to be rendered into Latin in order that the common people might understand it. This led to the making of the translations known as "Old Latin." This was not a single, standard version, but a translation of various Biblical books by various people, and there were several different Latin translations.

This situation led to the great Latin version of the Bible now known as the Vulgate, the work of Jerome. Jerome was the son of wealthy parents, and one of the best educated and most learned scholars of his time (he lived A.D. 346-420). It was natural that Pope Damasus should turn to him with the commission that he produce a reliable and consistent Latin version. In a short time Jerome revised the Latin translations of the Four Gospels and the Psalter. Later he revised the rest of the New Testament and part of the Old. After the death of Damasus, Jerome moved at the age of forty to Palestine, and there spent the rest of his long life in a monastery in Bethlehem, carrying on his biblical studies. Knowing that the Old Testament had been written in Hebrew, and that the Septuagint itself was a translation, he made a new translation of the Old Testament from the Hebrew.

Though Jerome lived to be more than seventy, he did not live long enough to see the popularity his version was to achieve. During his lifetime it met much opposition. Jerome had received his first lessons in Hebrew from a converted Jew, and later studied with a Jewish rabbi. Some of his critics said that his version was tainted with Judaism. Others were simply afraid of anything new. Jerome retorted by calling his critics "two-legged asses." His work slowly gained popularity by its merit, and the Roman Catholic Church at the Council of Trent (1546) declared it to be the authoritative Bible in matters of belief and morals. It is still the official version of that church, though in recent years Catholic scholars have given increasing attention to the study of the originals.

Jerome's version came to be known as the Vulgate. Its Latin was the "vulgar" Latin in the sense that it was the language of the people, not in sophisticated or classical style. It is not entirely certain that all of the books now printed as the Vulgate were translated by Jerome, but most of them were. The Vulgate has had tremendous influence, perhaps more than any other foreign-language translation.

One other ancient version may be mentioned briefly. A large segment of the Eastern Church spoke the language known as Syriac, an Aramaic dialect which is akin to the dialect spoken by Jesus. In the course of time translations were made into this language, the most important of which acquired the name Peshitta, which means "simple" or "common," with perhaps the same significance as vulgate. Little is known of the origin of the Old Testament, not even whether it was made by Jews or Christians. It was made in the first or second century A.D., and the New Testament version in the fourth or fifth century. The Syriac versions are often important to scholars as they seek to recover the original reading of the Hebrew or Greek, because they were made very early.

Early English Translations

During the centuries when these versions were being made, civilization in England lagged far behind that of the countries bordering on the Mediterranean. Legend has it that Joseph of Arimathea introduced the Christian faith in England, and carried the holy grail to that country. Though there were certainly Christians in England by the third century, we have little information concerning them. Christianity revived after the arrival of Augustine, the first archbishop of Canterbury, in A.D. 597.

No translation of the whole Bible was produced in England until much later, the time of Wyclif in the fourteenth century. Probably little need was felt for such a translation, for few people could read, and the priests used the Latin Vulgate. The story of renderings into English before the time of Wyclif is that of paraphrases of parts of the Bible, translations of a few books such as the gospels and the Psalter, and interlinear translations—Latin and English—made primarily for use by the priests.

The story begins in the seventh century with an illiterate cowherd, Caedmon, who put into Anglo-Saxon verse paraphrases of the stories told him by the monks at Whitby. In this way he told of the creation of the world, the exodus from Egypt, the wanderings of Israel, and the life of Jesus.

The Venerable Bede in the next century translated the Gospel of John into Anglo-Saxon. He is said to have finished the last sentence of the gospel just before he died, with the Gloria on his lips. King Alfred, the first ruler of a united England, was a scholar as well as king. He prefixed to his code of laws a translation from Latin of the Ten Commandments, and is reported to have begun a translation of the Psalms before his death (901).

In the ninth and tenth centuries a number of interlinear translations were made. The Latin Vulgate was used, between the lines of which were placed lines of a literal translation into English.

After the Norman conquest (1066), French was used by the upper classes and Latin by the learned scholars, and the development of English was retarded. But a few translations were made, more particularly of the Psalter.

The first complete Bible in English resulted from the work of John Wyclif, who inspired its making and did some of the translating. He has been called "the Morning Star of the Reformation," because he taught ideas that were to be held later by Martin Luther and the reformers of the sixteenth century.

John Wyclif was educated at Oxford University, and became master of Balliol College in that university. Toward the end of his life he served as rector of a church. Wyclif had an opportunity to observe the corruptions of the church from the inside. He protested against the interference by the pope in political affairs, and against the wealth of the church and some of its officials. He taught that the Scripture constitutes a sufficient rule of life, and that every man—whether he be layman or priest—has the right to read the Bible for himself. It was out of this belief that he encouraged the translation of the Scriptures into English.

Wyclif established an order of poor, wandering preachers to go forth among the people to carry his message, somewhat like the Franciscans of a later time. Wyclif's followers were called Lollards; the word probably meant "chanters," but it was purposely confused with a Middle English word meaning "loafers."

A translation of the Bible into English appeared near the end of Wyclif's life (he died 1384), and a revision of it soon after his death. It is not known how much of the actual translation was done by Wyclif himself; it is certain that he was the moving spirit behind it. Most of the translating seems to have been done by a colleague, Nicholas of Hereford, and John Purvey, Wyclif's secretary. The translation was made from Latin, and because the printing press had not yet been invented, all copies had to be written out by hand. The first version was far too stiff and literal and was made from inferior Vulgate texts; the second was freer in its renderings, and more satisfactory to read.

During his lifetime Wyclif aroused much opposition from the authorities of the church; in one year the pope issued five bulls ordering that he be arrested and examined. Oxford University usually stood by him, and he had many supporters in England. After his death, the Council of Constance in 1415 ordered that the writings of Wyclif be burned, and that his bones be dug out of the consecrated ground. His body was disinterred and burned to ashes, and the ashes cast into the river Swift. But his work lived on, and his version continued to be read. It was reported that some people paid as much as the equivalent of $200 for a manuscript copy of his version, and others gave a load of hay for a few chapters of James or other epistles.

The fifteenth century was barren of translations, but many things were occurring to set the stage for the long series of great translations that were to follow. Classical learning was being revived, and scholars were learning Greek and Hebrew. Manuscripts of the Bible were being discovered and studied. The printing press was invented by Johann Gutenberg, and the first book of any size to be printed was a Latin Bible (about 1455). This was to make an enormous difference in the dissemination of the Bibles that before long were to be translated. In 1488 the first Hebrew Bible was printed, and early in the next century the first Greek New Testament (1516). The ideas set in motion by Wyclif and his followers were to lead more and more to the demand that the Bible be made available to the common people. English was rapidly developing into a form suitable for literary expression, and was becoming what we call Modern English.

William Tyndale and the Sixteenth Century

William Tyndale was the outstanding hero in the history of English versions, and perhaps the most creative of all English translators. He gave to the English of our Bible the general stamp and structure that has lasted to the present. He possessed the learning, persistence, courage, and literary genius needed for the task he set for himself, but met a martyr's death before he could finish it.

Born about 1490, Tyndale was educated at Oxford and Cambridge. At the latter university he studied Greek under the famous Erasmus, editor of the first printed Greek New Testament. Early in life Tyndale determined to make a translation from the original into the language of the people. To a prominent churchman of his time he said; "If God spare my life, ere many yeares I wyl cause a boye that dryveth the plough shall know more of the scripture than thou doest!" Unfortunately, there was still opposition among the church authorities to the making of such a translation, and Tyndale discovered that he could not carry out his resolve in England. The bishop of London refused his request for aid, but he was befriended by certain London merchants.

Tyndale went to the continent, where he probably came into contact with Luther. In 1526 he published his translation into English of the New Testament, at Worms in Germany. This was not only the first *printed* English New Testament, but the first translation made from Greek. It was ironical that it had to be published outside of England on German soil. Subsequently, Tyndale published a revision of his New Testament, and also English translations of the Pentateuch and the Book of Jonah. He worked also on the books from Joshua to Second Chronicles, which were published after his death.

Tyndale's New Testament was popular with the people of England, but was condemned by the ecclesiastical authorities. The bishop of London ordered that all copies be collected and burned, and a cardinal said that no burnt offering could be more pleasing to God. The burnings only increased interest in the book, and some of the merchants conspired to buy as many copies as possible for the bishop of London, so that Tyndale got the money and the bishop had his bonfires.

Tyndale was betrayed by a friend to whom he had lent money, and was imprisoned near Brussels for a year and a half. In a letter written from prison, he requested a lamp for use in the evenings, and also a Hebrew Bible, Hebrew grammar, and Hebrew dictionary, that he might pass the time in study. When he was tried, Tyndale maintained that "faith alone justifies before God." He was condemned to die, and was put to death by strangulation and burning on October 6, 1536, with the prayer on his lips: "Lord, open the King of England's eyes!"

Tyndale was successful not only because he was a scholar with the learning necessary to translate from the original languages, but because he wrote English that was simple, straightforward and vigorous, the kind that was understood by the people of his land. He often used words of Anglo-Saxon origin. He set the pattern for the translations that were to follow, for he made the Bible speak not in the language of the learned few, but in the simple dialect of the common people. Some scholars have estimated that nine tenths of Tyndale's New Testament has survived in the King James Version.

It is one of the ironies of history that a year before Tyndale was burned at the stake, a Bible was being allowed to circulate in England that used as the basis of its New Testament and Pentateuch the translation made by Tyndale. That Bible was the first printed *complete* Bible in English, prepared by Miles Coverdale. His name is the next important one in our story.

Miles Coverdale was about the same age as Tyndale. He was educated at Cambridge and served as a secular priest. He had some Reformation ideas, and may have come in contact with Tyndale in Germany. But he was a less passionate person, with a gentler and more conciliatory disposition. Whereas Tyndale met martyrdom at about the age of forty-five, Coverdale was eventually made a bishop and lived to the ripe age of eighty, though he spent some of his life in exile from England and died almost penniless.

The difference in the treatment of Tyndale and Coverdale arose in part from the nature of the Protestant Reformation in England, and the varying relationships between the papacy and the English crown. Henry VIII (1509-1547) was given the title "Defender of the Faith" by Pope Leo X for writing a treatise against Luther. Later, however, when Henry wished to divorce his wife Catherine of Aragon to marry Anne Boleyn, Pope Clement VII refused to annul the first marriage. Henry proceeded to marry her anyhow, his divorce being recognized by the Archbishop of Canterbury, and subsequently the English Parliament passed an act which made the king the supreme authority over the English church; this happened a year before the martyrdom of Tyndale. Yet, Henry was Catholic in doctrine; he executed Lutherans for their beliefs, and Catholics for refusing to recognize his authority. His successor, Edward VI (1547-1553) promoted definitely Protestant beliefs and practices, and in his reign the first Book of Common Prayer was issued. A reaction set in under Queen Mary (1553-1558), who re-established the Roman Catholic Church and executed over three hundred Protestants. The religious situation became more stable under the long reign of Queen Elizabeth (1558-1603), with the re-establishment of the Church of England as the state church.

Coverdale's Bible of 1535, which was allowed to circulate in England even while Tyndale was in prison, was not his own translation made from the originals. He revised Tyndale's New Testament and made use of his published Old Testament translations; otherwise, though he apparently knew some Hebrew, he made the translation from the German of Luther and others, and the Latin of Pagninus and the Vulgate. The title page of some editions said that the Bible was "faithfully and truly translated out of Douche and Latyn in to Englishe" ("Douche" is German). The free circulation of his Bible was doubtless promoted by its fulsome dedication to Henry VIII and the fact that Coverdale signed his name to the prologue to distinguish it from Tyndale's. Coverdale's own translations in this Bible are distinguished by felicity in phrasing and smoothness in sentence structure, not by great accuracy, since they were not made from the original languages.

The next version of the English Bible was published in 1537 under the name of "Thomas Matthew." This was a composite work, consisting of Tyndale's revised New Testament and

Pentateuch, Coverdale's version of the books from Ezra through Malachi and the Apocrypha, and a previously unknown translation of the Old Testament books from Joshua through 2 Chronicles. It is most probable that the last-named were the translations made by Tyndale but not published in his lifetime, and that "Thomas Matthew" was a pseudonym for John Rogers. Rogers was a friend and follower of Tyndale, whom he met in Antwerp. He was so much influenced by the views of Tyndale that he left the Catholic Church, was married (and had eleven children), and moved to Wittenberg in Germany. Rogers seems to have been entrusted with the unpublished work of Tyndale, and included it in this edition. He edited the whole work to a limited extent.

This Bible was in one respect the first "authorized version." The title page says that it was "Set forth with the Kinges most gracyous lycence." King Henry probably was not aware of the fact that this version was largely the work of one who had been burned at the stake a short time before.

John Rogers himself met a martyr's fate under Queen Mary. In her reign the Roman Catholics returned to power, and Rogers was summoned to trial for his views. He maintained that the pope had no more authority than other bishops, and was condemned to be burned at the stake.

Taverner's Bible, 1539, was the only version in this century produced by a layman. He was a lawyer, and a brilliant Greek scholar who sometimes quoted the law in Greek. He was once imprisoned at Oxford for reading Tyndale's Testament. He revised Matthew's Bible, with relatively few changes. In the Old Testament they are very slight, but his knowledge of Greek led him to make more changes in the New Testament.

The Great Bible of 1539 was the work of Coverdale; it is usually considered the first authorized English Bible, because its preparation was authorized in advance. Matthew's Bible was an embarrassment to the church authorities when it became evident that so much of it was Tyndale's translation, and the situation was confused when Coverdale's earlier edition also was given the king's license. Coverdale was therefore commissioned by Thomas Cromwell, secretary to Henry VIII and Vicar General, to prepare an edition that would supersede both. But Coverdale did not translate the Bible anew from Hebrew and Greek. He revised his own previous version and Matthew's Bible, making use of various helps, such as the Latin translation of the New Testament by Erasmus, and a new Latin translation of the Old Testament by Sebastian Münster.

The Great Bible was so called because of its large size. The pages measured 16½ x 11 inches, and it was elaborately printed, with a fine woodcut on the title page which shows King Henry VIII, with Cranmer and Cromwell, distributing Bibles to the people, who cry "Vivat Rex [Live the King!]" and "God save the King." The title pages of the 1540 and later editions declared, "This is the Byble apoynted to the use of the churches." The Archbishop of York ordered all curates to provide a Bible for each church, and to have it chained in an open place in the church. The people eagerly gathered around these Bibles and read them; sometimes they read and argued so loudly even during the church services that they had to be quieted. The Bibles were expensive: the price of a Bible, well bound and clasped, was fixed at twelve shillings, equivalent to about four weeks' wages of a skilled laborer. Many were placed in churches, but few in homes.

The Great Bible went through seven editions, but toward the end of Henry's reign a reaction set in against the free and open reading of the Bible in English. In 1543 Parliament issued restrictions which forbade the reading of the Bible by women (except noble and gentlewomen), artificers, apprentices, journeymen, servingmen of the degrees of yeomen, husbandmen, and laborers, on pain of a month's imprisonment.

In 1546 a royal decree forbade anyone to have Tyndale's or Coverdale's New Testament. King Henry VIII, addressing Parliament with tears in his eyes, complained that "the book was disputed, rhymed, sung and jangled in every alehouse and tavern." Many Bibles were destroyed or mutilated. But Henry was succeeded in 1547 by Edward VI, who was devoted to the Bible and promoted its reading.

No Bibles were published in English in the reign of Queen Mary, for she re-established the Roman Catholic Church, as we have seen. Many of those who had promoted the translation and reading of the Bible were executed, including Archbishop Cranmer. Coverdale was among those who left England at this time. Many Protestant leaders and scholars fled to Geneva, where John Calvin was at the height of his influence. It was here that the next important English Bible was translated and published, to be known as the Geneva Bible.

The Geneva Bible was clearly a Protestant translation, and it did much to promote Protestant ideas. It was published in handy quarto size (9½ x 6¾ inches) and in a clear Roman type; the verses were numbered, and there were extensive notes, mostly explanatory in nature but some strongly polemic against Catholics.

The Geneva Bible was an excellent translation, more accurate than any other English Bible to this time. It made large use of Tyndale, so far as his work was available, and the revisers had better Greek texts from which to translate. The Geneva New Testament was largely the work of William Whittingham, brother-in-law of Calvin and minister to the English congregation in Geneva. He probably led a small group in the production of the Old Testament.

Because of its small and inexpensive size, its accuracy, and its helpful notes, the Geneva Bible had a wide circulation, and became the household Bible of the English-speaking world for several generations. Between 1560 and 1644, at least 140 editions of the New Testament or whole Bible were published, and it was popular even after the publication of the King James Version. It was the Bible of Shakespeare and the Puritans, and was well known in the early American colonies.

The Geneva Bible is sometimes called "The Breeches Bible," because of the rendering of Genesis 3:7, where it is said that Adam and Eve "sewed figge tree leaves together, and made themselves breeches." This rendering was not unique, however, for the word had been used previously by Wyclif.

The Geneva Bible was dedicated to Queen Elizabeth, but was not generally acceptable to the leaders of the Church of England because of its strong Protestant bias. A move was set on foot for a new Bible to be produced by the English bishops, led by the archbishop of Canterbury. This version was published in 1568, and is called The Bishops' Bible, because a majority of the translators were bishops. Though it received official sanction, it was uneven in quality. There was no general supervision, and the separate revisers were left to go their own way. Some were, of course, better scholars than others. While some followed the Great Bible closely, others followed the Geneva. The Bishops' Bible has been termed a backward-looking version, adding little to what had been done before. However, the second edition of it, 1572, was the official basis for the King James Version.

One note in the Bishops' Bible is of special interest to Americans. On Psalm 45:9, which mentions the gold of Ophir, this explanation appears: "Ophir is thought to be the Ilande in the West coast, of late founde by Christopher Colombo: from whence at this day is brought most fine golde."

In our discussion of the history of the English Bible, we have implied that Protestants usually favored the making of translations into English while Roman Catholics opposed it. This is true as a general statement, but the situation was not as simple as might appear.

The Bible used in the Roman Catholic Church was the Latin Vulgate, and its worship was in Latin. The attitude of the church in the Middle Ages toward translations into the vernacular of any country was generally one of distrust, especially of the whole Bible. Translations were allowed for missionary purposes, and among professing Christians translations of Bible portions were permitted as aids to devotion and for religious instruction. In the earliest period the Gospels and the Psalter were the portions most often translated.

There were a number of reasons for the Catholic attitude. Pope Gregory VII in the eleventh century explained that God wanted Scripture to be a secret in certain places, "lest, if it were plainly apparent to all men, perchance it would be little esteemed and be subject to disrespect; or it might be falsely understood by those of mediocre learning, and lead to error."[1] Sometimes it was held that the vernacular English was too rude and coarse a language to express the great truths of the faith. The church always felt that laymen as well as priests needed the authoritative interpretation of the Bible along with the text. In the time of Wyclif, some said that translating the Bible into the language of the masses was like throwing pearls before swine.

Yet there were some Roman Catholics who did not take this position. Erasmus, the Dutch humanist who had some Protestant ideas but died a faithful adherent of the Roman church, said that he wished that even women could read the gospel and the Epistles of Paul, and wrote: "We cannot call any man a Platonist, unless he have read the works of Plato. Yet call we them Christian, yea and divines, which never have read the Scriptures of Christ."[2]

---

[1]Quoted by Luther A. Weigle, *The English New Testament from Tyndale to the Revised Standard Version* (New York: Abingdon Press, 1949), p. 29. This is in a letter written by the pope to the king of Bohemia who had asked permission for his monks to recite the divine office in the Slavonic language.

[2]*Ibid.*, p. 33. Quoted from Erasmus' preface to his Greek New Testament of 1516.

In the events surrounding the break between the Roman church and the establishment of the Church of England, we must remember that many who refused to recognize the authority of the pope in Rome continued to adhere largely to the Catholic faith, rather than to the Protestant faith as represented by Luther, Calvin, and other reformers. There were various shades of Protestant belief. Translation of the Bible into the English language could serve to strengthen the national church in England, and there were some in that country who wished to use the Bible to create a strong English monarch, supported by the doctrine of the divine right of kings.

The situation was not simply that Protestants favored, and Catholics opposed, the Englishing of the Bible. Often the differences arose over the words to be used in translation, and over the notes that went along with the text. There were certain words which Protestants generally favored and Catholics opposed—for example, congregation instead of church, elder for priest, overseer for bishop, minister for deacon, image for idol, repentance for penitence, repent for do penance, and others. Around words such as these the Protestant-Catholic battles raged.

The notes that accompanied the text of the Bible often contained either Protestant or Catholic bias or polemic. For example, the Geneva Bible explained that the "angel of the bottomless pit" in Revelation 9:11 was the pope. On the other hand, the Rheims-Douai Version, to be discussed shortly, explained that the two masters of Matthew 6:24 which no man can serve are "God and Baal, Christ and Calvin, Masse and Communion, the Catholike Church and Heretical Conventicles."

Toward the end of the sixteenth century, Roman Catholics took steps to provide a version in English. This resulted in the production of the Rheims-Douai Version, sometimes known simply as the Douai Version.

This version was made by English Catholic exiles, as the Geneva Bible had been produced by Protestant exiles from England. Early in Elizabeth's reign, a Jesuit English college was founded at Douai in France. The New Testament version was published in 1582, at a time when the college was being conducted at Rheims. The college moved to Douai, and the Old Testament was published there in 1610, the printing of it having been held up for lack of funds. Most of the work on this Bible was done by Gregory Martin; he had been a fellow of St. John's College, Oxford, but renounced Protestantism and became a lecturer in the Catholic college.

The purpose of this version was to counteract the heresies of the Geneva Bible and other versions; it was also intended to provide Catholic preachers in English with a Bible from which they could quote. It was not at first officially sanctioned by the church, and was intended more for the priesthood rather than for laymen.

The Douai Version was made from the Latin Vulgate, not from the languages in which the Bible was written. The Catholics claimed that the Hebrew and Greek editions had been corrupted by Jews and heretics, and the Latin was accurately translated from the original languages when the texts were purer. The language of this version is a highly Latinate English, a far cry from the language of Tyndale. An extensive revision of the Old Testament was published in 1750 by Dr. Richard Challoner, with considerable improvements in the English.

Looking back to the time that Tyndale first published the New Testament in English while an exile in Germany, we must say that this was a most remarkable period in literary and religious history. It started with a version made by one who was a competent scholar and a literary genius, with the courage to pursue his task against great discouragements, and willing to give his very life to it. In the seventy-five year period that followed, no fewer than seven versions were produced, and the idea finally prevailed that the Bible should be made available for the average man in a language he could understand. In this way the Bible was unlocked, largely through the insistence of men of Protestant persuasion that the Bible proclaims the Word of God for all men. At the end of the period, grudging and partial assent to the idea was given by the Roman Catholics. The blood of martyrs and the many toilsome hours of patient scholarship had won the day.

The King James Version

When James I followed Queen Elizabeth on the throne (1603), England was a strong power in Europe, the nation was at peace and prosperous, and English literature was at the zenith of its golden age. The English church was definitely separated from Rome, but there were religious dissensions of various kinds—particularly between the Anglicans who were largely Catholic in doctrine, and the Puritans who were Protestants with Calvinistic beliefs. King James called a conference in his second year, "for hearing and for the determining things pretended to be amiss in the church." The only fruit of this conference, held at Hampton Court near London, resulted from a casual suggestion by a Puritan, John Reynolds, that a new translation of the Bible be made. James I eagerly adopted the idea. The king fancied himself to be a scholar and aspired to literary fame; he had written a paraphrase of the Book of Revelation, and had translated the Psalms into meter. James I appointed 54 men to make the translation (the names of 47 are now known), and urged them to the task. There is no record that he provided any funds, or that he did any of the work of translation; it has been said that for the version which bears his name he furnished "only enthusiasm."

Certain specific rules were laid down for the new version. The Bishops' Bible was to be followed as the basic version, but the following were to be consulted and used if they agreed better with the original text: Tyndale's, Matthew's, Coverdale's, the Great Bible, and Geneva. No marginal notes were to be used, except as necessary for the explanation of Hebrew and Greek words. The old "ecclesiastical words" were to be kept—e.g. church instead of congregation.

The translators were divided into six companies, and to each company was assigned a section of the Bible (including the Apocrypha). The companies met at Oxford, Cambridge, and Westminster, two at each place. Every member was expected to translate all of the section assigned his company, and then the members came together for consultation, to agree on a text. Suggestions were invited from scholars and divines who were not appointed to the committee. Then a smaller committee of twelve (two from each company) was appointed to go over the work of the various companies, and iron out discrepancies and settle difficulties. Finally, the whole was turned over to Dr. Thomas Bilson, bishop of Winchester, and Dr. Myles Smith, to prepare it for publication. The King James version came from the press in 1611.

The members of the committee included scholars of Oxford and Cambridge, and parish ministers. They were not all equally learned, but must have had varying gifts. Perhaps the most learned of all was Dr. Lancelot Andrewes, dean of Winchester, of whom it was said that he spent his holidays learning new languages, and that he might have been interpreter-general at the Tower of Babel.

The King James Version was not intended to be a fresh, new translation. It was officially a revision of the Bishops' Bible. Careful studies have shown that the version really owes most to Tyndale, the Geneva Bible, and the Rheims New Testament, in that order. The one individual whose work shines most through the pages of the King James Version is William Tyndale; his translation set the tone of simplicity, plainness of speech, and economy of words which characterize the version.

The language of the King James Version was not the language of 1611 in all respects. As a revision of earlier works, it retains some archaic and old-fashioned expressions. An oft-quoted sentence from the famous preface made clear the purpose: "Truly (good Christian Reader) wee never thought from the beginning, that we should neede to make a new Translation, nor yet to make of a bad one a good one . . . but to make a good one better, or out of many good ones, one principall good one."

This version should be called the King James Version rather than The Authorized Version. It was in fact the third or fourth, not the first, authorized version. It soon came to be the version most read in the churches, superseding the Bishops' Bible, but in the hands of the common people the Geneva Bible continued to be popular for half a century or more—probably because of its handy size, its full notes, and its clear-cut Protestant flavor. The King James Version was ecclesiastically a middle-of-the-road version, since the committee included both Anglicans and Puritans, though no nonconformists. It met some violent opposition. A great Hebrew scholar, Dr. Hugh Broughton, said of this version: "It is so ill done. Tell his Majesty that I had rather be rent in pieces with wild horses, than any such translation by my consent should be urged upon poor churches." (Since he was a cantankerous individual, he had been left off the committee on purpose, and his reaction may be the result of pique rather than considered opinion.) Some people complained that the new version supported the king's belief in witches. Various other criticisms were made, but by the middle of the seventeenth century it had won its way into the hearts and minds of English-speaking people by its sheer merit, and has remained the most beloved version since.

The King James Version was by no means perfect. It had some grievous faults. It is an uneven translation, and some of its inconsistencies are difficult to explain. No doubt some of the members of the committee were better scholars than others, and the task of harmonizing discrepancies and inconsistencies was not fully carried out. Some parts of the version are of high literary merit, but others are more obscure than they should be. The Hebrew and Greek texts on which the revisers had to depend were far from perfect. The Greek text was based mostly on late medieval manuscripts.

One fact concerning the King James Version is often overlooked by readers today: the version printed in 1611 was quite different from the one we read today. The spelling, of course, has been modernized, but many changes have been introduced from time to time, by editors and printers over whom there has been no effective control.

The greatness of the King James Version resulted from a happy combination of factors. It came at the climax of an 85-year period in which many translations of the Bible were made and there were great debates over numerous problems of Bible translation and interpretation. It was made in a time of great literature; Shakespeare did not die until five years after it was published. The committee of revisers were men of learning, dedicated to their task, and using for the first time in the history of English Bible translation the method of face-to-face conference. And, it appeared at a time when religion and religious tensions were a lively factor in English life.

English and American Revised Versions

The King James Version remained the supreme translation for two and a half centuries. It was used in homes and churches, and had great influence on English literature as well as on religion. In the middle of the nineteenth century, however, many scholars saw that the time had come for an official revision.

In the meantime many private translations were published. Of these we mention only three. John Wesley, father of Methodism, published his translation of the New Testament in 1755, when he was too weak to travel and preach but when, as he said, "blessed be God, I can still read, and write, and think." Alexander Campbell, a leader among early Disciples of Christ, issued in 1826 a new version with the title, *The Sacred Writings of the Apostles and Evangelists of Jesus Christ, Commonly styled the New Testament.* He based this version on the translation of three scholars of the Church of Scotland—George Campbell, James Macknight, and Philip Doddridge—making some changes in the interest of accuracy and readability. It went through six editions, selling at least 40,000 copies, but its value as a popular version was marred by Campbell's tendency to use ornate words of Latin origin in a somewhat formal style. Noah Webster, of dictionary fame, published in 1833 a translation of the Bible, using special care to employ words in common usage at the time.

There were several reasons why a movement began in the Church of England for an official revision of the King James. Perhaps the principal reason was that many early manuscripts of the New Testament had been discovered, including the fourth-century codices mentioned above (p. 286), which made it possible to establish a far more accurate text of the Greek New Testament than was possible for the King James revisers. Then, of course, much progress had been made in various areas of biblical scholarship, and changes had occurred in English so that the King James was becoming more and more obscure and archaic. In 1870 the Church of England, through the Convocation of Canterbury, took steps to form a committee of 54 to revise the King James Version. The committee included nonconformists as well as members of the established church, one being a Unitarian. Shortly, American scholars were invited to form a committee to work with the English group; twenty-three Americans served on the committee, but they did not meet with the English scholars, all of their consultations being carried on by correspondence.

The English Revised Version of the New Testament was published in 1881, and the Old Testament four years later. The New Testament met with a great response, three million copies being sold in the first year. Two Chicago newspapers printed the entire New Testament on a single day, shortly after publication. The Old Testament met with less enthusiastic reception, and before long severe criticisms of the entire project were made.

Many of the proposals made by the co-operating American committee were rejected by the English scholars, but a list of the most important ones were published as an appendix in the English Revision. The American committee had agreed to withhold publishing its own version for fourteen years, but several unauthorized versions incorporating American preferences were published. In 1901 the committee officially published the American Standard Version, a new revision of the King James that went beyond merely incorporating the preferred readings of the Americans.

Both the English and American Revisions were widely used, and were recognized as more accurate translations than the King James. Yet, there were many criticisms. Some of these arose simply out of reaction against anything different from the King James Version. The two important criticisms were: first, the revisers attempted to use the Elizabethan English of the King James Version, and actually became in some instances more archaic than the King James; and second, the revisions were often overliteral. The first criticism was more appropriate for the English Revision than the American. As for the second criticism, we may note that Charles H. Spurgeon, the London preacher, said that the New Testament in this version was "strong in Greek, weak in English."

The Revised Standard and other Modern Versions

Dissatisfaction with the American Standard Version, rapid progress in biblical scholarship, and increasing recognition of the archaic nature of the King James Version led to the making of the Revised Standard Version. This is the only version in the Tyndale-King James tradition which has been made on the initiative of a large group of American churches, by American scholars. It resulted from official action of the International Council of Religious Education, a co-operative organization of forty Protestant denominations in the United States and Canada. The copyright of the American Standard Version passed to that Council in 1928, and it appointed a committee to have charge of the text and consider whether a new version was desirable. The committee reported favorably on the latter question, and the Council authorized the version in 1937, specifying that the version should "embody the best results of modern scholarship as to the meaning of the Scriptures, and express this meaning in English diction which is designed for use in public and private worship and preserves those qualities which have given to the King James Version a supreme place in English literature." The New Testament appeared in 1946, the Old Testament in 1952, and the Apocrypha in 1957. The interdenominational committee responsible for this version consisted of 37 members, with an advisory board of fifty members. When the National Council of Churches was formed in 1950, the Council which had originally authorized the version was merged with other bodies to become the Division of Christian Education.

The Revised Standard Version attempted to make full use of the resources of modern biblical scholarship, as the American Standard Version had done, but it went beyond the latter in using English which is in current usage in America—not slang, of course, but the living language of educated people today. Nevertheless, it is not a completely fresh and new version, for it attempts to remain within the tradition established by Tyndale and continued through the King James and the English and American Revisions.

When the whole Bible in this version was published in 1952, it met with a mixed reaction, as all versions have. It was widely acclaimed in many quarters for its scholarship and clarity, and many copies of it were sold. In other quarters it was condemned for its "modernism," and copies of it were publicly burned. This version has withstood criticism, and has been widely adopted in the pulpits of America and in the educational literature of many denominations. It has been acclaimed in England as well as the United States, and has been praised by Roman Catholic as well as Protestant scholars.

The Standard Bible Committee is a permanent committee of the National Council of Churches. It meets from time to time to make minor improvements or corrections in the Revised Standard Version, so that it may continue to be up-to-date both in its scholarship and in its diction. Though it is not a perfect version (and no version is perfect!), it is perhaps the best version for the average reader in America today.

Every reader of the Bible, however, can profit from consultting other translations, of which a large number have been produced in the twentieth century. Space is not available to mention all of them, and the following list is necessarily brief.

The whole Bible has been translated by James Moffatt (1924); the New Testament is an excellent translation, giving the meaning accurately in graceful English, but the Old Testament is often too free in its rendering of the Hebrew. One of the most useful versions is *The Bible: An American Translation,* published by the University of Chicago Press, sometimes known as the Smith-Goodspeed version. The New

Testament and Apocrypha were translated by E. J. Goodspeed, and the Old Testament by a small group of scholars under the lead of J. M. P. Smith. There have been many translations of the New Testament, such as *The Twentieth Century New Testament* (1904) by a group of scholars, *The Centenary New Testament* of Mrs. Helen Barrett Montgomery (1924), and the translations of R. F. Weymouth (1903), and J. B. Phillips (1947-58). The last-named often puts the New Testament into striking modern phrases that vigorously convey the meaning. *The Basic Bible* (1950) is remarkable in that it puts the whole Bible into a vocabulary of only 1,000 words— the 850 words of basic English plus 150 words necessary for the Bible. J. B. Phillips has also translated Amos, Hosea, First Isaiah, and Micah in *Four Prophets* (1963).

The New English Bible was published in complete form, with the Apocrypha, in 1970. It is a version sponsored by several denominations in England and Scotland. It is a fresh, new translation which attempts to present the Bible accurately and clearly in contemporary speech. It does not claim to be in the Tyndale-King James tradition, and is intended for private reading and religious education rather than for use in public worship. An unusual feature is that, in addition to the biblical scholars who work on it, there is a panel of experts in literary usage. While this version occasionally uses words with specifically British meanings, it can be read with great profit by Americans.

A Jewish version of the Old Testament was published in 1917 by the Jewish Publication Society of America; this version is now in the process of revision. The first part of the revised Jewish version was published early in 1963 as *The Torah: The Five Books of Moses.*

Roman Catholic scholars have been active in the publication of new translations, especially since the papal encyclical of Pope Pius XII in 1943 which encouraged the study of the Bible and the making of translations from the original Hebrew and Greek. Ronald Knox translated the whole Bible into highly readable English (1950), working primarily from the Latin Vulgate with some consultation of the originals. *The New American Bible* appeared in complete form in 1970. Parts of it had been published earlier as The Confraternity Edition. Four Protestant scholars assisted in the final stage of the translation. *The Jerusalem Bible* was published in 1966. It is based on a French version made by a committee of which the chairman and some of the translators were on the faculty of the École Biblique in Jerusalem—hence its name. Six Catholic scholars have been members of the Revised Standard Version Committee since 1969.

The Meaning of the Story

We began this chapter by raising the questions: Can we really understand the Hebrew and Greek in which the Bible was written? Can we rely on the English translations that are available for our reading today? The answer to both questions is, Yes—but this answer cannot be unqualified and absolute.

No book from ancient times has been so often and so reverently copied, studied, translated, and interpreted as the Bible. We have far more Hebrew and Greek manuscripts of the Bible than of any other ancient book. Hebrew and Greek have never been completely "dead" languages, for they have always been read and used by some people—even if only by scholars in their studies—and the modern spoken Hebrew in the land of Israel and the native tongue of Greece are descended from those ancient languages. The Bible has been read and studied by all kinds of people, and for many different purposes. The results of all of these facts is that we *can* have confidence in the translations that are available to us, for it *is possible* to understand the languages in which the Bible was written.

We have seen that, though new versions have been needed from time to time, nearly every new translation has been attacked or severely criticized. Early translators were burned to death; recently, gentler critics have burned the new translations. Harsh criticism met the publication of the King James Version before it became widely used and beloved, and there was violent opposition to Jerome's Vulgate which was to become the official Bible of the Roman Catholic Church and be placed in some respects above the Bible in the original languages. Such opposition has grown largely out of distrust of that which is new and different in an area of life so personal and so important as religion. Fortunately, there have always been translators ready to bear the brunt of the attacks because of their conviction that the Bible must be understood, and must be made available in the vernacular.

Our story should convince us, however, that no translation is perfect, and that the process of searching for new manuscripts, of studying and interpreting the Bible, and of rendering it into the language of everyday life must continue. In the future new manuscripts will be uncovered that will lead us back closer to the autographs of individual books. Progress will be made in understanding Hebrew and Greek, and in interpreting the Bible correctly. English will change as long as it is a living, spoken language. Better and more perfect translations will be published.

Tyndale wrote in the prologue to the first printed English New Testament: if other men "perceive in any places that I have not attained the very sense of the tongue, or meaning of the Scripture, or have not given the right English word, that they put to their hands to amend it, remembering that so is their duty to do. For we have not received the gifts of God for ourselves only, or for to hide them: but for to bestow them unto the honoring of God and Christ, and edifying of the congregation, which is the body of Christ."

IX

the authority
of the bible

WHAT AUTHORITY DOES THE BIBLE HAVE FOR twentieth-century Christians? In the preceding chapters we have emphasized the historical nature of the Bible. It was produced by many persons over a long period of time, and the modern reader who wishes to understand it must approach it from a historical perspective. The Bible was completed about two thousand years ago, and it represents a selection from a large number of individual books that might have been included in its covers. Those who wrote the Bible lived long ago and far away. How can a book such as this have decisive authority for Christians in twentieth-century America?

Let us begin by admitting that virtually all Christians base their beliefs and practices upon the Bible in one way or another. This is true of both Protestants and Catholics of all stripes, and of Christian groups that do not like to be included in either category. The Protestant reformers of the sixteenth century set up "Scripture alone" as the authority, but Roman Catholics also believe that their faith and practices rest upon the Bible. The principal difference is that Roman Catholics place tradition alongside Scripture as authoritative, and believe that the church is the official interpreter of Scripture, since—they maintain—it was the church that produced Scripture in the first place. Those Christian groups which have put less emphasis on the authority of Scripture than others have been the highly individualistic and mystical groups, such as the Quakers, who have laid stress on direct guidance of the Spirit. Yet even they accept the authority of the Bible in many matters, and find in the Bible a basis for their views.

If this statement is true, then it poses for us a difficult question: how can the Bible be the basis of authority for so many groups of Christians whose beliefs and practices differ so widely from one another? Surely there must be different ways of viewing the authority of Scripture.

It is important, therefore, for every reader of the Bible to straighten out his own thinking about the authority of the Bible, deciding what the Bible *is*, and what it *is not*, and in what ways he can follow it as authoritative for his own life. Rather than be dismayed by the great variety of ways in which the Bible has been interpreted and followed in the past, he must accept the challenge to decide for himself what authority the Bible really has for him. As he does this, his decision must rest upon a knowledge of what is in the Bible and what it actually says, not upon what others have said about it. Any doctrine or theory regarding its authority should be *derived from* the Bible and a genuine knowledge of its contents, and not be *imposed upon* the Bible because of what someone else tells us we ought to believe about it. A discussion of the authority of the Bible properly belongs at the end of a book about the Bible rather than at the beginning.

Because this decision is highly personal, the present writer proceeds to discuss the authority of the Bible with some diffidence. He does not wish to impose upon anyone his own theory concerning the Bible's authority. The following discussion must be read, therefore, as a series of suggestions that arise out of one person's study of the Bible. They are, we believe, consistent with the point of view taken throughout the present volume, but they are intended to stimulate the reader's own reactions, not to suggest that he accept in full the attitude here expressed.

What the Bible Is Not

Before discussing in an affirmative way what the Bible is and what authority it may have for us, we must clear the ground by saying what the Bible is not. There are false ways of viewing the Bible and its authority.

(1) The Bible is not a good-luck charm, a fetish, or an idol. Many Christians seem to feel that the Bible is a book that is "nice to have around the house," for some kind of bad fortune may result if there is no copy of it around. It is looked upon in somewhat the same manner as a rabbit's foot or horseshoe, expected to bring good luck just by being there.

Many altars of Christian churches contain an open Bible, in addition to or instead of a cross. When so placed, the Bible should be a symbol of the "open Bible" available for every Christian to read; it should not be an object of worship. Worship of the Bible itself, or of some doctrine about the Bible, is a dangerous form of idolatry.

The Bible is not a fetish. It is a book made up of pages that have words upon them. Those words were meant to be read— either silently in private, or aloud in public. Only when the Bible is read and listened to can it have value and authority. No age has ever had as high a rate of literacy as ours, but if we use our ability to read only for comics and sport pages, what does it profit us? We have the possibility of reading the Bible more widely and more intelligently than ever before in history. It is a pity if we look upon it as an idol to be worshiped, rather than as a book to be read.

(2) The Bible is not a complete, detailed blueprint for our individual lives, telling us everything that we must believe and do; nor is it a blueprint for the church, describing in every detail its organization and its ongoing life.

The Bible has very often been taken in this way. Individuals and churches have found in the Bible support for many different patterns of life and structure, and have argued endlessly over details that seemed to them important. Separate groups have been able to support their points of view out of Scripture, but usually by lifting out of the Bible certain teachings or certain instructions while ignoring others. Parts of the Bible are interpreted very literally, while others are ignored or explained away.

The way out of this dilemma is to see that the Bible does not offer blueprints, but rather principles and guidelines. It sets forth a way of life, a spirit by which men may live together and before God, and above all it sets before us an Object of faith. A fundamental text for all to remember is: "the letter killeth, but the spirit giveth life" (2 Cor. 3:6 KJV). Much fanatacism can be avoided if we look at the Bible as a whole, and seek to appropriate its underlying spirit and its overarching purposes. This will give us a tolerance and understanding of others who differ in details but are akin in purpose and intention.

(3) The Bible is not a book that is verbally inspired in all of its parts, and therefore wholly infallible and inerrant. It is not a book that is all on an equal plane of inspiration and authority, and therefore to be accepted or to be rejected as a whole.

There is no doubt that many people hold to this view of the Bible, or think that this is the view they ought to hold. It is proclaimed in many quarters, and many Christians therefore think they must look at the Bible in this way. Some have lost their Christian faith when they came to believe that they could not accept the Bible in this manner, and could find no other acceptable way of looking at it.

Because this view is so widely held, we wish to set down several specific reasons why we think it is false and misleading.

(a) In previous chapters we have seen that the Bible has come down to us in copies of copies of copies of the originals; we do not have a single book, not even a single word, of the Bible in the handwriting of its first author. For practical purposes this fact is not very significant, for we do know the Bible well enough to have much confidence in the Hebrew and Greek texts that are now available, and in the translations made from them. But in all honesty we must admit we do not have all of the original words of the Bible, and this admission is very significant for any theory of complete infallibility or inerrancy. If we do not really know *all* of the original words, how can we say that they are wholly infallible and are equally inspired?

(b) Another honest admission must be made by scholars who study the original texts: in some cases we do not know the precise meaning of some words and some passages in the Bible. Many of these are of little importance, but some are passages that have been considered of crucial significance in Christian history. An outstanding example is Job 19:25-27. This is the passage that begins, "For I know that my Redeemer lives," but after one has read those words he runs into great difficulties in translating and understanding the following lines. Scholars have debated endlessly whether the words refer to resurrection or not, whether the redemption comes before death or after death, and who the Redeemer is— whether God or a mediator between man and God. The text is in reality so obscure that no scholar can be sure of the original meaning. It is not surprising that the Revised Standard Version has a note on Job 19:26 which says, "The meaning of this verse is uncertain." In the New Testament a striking example of our ignorance of the precise meaning of a single Greek word is found in the Lord's Prayer. It is the little word *epiousion* in the phrase, "Give us this day our *daily* bread." No one can be entirely sure that it really means "daily"; it may mean "for the morrow," or something else. Most scholars would agree that "daily" gives the idea expressed in the word, but they are not entirely certain.

Again, we must say that these points are not of really great significance in the Bible as a whole, but they are fatal for any theory of the complete verbal inspiration and infallibility of Scripture. If we do not know what every word means, how how can we say in all honesty that they are infallible?

(c) More important is the simple fact that the Bible, when taken as a whole, contains internal contradictions and inconsistencies. Some of these have to do with historical matters, while others have to do with religious teachings. For one who loves the Bible, it is painful to point these out, for they have been too often listed by disbelievers and agnostics. But Christian honesty compels the reader to admit that they are present.

In both the Old and New Testaments there are historical books that come from different hands and different times, covering the same periods and same facts, but without always agreeing in detail. First and Second Chronicles cover much of the same history as 1-2 Samuel and 1-2 Kings; indeed, the last-named books were used as sources by the editors of 1-2 Chronicles. Historical statements in these two sets of narratives sometimes differ, and the editors of 1-2 Chronicles present certain individuals in quite a different light from the earlier books—most notably King David, whose faults are ignored and whose virtues are extolled and exaggerated.

In the New Testament, there are some historical inconsistencies between the first three Gospels (the Synoptic Gospels) and the Gospel of John. They differ regarding the time in the life of Jesus when the cleansing of the temple took place, and regarding the date of the crucifixion. At many small points there are differences between the Four Gospels that should not be simply ignored or explained away.

More important than these historical discrepancies are the differences in religious teaching or religious outlook of various parts of the Bible. In the Old Testament the book of Esther presents a form of narrow nationalism that is unworthy of the best that can be found in both the Old and New Testaments. The author of the book of Ecclesiastes was unorthodox in his own time, and is unorthodox when compared with the rest of the Bible. No Christian today literally believes the following: "The fate of the sons of men and the fate of the beasts is the same; as one dies, so dies the other. They all have the same breath, and man has no advantage over the beasts; for all is vanity" (Ecclesiastes 3:19).

The Old Testament is valuable for the Christian, but it contains some teachings that are sub-Christian, and the New Testament itself contains teachings that are sub-Christian when compared with the best in that Testament.

(d) The Bible contains statements that cannot be reconciled with known facts of history, or with prevalent scientific beliefs of our day. We have been concerned in the last point with internal inconsistencies of the Bible; here we are concerned with inconsistencies between the Bible on the one hand and modern science and history on the other.

A striking example of a historical inaccuracy in the Old Testament is found in Daniel 5:30-31. Those verses say that Darius the Mede received the kingship of Babylonia from king Belshazzar, when the latter was slain. "Darius the Mede" was not the king who overthrew the Babylonian kingdom upon the death of Belshazzar. One of the best-known facts of history is that Cyrus the Persian conquered Babylon and overthrew the kingdom that had been ruled by Belshazzar and his father. This is a simple historical fact that cannot be refuted. There are similar errors that could be cited from the book of Daniel and some other biblical books.

Perhaps more important for the average reader of the Bible is our assertion that the Bible contains statements that cannot be reconciled with modern science.

The history of the warfare between science and biblical religion is a long and often tragic story. From one point of view the scientists have steadily won, and the defenders of the Bible have steadily lost or continually retreated. It should be entirely clear now that we cannot harmonize many statements and viewpoints of the Bible with scientific views generally held today. The account of creation in Genesis—or, in reality, the two separate accounts in Genesis 1 and 2—cannot be harmonized with views held by scientists today concerning the origin of the world. The accounts in Genesis of a worldwide flood and of the origin of languages at the tower of Babel do not appear credible to modern scientists and linguists. The whole modern view of the universe is very different from that held in biblical times, when men conceived of a three-storied universe, with heaven above, hell (or Sheol) beneath, and a flat earth between. The modern conception of natural law makes it difficult for many twentieth-century men to accept literally all of the miracles of the Bible.

We should not expect the Bible to contain modern scientific views, and we should not expect to be able to harmonize modern science with the scientific viewpoints held in ancient Israel and early Christianity. The warfare between science and religion has been largely unnecessary. The Bible is not primarily a manual of science or book of history. It is a religious book. God alone is infallible. In revealing himself through biblical writers God has made use of men who were human, and therefore fallible, who necessarily held the scientific views of their day.

After saying this, however, we must go on to say that it is wrong to deify science or idolize modern scientists. We can be certain that some of our present scientific viewpoints and beliefs will not stand the test of time; there is little doubt that many will be superseded. Nevertheless, it is not probable that we shall return to the scientific viewpoints held in biblical times.

(e) It is not true, as some people say, that the Bible claims full infallibility for itself. The passages most often quoted to prove this are 2 Timothy 3:16; 2 Peter 1:21; and Revelation 22:18-19. Anyone who will read these passages carefully will see that they do not claim complete infallibility for *all* of the Bible; at most they claim inspiration for a part of the Bible, and inspiration does not necessarily imply the kind of infallibility and inerrancy which some want to attribute to the Bible.

In the Old Testament, some of the prophets on occasion changed their points of view, and even some of their predictions. In the New Testament, Paul sometimes made it clear that he spoke his own opinion, not the command of the Lord (1 Corinthians 7:12, 25).

Even if the Bible did claim for itself complete infallibility, and inspiration in every jot and tittle, would we have to accept the claims of the Bible for itself? Would that not be completely circular reasoning?

(f) Our final argument against this view of Scripture is that no one ever really accepts the whole of the Bible as completely inspired and utterly infallible. Everyone makes a selection within the Bible of that which is most important to him, and emphasizes certain parts at the expense of others. Contradictions are reconciled and difficulties are banished either by allegorical interpretations or by simply ignoring parts of the Bible. Most of those who hold strongly to the view of literal inspiration and entire infallibility do so either because they feel that they are expected to do so, or because they wish to protect some of their most cherished beliefs from criticism. The dogma of verbal inspiration or complete infallibility "does less than justice to the Bible itself, in the interests of a theory about the Bible," as C. H. Dodd has well said.[1] When we speak of infallibility, we should confine that word to God alone; man in his finiteness is never sure that he knows God in an absolute and unconditioned manner. When we speak of inspiration, we should apply it to men and events rather than to written words. Inerrancy is a word that is appropriate to the religion of the Bible at its best, not to its history and science.

What the Bible Is

If we would understand the authority and meaning of the Bible for our own lives in our time, we must try to see what the Bible really is, if it is not any of the things we have described above. There are various ways of describing it in a positive way, but we believe that the following is one of the best.

The Bible is a record of God's disclosure of himself to men both in his acts in history and in his speaking to men; it is also a record of men's response to that disclosure—in what they both did and said, whether in faith or in rebellion, whether they understood him correctly or not.

---

[1] *The Authority of the Bible* (Harper Torchbooks; New York: Harper & Brothers, 1958), p. 12.

The Bible is not primarily a set of statements or propositions about God, but rather a record of God's revelation of himself on the stage of history. That history is found especially in the life of Israel, God's chosen people in Old Testament times; in the whole of the Christ event—his life, his teachings, his death, and his resurrection; and in the history of the early Christian community. The history of the Bible is sometimes called sacred history or salvation-history (a translation of the German *Heilsgeschichte*). It is a special type of history in that it relates what God has done for man and his salvation, but it is not divorced from universal history. The early pages of Genesis tell of the history of mankind before the choice of Abraham as one through whom all of the nations of the earth would be blessed. The Bible recognizes that God may act in the history of other nations (Amos 9:7), and that God's power and deity were known to mankind through his work of creation (Romans 1:19-21). But God disclosed himself in the history of Israel and of early Christianity as nowhere else.

In this salvation-history certain "mighty acts" of God stand out above others. In the Old Testament the Hebrews emphasized the exodus from Egypt as God's mightiest act of redemption, for in it they saw their release from the house of bondage into a new freedom that led to the covenant at Sinai and the settlement in the land of Canaan. They saw the hand of God in all of their history, even in the acts of judgment which led them into exile and into suffering.

For the Christian, the culmination and climax of God's revelation of himself in history is to be seen in the whole of the life of Jesus Christ—his birth in a stable, his life of humility and sacrifice, his teachings, his crucifixion on a cruel cross, his resurrection and ascension. God continued to act through the early Christian community as it sought to understand the meaning of Christ for its own life.

When we wish to know the nature of God, we look at what he has done, for his nature is revealed in his actions. He has revealed himself to be a God of both mercy and judgment, a Sovereign of the nation (or the church) and the individual, a Ruler of both history and nature, a God who at all times is concerned for man and his redemption.

Yet the Bible contains more than a record of what God has done in history; it records also what he has said—or, to be more precise, what men believed God said, and their interpretation of the significance of what God has done. In the Old Testament the prophets in particular spoke in the name of God, often prefixing their utterances with "Thus saith the LORD." We should think of them as inspired men who spoke as they believed God had spoken to them, but we do not have to view as the very word of God everything they said. In the New Testament God speaks to us especially through Jesus' teachings, as well as through his life. The author of Hebrews expresses the matter in this way: "In many and various ways God spoke of old to our fathers by the prophets; but in these last days he has spoken to us by a Son, whom he appointed the heir of all things, through whom also he created the world" (Hebrews 1:1-2).

We have said that the Bible is not only a record of what God has done and said to reveal himself, but also a record of men's response to him. In this way the Bible reflects human life, sometimes at its best, often at its worst. It does not fail to record the rebellions and failures of men as well as their obedience and fidelity. The Hebrew people are often depicted as disobeying their God and calling down upon themselves the judgments of the prophets. In the New Testament, the disciples of Jesus fled at the time of the crucifixion, deserting the one who had been their master. In the history of the earliest Christian community there were dissensions and misunderstandings, and even some of the outstanding leaders quarreled among themselves. The hope which the Bible offers to men in this world is that God can break through their rebellions and their sins to redeem them for himself.

Finding Authority in the Bible

With this kind of understanding of the nature of the Bible, how can we find authority in it for ourselves? How can we read it in such a way as to see its relevance for our life in the twentieth century? There are several specific suggestions that we can make in order to help the reader answer these questions for himself.

(1) The goal and purpose of our reading of the Bible should be to lead us to know the God who has disclosed himself in its history and within its words. It is not sufficient that we *know about* God, that we have an intellectual understanding of what the Bible says concerning him. We should have an encounter with the God who is revealed there, as we associate in our reading with those who found him in the past, and as we read the record of his actions in history.

We often approach the Bible with only an antiquarian interest, going to its pages as we would go into a museum. Or we read it merely to derive information from it. If we read the Bible as we ought, we shall come to know God for ourselves, believing that the same God who acted in ancient times works also in our lives, both individual and corporate, as we surrender ourselves to him.

As one reads the Bible in order to *know* God, he cannot predict in advance that he will really succeed, and if he does succeed, he cannot predict what God will say to him. If he goes to the Bible only to buttress beliefs long held or to seek support for his own prejudices, he will hardly come to know the God of the Bible. He is more likely to find in the Bible a challenge to a new way of life, to new forms of fidelity, to knowledge of a God he has not known before. He may find deepened security and profounder hope, and he may find courage to respond to the God who challenges him within the pages of the Bible. He must be prepared to have God *meet him* in God's own way.

(2) The Christian reader will encounter God especially in the life of Jesus Christ, as the climax of God's disclosure of himself and as the incarnation of God. Christ will become the object of his faith, and the standard by which he as a Christian will read the whole Bible. He can come to read the Bible as Paul read his Bible, when he found that Christ was the key to its understanding. This does not mean, of course, that he must read Christ into every page of the Old Testament by a false allegorizing; the Old Testament can contribute in many ways to his understanding of the life of Christ, but Christ will become the norm by which he understands the whole of the Scripture.

(3) Rather than assert that the Bible *is* the word of God, it is better to say that the Bible *contains* the word of God. Even more appropriate is the statement that the Bible may *become* for us the word of God as we read it. The first assertion is misleading because it implies that the whole of the Bible is in some objective way the word of God. We have seen that the whole Bible is not all on the same plane; some of it is sub-Christian, and thus is not the very word of God.

The other statements are more adequate because they insist that the reader must find the word of God within the words of the Bible as he reads them. He cannot do so if he reads in a passive manner; he must read expectantly, with the eyes of faith. As he does so, the word of God may speak to him, and he may hear that word. Some parts of the Bible may not be to him God's word. If he does not hold a false theory of verbal inspiration or of complete infallibility, he will not be disturbed by his failure to find God's word in some pages of the Bible.

The reader who approaches the Bible seeking to find within it God's word for himself must bring questions to it, and must expect to find answers within it. In this way he can enter into a dialogue with the Bible. If he listens, he may hear God speak to him within its pages, and he may speak in response.

"The Bible reading of all enlightened Christians," wrote Alexander Campbell, "generally terminates in a sacred dialogue between the Author and the reader."[2] This can happen if the reader approaches the Bible with the historical method, seeking first to understand what the authors of the Bible meant to say in their own time. Behind the authors of the Bible he may then hear the Author of the truth within the Bible, and carry on dialogue with him. In such a manner the Bible may become for the individual reader or hearer the word of God.

(4) As we search within the words of the Bible for the word of God, nothing can exempt us from the difficult task of "translating" the word of God in the Bible into terms that are meaningful in our own time and relevant to our needs.

We are not concerned here with that kind of linguistic translation which seeks to transfer the words of the Bible from the original Hebrew and Greek into modern English or some other modern tongue. We are concerned with the translation of the thought-forms of the Bible into the thought-forms of our day, and with the application of the spiritual and moral insights of the biblical authors into terms and principles that have relevance to modern problems and twentieth-century needs. It is never sufficient for us simply to archaize ourselves, and turn the calendar back to one of the centuries B.C. or the

---

[2] *Millennial Harbinger*, 1839, p. 38.

first century A.D. We may begin by doing that, but we should not be satisfied to remain in an ancient past.

A few examples will illustrate our meaning better than abstract discussion.

We have seen that in biblical times men thought of their universe as having three stories: heaven above, hell (or Sheol) beneath, and a flat earth on which men live. They believed that angels might descend from heaven to this earth, and that some men ascended direct to heaven; they thought at certain times that this earth contained a great host of demons, who caused disease and much trouble for man. They pictured this earth as the center of the universe, with the sun rising in the east and setting in the west as it went on its journey around the earth.

This is not the kind of universe in which we believe we live. Our universe has expanded immeasurably. Our earth is now known to be only a small planet in a solar system, revolving on an axis as it makes a journey around the sun. Our universe is made up of numberless constellations and galaxies, and it is not wholly improbable that life like ours exists on some other planets. We cannot locate heaven above and hell beneath. Only the most densely ignorant can now believe that our earth is flat, after several men have sped in orbit around this earth. We do not believe literally in demons as the cause of disease, nor do we have any experience with angels.

All of this means that, if we are to read the Bible intelligently so that it may become for us the word of God, we must translate many things within the Bible into the thought-forms of our time. Our understanding of the kind of universe within which we live will influence our understanding of the nature of heaven and hell, of resurrection and ascension, of the plausibility of some of the miracles recorded in the Bible, of the second coming of Christ, and many other things. It should lead us to seek to discover in the Bible that which is of lasting and permanent significance, as distinguished from the temporary thought-forms within which it is expressed.

Again, we may illustrate the need for translation by thinking of the message of an Old Testament prophet such as Amos. He lived in the middle of the eighth century B.C. His book contains some predictions regarding the future, but they are not the most important sections of it. Amos was a preacher to the people of his own time. As he observed the life of his day, he saw much injustice taking place. The wealthy were oppressing the poor; judges were taking bribes to convict the innocent and let the guilty go free; merchants were giving short measure and charging excessive prices. Many people were substituting a formal and sometimes elaborate worship of God for moral obedience. Amos called upon the people of his age to seek justice and righteousness, and to obey God's moral laws, if they wished to escape God's judgment upon them.

If we ask what is the relevance of this prophet's message for our day, we shall see that it is necessary for us to compare the conditions of our own time with those of the eighth century, and then consider how Amos' message is applicable, and in what respects it is not applicable. Does social injustice occur in our society? How similar are conditions in our highly industrialized, urban life to those in the relatively simple society in which Amos lived? Can we call upon men to give voluntary obedience to God, and thus be honest and forthright in all their dealings, or must the government in some areas force them to do so? Does God desire and demand justice and righteousness in our day as he did in Amos'? These are some of the questions we must consider as we attempt to translate the message of Amos into meaningful terms for the twentieth century. At some points we may see that he has no message for us, but at others we may see that he spoke in truth the word of God.

As we translate the meaning and message of the Bible for our own lives, we may feel the need in some areas to go beyond the specific teachings of the Bible. If we have a true encounter with the God of the Bible, we may see that his will for our lives is not the same as it was for biblical times, or that we comprehend that will differently. For example, the whole of the Bible takes for granted the institution of slavery. This is true of the New Testament as well as the Old. In ancient Israel slaves were not as numerous as in ancient Greece. The reason may not have been wholly a humanitarian one; it was often cheaper to employ free labor than to support slaves. Slavery existed in Palestine in New Testament times. Masters were often exhorted to treat their slaves with kindness. Yet, when Paul wrote to Philemon concerning the runaway slave Onesimus, he did not admonish Philemon to free him, but rather to treat him as a brother. Through many centuries of the Christian church slavery was defended as not only legal but desirable. Yet, in most Christian lands today slavery is not practiced, and we have come to see that it is not consistent with the biblical teaching of the equality of all men as creatures of God (Job 31:13-15) and as brothers in Christ.

Likewise, the Bible usually portrays women as occupying a role distinctly inferior to that of men. Again, this is true of the New Testament as well as the Old. But in Christian lands, where the gospel has been taken seriously, women have been accorded more and more equality with men and given a higher status in society. Most of us who follow Christ no longer take literally the admonitions of the Apostle Paul concerning the place of women in the home and in the church. Yet, we can find in the Bible, especially in the teachings and attitude of Jesus, implications for giving women a higher status and for according to them treatment as individual persons in the sight of God.

(5) In our understanding of the authority of the Bible, there are always two elements that are important, and neither can be neglected. One of these is the subjective, highly personal element; the other is the objective element, which comes to us through tradition. Speaking very generally, the first is the emphasis made by Protestants, whereas the second is the Catholic emphasis. In a well-rounded understanding of the Bible, both must be kept.

The Protestant reformers rebelled against the belief that the church is the official interpreter of the Bible, and that the pope and church councils had the right to determine what the Bible meant and what Christians therefore ought to believe. Luther and the other reformers insisted that the common man must be able to read the Bible for himself, in his own tongue, and secure from the Bible a message for his life. The conscience and understanding of the Christian man and not infallible officials at the top of the church were to decide what the Bible meant.

There are various ways of putting this emphasis. Samuel Taylor Coleridge once wrote: "Whatever *finds* me, bears witness for itself that it has proceeded from a Holy Spirit."[3] The Quaker sought in the Bible that which would "speak to his condition." Some have said that those parts of the Bible are *inspired* which are *inspiring* to the reader.

The classical Protestant way of expressing this is to say that the word of God will find acceptance in the hearts of men when it is sealed by "the inward testimony of the Spirit." The reader of the Bible must have his own conscience and understanding instructed by the Holy Spirit. This was especially

---

[3] "Confessions of an Inquiring Spirit," Letter I.

stressed by John Calvin, who insisted that the same Spirit who spoke through the prophets can penetrate into our own hearts to convince us that what they said was of divine origin.

This is what we have called the subjective or personal element in the reading of the Bible. The individual Christian must hear God speak to him in the Scriptures; otherwise, he does not really hear God's word. As I read the Bible I must ask: "What does this mean to *me?* What does God say to *me* as I read or hear Scripture?"

There is a certain danger in this approach if it is the only approach that we make in searching for the word of God within the words of the Bible. Many fanatics have heard what they believed to be the word of God in Scripture, and have gone forth to commit iniquities in the name of Scripture. Therefore, we must not leave out the second element which we have called objective, or the voice of tradition.

We do not mean that the Protestant Christian must submit to the pronouncements of the head of a great church, to the decisions of councils that have taken place throughout history, or to long creeds in which men have sought to set forth the "faith once for all delivered to the saints." The Protestant should not, however, ignore all that others have said in the past as they have read and studied the Bible, and as they have found the word of God within its pages. There have been in the past spiritual geniuses and learned scholars, men of devotion and learning, who have read and studied the Scripture long and carefully. We can ignore what they have found only at our peril.

When we are willing to listen to some extent to the voice of such men, we can be saved from fanaticism, from confusing our own feeble ideas with the testimony of the Holy Spirit, and from the danger of false and one-sided emphases in our faith and practices.

The Roman Catholic Church insists that the church has the right to interpret the Bible, because the church produced the Bible. It also places the authority of tradition alongside that of Scripture. It is not correct to say that the church produced the Bible. It is more nearly correct to say that the Bible and the church have derived from a common source—from the experience and faith of those who came to know Jesus Christ, and felt the power of his saving personality and work. Thus, the Bible can usually be best understood and its truth appropriated by the individual within the fellowship of the church —not an authoritarian church which prescribes what he must believe, but a fellowship of free individuals committed to Jesus Christ who are searching together for the truth of God.

The great reformers in the history of the Christian church have gone to the Bible to renew their lives and their devotion at the sources of our faith. For this we should be grateful, and we should hope that in the future there will be others who will go back to the same springs of faith and inspiration. Yet those who have truly reformed the church have not read the Bible with entirely new eyes, as if they had never seen it before. They knew the traditional interpretations, and knew how the Bible had been interpreted before them. Their purpose was to correct and purify the traditions in the light of a fresh study of the Scriptures for themselves, but they could not ignore all that others had said.

Our reading of the Bible should then be highly *personal*, but it need not be wholly private. It should be personal in that we must read it for ourselves and find in it the word of God for our own needs and our own times; we are under no compulsion to accept the external authority of other men and subscribe to their interpretations. We should always pray for the "inward testimony of the Spirit" as we read. But if we do this, our reading will not be wholly private, unconcerned with what the Bible has meant for others and what today it speaks to our fellow Christians. If we combine both of these attitudes, we shall be saved from fanaticism and dogmatism, and set free to have security in Christ without prejudice and intolerance.

The authority of the Bible is, in sum, the authority of the love and will of God as they lay hold upon us in the pages of Scripture. It is not a secondhand authority, or one that is imposed by men above. It is the authority which we find in the Bible as we come to it and seek answers to these questions: What did the original authors of the Bible intend to say? To what extent did they express the will and purpose of God? What does God say to *me* as I seek his word within the words of the Bible? And, finally, can I accept the love of God and follow his will as I find them in Scripture?

Many Christians will say that the Bible is not the only source of the word of God, the only medium through which he speaks to men. Many find him as they read the Book of Nature; some believe that he speaks directly to men today as he did of old; others say that God cannot be wholly absent from the scriptures of other religions. For the Christian, however, the Bible will always speak a word that is decisive and that is seminal, out of which will come fresh apprehension of the truth which comes from the Author of all truth. John Robinson spoke well when he said to the Pilgrim fathers as they departed from Holland:

"The Lord hath more light and truth yet to break forth out of His holy word."

appendix

Suggestions For Further Reading

The following is a brief, selected list of books for further reading. Many are available in paperback, and should be easy to secure.

I. GENERAL

The Interpreter's Bible. Edited by George A. Buttrick and others. Twelve Volumes. New York and Nashville: Abingdon Press, 1952-57. An excellent detailed commentary on all of the books of the Bible.

Peake's Commentary on the Bible. New Edition, Edited by Matthew Black and H. H. Rowley. London: Thomas Nelson and Sons Ltd., 1962. Best one-volume commentary on the whole Bible.

Hastings' Dictionary of the Bible. Revised Edition by Frederick C. Grant and H. H. Rowley. New York: Charles Scribner's Sons, 1963. Best one-volume dictionary of the Bible.

339

II. THE OLD TESTAMENT

Bernhard W. Anderson. *Understanding the Old Testament*. Englewood Cliffs: Prentice-Hall, Inc., 1957.

John Bright. *A History of Israel*. Philadelphia: Westminster Press, 1959.

H. H. Rowley. *The Faith of Israel*. London: SCM Press Ltd., 1956.

III. THE NEW TESTAMENT

Morton Scott Enslin. *Christian Beginnings* and *The Literature of the Christian Movement*. New York: Harper and Brothers, 1956 [1938]. Harper Torchbooks (paperback).

Günther Bornkamm. *Jesus of Nazareth*. Translated by Irene and Fraser McLuskey with James M. Robinson. New York: Harper and Brothers, 1960.

Adolf Deissmann. *Paul: A Study in Social and Religious History*. Translated by William E. Wilson. New York: Harper and Brothers, 1957 [1927]. Harper Torchbook (paperback).

Rudolf Bultmann. *Theology of the New Testament*. Translated by Kendrick Grobel. Two Volumes. New York: Charles Scribner's Sons, 1951-52.

IV. HISTORY OF TEXTS AND VERSIONS

Ira Maurice Price. *The Ancestry of Our English Bible*. Second Revised Edition. New York: Harper and Brothers, 1949.

Herbert Gordon May. *Our English Bible in the Making*. Philadelphia: Westminster Press, 1952.

V. APOCRYPHA

Bruce M. Metzger. *An Introduction to the Apocrypha.* New York: Oxford University Press, 1957.

G. Vermes. *The Dead Sea Scrolls in English.* Penguin Books, 1962. Paperback, containing excellent introduction to the scrolls and translation of most of the texts which have been published.

VI. AUTHORITY OF THE BIBLE

Robert H. Bryant. *The Bible's Authority Today.* Minneapolis: Augsburg Publishing House, 1968. A thorough study of the subject, both historical and constructive.

C. H. Dodd, *The Authority of the Bible.* New York: Harper and Brothers, 1958 [1929]. Harper Torchbook (paperback).

index to
scripture passages

General Index

A

Abraham, 52-6, 94, 149, 153, 238
Acts of Paul, 154, 266
Acts of the Apostles, 174, 175, 185-6, 188, 202, 203, 226, 268, 270, 271, 272, 273, 276
Additions to Daniel, The, 144
Additions to Esther, The, 142
Adler, Mortimer J., 13-4
'adonay, 90
Agrippa, 161-2, 191
Akiba, Rabbi, 163
Alexander the Great, 82, 285
Alexandria (Egypt), 84, 130, 131, 163, 288
Alfred, King, 292
Allegorical interpretation, 31-3
American Standard Version, 45, 90, 310-11
'ammê hā-'āretz, 168
Ammonites, 67, 68
Amorites, 61
Amos, 27-9, 43, 74, 96, 101-02, 113, 333
Amphictyony, 63
Andrewes, Lancelot, 306
Angels, 136, 165-6, 167, 332
Antichrist, 208-09, 211
Antioch, 188, 202

Antiochus III, 84
Antiochus IV Epiphanes, 84, 85, 125, 126, 127
Antipas, Herod, 161, 180
Apocalypse of Paul, 155
Apocalypse, apocalyptic, 32, 34-5, 85, 114, 138, 147, 165, 210, 216, 242, 261, 263
Apocrypha, New Testament, 153-7
Apocrypha, Old Testament, 121-46, 147n, 159, 165, 264-5, 278-80
Apostolic Council in Jerusalem, 190, 198, 230
Aramaic, 82, 153, 169, 178, 205, 284, 285, 291
Arameans, 56, 73
Archaeology: definition of, 39; purpose of, 40; relationship to higher criticism, 40; discoveries relating to conquest of Canaan, 62; relating to divided monarchy, 73
Archelaus, 161
Ark of Yahweh of hosts, 64-5, 68, 70
Armageddon, Battle of, 153
Artaxerxes I, 80
Ashera, 61, 74
Ashtoreth, 61
Assyrian empire, 72, 73
Athanasius, 272
Authorship of Biblical books, 25

353

B

Baal, 61, 64, 72, 74
Babel, Tower of, 324
Babylon, Babylonia, 75, 76-9, 134, 140, 141, 145, 208, 210, 323
Baptism: of Jesus by John, 175, 178, 223; of Paul, 187; in the kerygma, 228-9; in Paul's message, 236-7
Bar Cocheba, 162-3
Barnabas, 173, 188, 205, 273. *See* Letter of Barnabas
Baruch, 140-1, 147
Basic Bible, The, 313
Bathsheba, 67, 69
Beatty papyri, 286, 287
Bede, Venerable, 292
Bel and the Dragon, 144, 145-6
Belshazzar, 85, 140, 323-4
Bettenson, Henry, 269*n*, 271*n*
biblia, 255
Bishops, in Pastoral Epistles, 204-05
Bishops' Bible, 301, 305, 307
Bodmer papyrus, 286
Broughton, Hugh, 307
Bultmann, Rudolf, 237

C

Caedmon, 292
Caesarea, 191, 198
Caesarea Philippi, 161, 180, 222
Caird, G. B., 177*n*
Caligula, Gaius, 161
Calvin, John, 300, 336
Campbell, Alexander, 309, 331
Canaanites, 70, 83; meaning of term, 61; religion of, 61-2; Hebrew conquest of, 62-3; influence of religion on Hebrews, 63-4; defeat by David, 68
Canon, 26, 122, 154, 209; idea of canon of Scripture, 255-8; formation of Old Testament canon, 258-65; formation of New Testament canon, 266-76; factors in for-mation of, 276-8; Christian's attitude toward, 278-81
Catholic Epistles, 203, 206-09
Catholics, Roman, 122-3, 124, 128, 139, 142, 145, 147*n*, 255, 265, 272, 290, 298, 300-05, 313-14, 317-18, 335, 337
Chaldean empire, 72, 73
Challoner, Richard, 304
Charles, R. H., 147*n*
Christ, 141, 200-01 *et passim;* in the Old Testament, 33; meaning of the term, 112, 220; in Paul's theology, 233-9; in John's theology, 243-5. *See* Jesus, Messiah
Chronicler, The, 51, 80
1-2 Chronicles, 48, 51, 142, 279, 322
Church, 174, 189, 193, 200-02, 206, 252, 274, 318, 335, 337; early organization of, 204-05; in Paul's theology, 240-1; in John's theology, 246-7
Circumcision, 84, 190, 197, 205
Codex, 271. *See* Sinaiticus, Vaticanus
Coleridge, Samuel Taylor, 126, 335
Colossians, 193, 198, 199-200, 268
Confraternity Edition, 314
Corinth, 188, 189, 195, 196, 198
1-2 Corinthians, 195-6
Covenant, 63, 119, 259; making of, at Sinai, 58-60; festival of covenant renewal, 64; new covenant of Jeremiah, 76, 88, 213; key concept of Old Testament, 88; covenant election of Israel, 101; terms of, 116; in Qumran community, 151-2; the new covenant in Christianity, 213-14, 252
Covenant Code, 117
Coverdale, Miles, 296-300, 306
Creature, new, in Paul, 234, 236
Criticism: meaning of term, 19; lower criticism, 18-22; higher criticism, 22-31
Cromwell, Thomas, 299
Crucifixion, 164, 175, 177, 183, 251, 323, 328
Cyrus, 51, 78, 79, 93, 145, 324

D

Damascus, 68, 73, 187, 290
Daniel, 32, 35, 44, 85, 114, 138, 144-6, 147, 165, 255, 261, 264
Darius, 80, 82, 137, 323
David, 25, 51, 52, 63, 66, 81, 91, 113, 228, 233, 322; reign of, 67-9
Dead Sea Scrolls, 150-3, 167, 243, 284. *See* Qumran
Decalogue, 117. *See* Ten Commandments
Demonic powers of universe, 231, 235
Demons, 136, 165-6, 179, 217, 332
Deutero-Isaiah: *see* Isaiah, Second
Deuteronomic Code, 117
Deuteronomist, Deuteronomic editor, 50, 66, 72-3, 77, 93, 260
Deuteronomy, 44, 50, 75, 259, 277
Diaspora, 163, 169
Diatessaron, 271
Dillenberger, John, 280*n*
Docetism, 203. *See* Gnosticism
Dodd, C. H., 227, 326
Domitian, 202, 210
Douai Version, 303-04, 306
Dualism: in apocalyptic view of history, 114; in Dead Sea Scrolls, 151-2; in John, 243

E

E (The Elohist), 49, 77, 259
Ecclesiastes, 16, 44, 71, 83, 122, 130, 146, 147, 263, 264, 274, 278, 279, 280, 323
Ecclesiasticus: *see* Sirach
Edom, 53, 60, 68
Edward VI, 297, 300
Egypt, 56-7, 71, 73, 128
Elders, 204-05
Elijah, 74, 111
Eliot, Charles W., 14
Elisha, 74
Elizabeth, Queen, 297, 301, 305
Elohist, The: *see* E.

England, Church of, 291; attitude toward Apocrypha, 124; attitude toward English translations, 296-7, 303
English Revised Version, 309-10
Enoch, 111
Enoch, Book of, 147-8, 165, 166, 224
Enslin, Morton S., 240, 274*n*
Ephesians, 193, 203, 268, 280
Ephesus, 188, 189, 192, 195, 196, 198, 199, 201, 202, 242
Ephraim, 72
epioúsion, 322
Erasmus, 15, 294, 299, 302
Esau, 53
I-II Esdras, 123, 265
I Esdras, 137-8
II Esdras, 138-40, 165, 279
III Esdras, 137
IV Esdras, 139
Essenes, 151, 167-8, 243
Esther, Book of, 82, 134, 143-4, 146, 150, 255, 263, 264, 278, 280, 323
Eternal life, 247-50, 252. *See* Immortality
Ethics: Nature of Biblical ethics, 16-17; of Old Testament, 115-20; of Judaism in New Testament era, 166; of Sermon on the Mount, 218-9; of Paul, 238-40; of New Testament, 252-3
evangélion, 170, 227
Exodus, Book of, 48, 149
Exodus from Egypt, 57, 327; return from exile a new exodus, 93
Ezekiel, 44, 76, 263
Ezra, Book of, 51, 137
Ezra the scribe, 51, 80-1, 137, 147, 258, 259, 260, 263, 264, 277

F

Faith, reading with "eyes of faith," 41-2; miracles of Jesus and, 179; in the Pastoral Epistles, 204; in Jude, 209; in Paul, 231-3; in John, 246

U

V

W

Y

Z

Notes